strategic management

strategic management

2nd edition

philip sadler

mba **masterclass**

**KOGAN
PAGE**

London and Sterling, VA

First published in 1993, authors James C Craig and Robert M Grant

Second edition published in Great Britain and the United States in 2003 by Kogan Page Limited, author Philip Sadler

120 Pentonville Road
London N1 9JN
UK
www.kogan-page.co.uk

22883 Quicksilver Drive
Sterling VA 20166–2012
USA

ISBN 0 7494 3938 6

British Library Cataloguing in Publication Data

A CIP record for this book is available from the British Library.

Library of Congress Cataloging-in-Publication Data
Sadler, Philip, 1930-
  Strategic management / Philip Sadler. – 2nd ed.
    p. cm. – (MBA masterclass series)
Rev. ed. of: Strategic management / James C. Craig. 1st ed. 1993.
Includes bibliographical references and index.
  ISBN 0-7494-3938-6
  1. Strategic planning. I. Title. II. Series.
  HD30.28.S224 2003
  658.4'012–dc21
                                    2002154764

Typeset by Saxon Graphics Ltd, Derby
Printed and bound in Great Britain by Biddles Ltd, Guildford and King's Lynn
www.biddles.co.uk

Contents

The series editor

Philip Sadler is a Vice President of the Ashridge Business School where he was chief executive for 20 years. He now divides his time between writing, speaking, consultancy and voluntary service. He is a Fellow of the International Academy of Management, a Companion of the Institute of Management, a Fellow of the Institute for Personnel and Development, a Fellow of the Institute of Directors, and a Patron of the Centre for Tomorrow's Company.

He has been awarded the honorary degrees of DSc (City University) and DBA (De Montfort University). He holds the Burnham Gold Medal of the Institute of Management and was appointed CBE in 1986.

His recent books include *Managing Change* (1995), *Leadership* (1998), *The Seamless Organization* (2001) and *Building Tomorrow's Company* (2002).

THE *MBA MASTERCLASS* SERIES

The new *MBA Masterclass* series is designed to meet the needs of both MBA students and experienced managers looking for a refresher course in a particular subject.

Authoritative but practical, these titles focus on MBA core subjects as well as covering the latest developments in management thinking and practice.

Written by international academics, consultants and practitioners, this series is an ideal companion for any busy MBA student or manager.

Current titles published in the series:

Leadership
Intercultural Management
Strategic Management

And still to be published:

Project Management
Branding
Finance and Accounting
Human Resource Management

To obtain further information, please contact the publisher at the address below:

Kogan Page Limited
120 Pentonville Road
London N1 9JN
Tel: +44 (0) 20 7278 0433
Fax: +44 (0) 20 7837 6348
www.kogan-page.co.uk

Introduction

This book is aimed at two overlapping audiences. For aspiring or actual MBA students I have tried to include references to the most important work by both academics and consultants since the topic of strategy first became salient in the 1950s. For practising managers facing strategic decisions I have tried to use common-sense language where possible, avoiding undue reliance on jargon. I have also tried to illustrate points in the argument with relatively recent and familiar examples of both good and bad practice.

On the surface the notion of business strategy would seem to be quite straightforward and uncomplicated. Surely it is just a matter of deciding some medium- to long-term goals, bringing together the resources, human and material, that will be required if they are to be achieved, devising a plan and schedule for implementation, and then just getting on with it.

In practice, however, and especially in large, multi-business companies, it is not at all straightforward. There are several reasons why this is the case.

First, by definition, a strategy is something that unfolds over time; during that time period the environment is changing with great rapidity and can invalidate the assumptions on which the plan was based.

Secondly, there are often sharp conflicts between the requirements of the strategy and the imperatives of short-term profitability or even survival.

Thirdly, as research has shown, in practice strategy formulation is usually far from being the rational, objective process that the textbooks prescribe. It is subject to distortion from such factors as the machinations of organizational politics, the existence of mindsets linked to particular corporate cultures, and 'fashions' in management theory.

Fourthly, there is the tendency of people with a high level of intelligence and formal education to eschew the simple approach and overcomplicate things – a tendency symbolized by the growth of the use of jargon.

Finally, implementation is certainly not always a smooth process; successful implementation is a function of many interacting variables among which the quality of leadership is paramount.

Unravelling this complexity has involved a massive output of writings by management experts in the business schools and management consultancies. A whole industry of strategy consultants has grown up, peddling a wide range of analytical techniques and methodologies. These consultants command fees commensurate with the importance of the issues they are dealing with, but which often seem extravagant when related to the outcomes. Fashion has followed fashion and no doubt there will be many more 'flavours of the month' in the future. Nowadays it is rare indeed for the directors of a major company to sit down and debate strategy and reach consensus without the aid of a large planning staff and a whole army of bright young MBA graduates from a consulting firm to aid them. It is considered impolite to ask what these highly rewarded directors are actually paid to do.

In the large, multi-business company a further source of complexity is that there are two distinct levels of strategy. At the level of the corporate head office or holding company some fundamental strategic decisions need to be made:

▌ What is the company's mission or purpose and what are the values and principles that should govern the behaviour of members of the organization?

▌ What are the desirable characteristics of the company's culture?

▌ What industries or market segments should it enter or leave?

▌ What form of organization structure and what kind of control systems would best support the strategy?

▌ How can value be added through such things as brand strength, image and reputation?

There are also some key decisions to be taken that have strategic implications, such as the appointment of the chief executives of the operating divisions.

At the level of the business unit or subsidiary the main strategic issue is how to achieve a sustainable competitive advantage in the particular product/market field in which the division operates. (This level is generally known as business strategy or competitive strategy as distinct from what takes place at head office, which is referred to as corporate strategy.) It involves identifying correctly the critical success factors (CSFs) in a particular market and so managing the business as to meet these more successfully than competitors.

This book covers both corporate and competitive strategy. (In the case of a single-business company, of course, they merge into each other.)

As will be shown in Chapter 1, the literature on strategy falls into two broad groupings. On the one hand there is *prescriptive* writing – the 'how to do it' approach. Prescriptions range from highly formal and analytical methodologies involving huge amounts of data collection and analysis to the 'visionary' approach that urges the importance of 'dreaming ahead' and going for BHAGs (big, hairy, audacious goals).

On the other hand there is the *descriptive* literature, which attempts to portray what actually goes on in the processes of strategy formulation and implementation. As with all human activities, different observers focus on different aspects of the activities they are observing.

Another useful distinction is that between 'intended' strategy and that which is actually implemented – usually referred to as the 'realized' or 'emergent' strategy. There are several reasons why the two diverge. One is simply a failure in implementation; another is the intervention of an unanticipated change in the environment such as the tragic events of 11 September 2001. More often, perhaps, it is simply an inherent quality of a process that takes place over time, involving large numbers of actors, many of whom change as the process unfolds.

There is much to be learnt from both approaches. It is useful to study the various prescriptions on offer and to select that which appears best to meet the needs of a particular organization in a particular context. At the same time it is important to be aware that real life is always much messier than the theory and that the process of strategic management involves working through particular issues facing a particular company in a given business context rather than picking a ready-made approach off the shelf, no matter how illustrious its pedigree.

The changing context of strategy formulation

Back in the late 1960s and early 1970s a number of original thinkers such as Peter Drucker, Daniel Bell and Alvin Toffler drew attention to certain emerging trends that were going to result in radical changes to the structure of Western industrial economy and society. Among these trends the most important were:

▌ the decline of 'smokestack' manufacturing industries and the growth of services, in terms of both employment and share of gross domestic product;

▌ the rise in the proportion of women in the active workforce;

▌ the increase in the proportion of the workforce who could be described as 'knowledge workers';

▌ the way in which information technology was ushering in a new industrial revolution;

▌ the increasing globalization of markets.

These thinkers were not using crystal balls and peering into the future. They were looking at trends that were already established. Their ability to see how important these trends were for the future of business and to draw out their implications was a function of the fact that these thinkers were, in the words of Prahalad, 'able to escape the gravitational pull of the past'. Regrettably, this is a mental capacity shared by very few people in the profession of management. Most managers cling to the conventional wisdom of the past in the same way that Linus clings to his security blanket. 'If you want to escape the gravitational pull of the past, you have to be willing to challenge your own orthodoxies, to regenerate your core strategies and rethink your most fundamental assumptions about how you are going to compete' (C K Prahalad, 1999, speech to annual conference of Chartered Institute of Personnel and Development).

Those with imagination and who think creatively are seeking to be ahead of the game. They are searching for tomorrow's big idea. To be ahead of the game calls for the ability to think outside the box – indeed the ability to recognize that the box does not exist except in our minds. For managers to be able to think in this way their development needs to include processes that enhance and bring out their inherent ability to think creatively.

As we entered the 21st century there was a rush on the part of business to exploit the new opportunities thrown up by the Internet. Investors were scrambling to invest in dotcom companies that had yet to make a profit. Blue-chip companies in what has become known as the old economy were reeling as their shares went into relative decline. As we now know much of that investment was ill considered and was more to do with following the herd than thinking creatively. It is at times like these when almost everybody is looking in one direction that the creative mind starts looking elsewhere.

Clearly, the revolution in information technology has come about largely as a result of some highly creative thinking on the part of relatively few people. Yet its application to e-commerce may not, in the end, constitute its most important impact on our world. We may find that even greater consequences follow from its impact on the design of organizations and on the way they function. In traditional organization hierarchies some of the layers of management were not there to make decisions or supervise operations; their function was rather to act as relays for information, rather like boosters on a telephone cable to collect, amplify, interpret and disseminate information. Modern technology does a better job and tomorrow's technology will do it even better. A new principle, the span of communication, is taking the place of the old span of control. The number of people reporting to an executive is now limited only by the subordinates' willingness to take responsibility for their own communications and relationships. Those subordinates can be located in any part of the world. Being connected replaces being in control.

Turning from opportunities to threats, the dangers associated with climate change and depletion of natural resources may finally reach the top of the agenda in the coming decade. At the World Economic Forum at Davos in 2001 this issue came first in a delegate vote on the most important issues currently facing business – ahead of problems to do with the world's financial systems.

Another important development in the past few years has been the growing acceptance by companies, particularly large global enterprises, of the need to set objectives in the field of corporate social responsibility as well as financial ones and to measure and report on the extent to which they are being achieved.

This acceptance is reinforced by strong expressions of public opinion in anti-capitalist and anti-globalization demonstrations and by changes in company law.

Finally, events such as the collapse of the Enron empire and the associated demise of Andersen have reminded business leaders that failure to put shareholders' long-term interests at the top of the agenda and failure to observe basic ethical principles can not only lead to corporate collapse but also to the very real possibility of prison sentences.

These developments mean that strategy formulation in the first decade of the 21st century is a very different process and has a very different agenda from those featuring in the classic writings on strategy in the last quarter of the 20th century. In today's business environment the achievement of sustainable growth in shareholder value is about much more than positioning in the market and portfolio selection. It is increasingly about good corporate governance, reputation building, the ability to attract and retain top talent and relationships with stakeholders. These important themes will be explored in depth at various points in what follows.

At the end of the book are two case studies, Tesco and Marks and Spencer, which have been chosen to illustrate best practice and worst practice respectively.

Part 1

Strategic management and its context

Introduction to strategic management

THE ELEMENTS OF STRATEGY

Strategy is a highly complex concept and attempts to define it adequately within the compass of a sentence or two are almost certainly going to miss out some key elements. Among the many definitions in the literature can be found a number of words and phrases that are all linked in some way with the notion of strategy:

▌ purpose or mission;

▌ policies;

▌ defining what business the company is in;

▌ defining what kind of company it is;

▌ objectives or goals;

▌ strengths and weaknesses;

▌ opportunities and threats;

▌ key success factors;

▌ key decisions;

▌ capabilities or competences;

▌ planning and scheduling;

▌ implementation;

▌ sustainable competitive advantage.

Purpose or mission

This is, in effect, a statement of why the company exists. Company statements of purpose tend to fall into three groups:

▮ The purpose is to create shareholder value.

▮ The purpose is to meet the needs and expectations of all the stake-holders – employees, customers, suppliers and the community as well as investors.

▮ The purpose is of a higher order in that it is aspirational and idealistic, or challenging and inspiring.

Each of these three approaches is discussed further in Chapter 3.

Policies

In the context of company strategy, policies are guiding rules or principles that are regarded as an integral part of the company's 'success model'; that is to say, they are practices or ways of doing things, often long established, that are seen as indispensable parts of the company's formula for achieving a sustainable competitive advantage.

A simple example will make this clear. Marks and Spencer has long practised the policy of unquestioningly accepting returned goods and refunding customers' money. This practice is one among a number that the company believes have been important factors in its long-term success.

It is also the case that until relatively recently the company refused to accept credit cards. This policy was believed by many outsiders to be seriously mistaken and a contributory factor in the company's loss of market share in recent years.

Defining what business the company is in and defining what kind of company it is

Decisions about corporate purpose and company policies are closely linked to two key sets of strategic decisions – what business the company is in or is to be in and what kind of company it is or is to be.

Decisions of the first kind are to do with choice of industry or industries in which to operate and which sectors or niches within broad industry groups to focus on. Decisions of the second kind are to do with the difficult and intangible area of corporate culture.

Both sets of decisions are complex and will be treated at some length in later chapters.

Objectives or goals

These terms tend to be used interchangeably. Strategic objectives are normally ones to be achieved over the medium to long term. They may be financial such as a certain increase in earnings per share or non-financial such as a percentage increase in market share. In theory they should be capable of being quantifiable and hence susceptible to measurement.

Opportunities and threats

An important part of the strategic process is the identification of opportunities in the market-place. These are then matched with the company's capabilities. The competitive environment is also scanned for potential threats to the competitiveness of the business.

Key success factors

These are the things that a business must be able to do exceptionally well if it is to attain a leading position in a particular market. For example, in the highly competitive world of the major supermarkets the key success factors include:

- site location and acquisition;
- average store size;
- IT systems linking point of sale to logistics;
- accurate and rapid feedback from consumer research;
- purchasing power.

Key decisions

Strategic decisions are ones that are of fundamental importance to the business, but will not prove to have been right or wrong for some considerable time. For example, the decision to make an acquisition of another company will normally take at least two to three years before a realistic view can be taken as to whether or not it was a sound decision. Strategic decisions are normally such that they are irreversible or at least can only be reversed at considerable cost.

Among the most important decisions are ones to do with the *allocation of resources*, particularly the allocation of capital. An obvious example is the choice between funding organic growth and funding growth by acquisition.

Capabilities or competences

These are the distinctive competences that are difficult for competitors to copy and which are linked to the achievement of a competitive advantage in a particular market.

Hamel and Prahalad (1994) introduced the concept of core competences. These are defined as bundles of skills and technologies that enable a company to provide a particular benefit to customers. To be considered a core competence a skill must pass three tests:

■ It must make a disproportionate contribution to customer value.

■ It must be competitively unique.

■ It must be applicable to a range of products.

They argue that the firm should be regarded as a collection of core competences rather than a portfolio of assets.

Kay (1993) identifies four basic kinds of distinctive capability:

■ *Architecture*, ie a network of relationships within or around the company. Internal relationships are with or among employees; external ones are with suppliers, customers or joint venture partners. Architecture depends on the ability of the company to build and sustain long-term relationships and in this way to create a favourable operating environment that cannot easily be replicated by competitors.

■ *Reputation*, which is particularly important in markets where product and/or service quality is important but can only be demonstrated over relatively long periods of time.

■ *Innovation* and the ability to exploit it so as to gain a sustainable competitive advantage.

■ *Strategic assets*. These are of three main types – natural monopolies, cases where the costs of infrastructure have already been incurred so that new entrants benefit from an advantageous cost structure and cases where companies benefit from regulations or licensing requirements that restrict entry to the market.

Implementation

A sound strategy is of little value if implementation is weak. Implementation begins with *planning* and *scheduling*. It involves decisions about such things as *organization structure*, the *allocation of resources* and the level of *risk* that is acceptable. It also involves leadership as well as managerial skills, particularly when, as is often the case, the adoption of a particular strategy involves major organizational change.

Sustainable competitive advantage

This is what the strategy is designed to achieve – a position in the market such that the company is not only able to earn a higher profit margin than its competitors, but is able to sustain that position over a significant period of time.

In the world of the 21st century the 'significant period of time' may be quite short, particularly in the case of industries characterized by rapid technological developments. The implication is that, depending on the speed of change that characterizes a market, companies will need to carry out strategic reviews at appropriately frequent intervals.

CORPORATE AND COMPETITIVE STRATEGY

In the large, multi-business company there are two distinct levels of strategy. At the level of the corporate head office or holding company some fundamental strategic decisions need to be made:

▌ What is the company's mission or purpose?

▌ What are the values and principles that should govern the behaviour of members of the organization?

▌ What are the desirable characteristics of the company's culture?

▌ What industries or market segments should it enter or leave?

▌ What form of organization structure and what kind of control systems would best support the strategy?

▌ How can value be added through such things as brand strength, image and reputation?

There are also some key decisions to be taken that have strategic implications, such as the appointment of the chief executives of the operating divisions.

Decisions of this type fall under the heading of corporate strategy.

At the level of the business unit or subsidiary, however, the main strategic issue is how to achieve a sustainable competitive advantage in the particular product/market field in which the division operates. This is generally known as business strategy or competitive strategy. It involves identifying correctly the critical success factors (CSFs) in a particular market and so managing the business as to meet these more successfully than competitors.

For example, the highly successful US commuter airline SouthWestern identified the following CSFs:

▌ low-cost, no-frills fares leading to high load factors;

▌ friendly, courteous, cheerful staff with strong commitment to their company;

▌ high standards of teamwork without rigid job demarcations;

▌ remarkably quick turnround times giving increased aircraft utilization;

▌ an egalitarian culture symbolized by relatively modest (by US standards) top management remuneration;

▌ very careful screening of recruits at all levels from baggage handler to aircrew.

Kay (1993) makes the distinction between corporate and business strategy clear by the examples he uses. He cites the following as typical issues at the corporate level:

▌ Was Benetton, a knitwear manufacturer, right to move into retailing?

▌ Should Saatchi and Saatchi have attempted to build a global advertising business?

▌ What segment of the car market was the right one for BMW?

At the business or competitive strategy level he mentions:

▌ Should Eurotunnel offer a premium service or use its low operating costs to cut prices?

▌ How should a European airline react to increasing deregulation?

▌ How should Honda have approached the US motorcycle market?

SCHOOLS OF THOUGHT IN STRATEGIC MANAGEMENT

Having researched the literature thoroughly, Mintzberg, Ahlstrand and Lampel (1998) identified 10 key schools of thought, which they then classified into three groupings.

The first they call *Prescriptive Schools*, ones that are 'more concerned with how strategies should be formulated than with how they necessarily do form'. This grouping comprises the *Design*, *Planning* and *Positioning Schools*.

They then describe a second main group, which are termed *Descriptive Schools*, comprising *Entrepreneurial*, *Cognitive*, *Learning*, *Power*, *Cultural* and *Environmental Schools*. These set out not to prescribe how strategy should be made but rather to describe how it is made in practice.

The final group comprises just one school, the *Configurational*.

The Prescriptive Schools

The Design School

This approach sees strategy formulation as a conceptual process. It has been generally associated with the Harvard Business School. One of the earliest works was Selznick's *Leadership in Administration* (1957). Selznick introduced the notion of distinctive competencies. This school's basic text is *Business Policy: Text and cases* (1965) by Learned *et al*. Better known today is Alfred Chandler's *Strategy and Structure* (1962).

More recently this approach has been represented in the SWOT model (Strengths, Weaknesses, Opportunities, Threats), which effectively marks the position of this school in spanning the process of strategic management, from the recognition of environmental influences on the business in the form of opportunities and threats, and the need for an objective appraisal of the strengths and weaknesses of the business compared to competitors.

Mintzberg, Ahlstrand and Lampel (1998) offer a number of critical comments on this approach:

▌ It ignores the process of incremental learning and the 'emergence' of strategy.

▌ It ignores the influence of the existing structure and culture of the organization.

▮ The role of the chief executive is overemphasized.

▮ It is questionable how far an organization can determine its own strengths and weaknesses.

▮ It leads to inflexibility and cannot cope with environmental turbulence.

▮ It creates an artificial separation between strategy formulation and implementation.

The Planning School

This stems from the work of Igor Ansoff (1965) whose book *Corporate Strategy* is another classic text in the field. Another major contributor is George Steiner (1969) with *Top Management Planning*.
The stages in the planning model are:

▮ Set objectives.

▮ External audit, including scenario building, industry analysis and competitor analysis.

▮ Internal audit, ie strengths and weaknesses.

▮ Strategy evaluation. Several possible strategies are delineated and evaluated with the aim of selecting the best. The comparisons are made chiefly in financial terms using such techniques as risk analysis and the various methods associated with calculating shareholder value.

▮ Strategy operationalization. This involves a whole hierarchy of strategies and sub-strategies. Long-term plans sit on top, followed by medium-term ones and short-term annual operating plans, each with associated targets and budgets.

▮ Scheduling – the timetabling of the whole process.

Along with the planning approach came the planners – new senior management positions – whose task was to prepare strategic plans for top management's approval.

Mintzberg and his colleagues argue that the planning approach 'ran into trouble in the early 1980's when the activity was cut back in many companies. Most dramatic was its emasculation at General Electric, the company that "literally wrote the book on the subject".'

Despite this one of the major journals in the field still carries the title *Long Range Planning*, while the UK association known as the

Strategic Planning Society commands healthy support. Mintzberg's book (1994) *The Rise and Fall of Strategic Planning* tells the full story.

The Positioning School

This approach dates from the publication, in 1980, of Michael Porter's *Competitive Strategy*. The new idea was that only a few key or *generic* strategies are desirable or defensible in any given industry. Mintzberg summarizes the premises of this school:

▌ Strategies are generic positions in a market-place.

▌ That market-place is economic and competitive.

▌ The strategy formulation process is therefore one of selection of a generic position based on analysis.

▌ Analysts (in practice usually consulting firms) play a key role.

▌ Strategies come out of this process 'full blown'.

Porter's work includes, as well as his concept of generic strategies, a framework of analysis known as the Value Chain. The origins of this school are traceable to classic works on military strategy such as Sun Tzu's *The Art of War* (1971) and Clausewitz's *On War*, the link being the treatment of the market-place as a battlefield.

The development of this school is associated with the growth of specialized consulting firms in the strategy field, ones like The Boston Consulting Group with their Growth-Share Matrix and The Experience Curve and PIMs with its large empirical database.

In their critique of this school Mintzberg and his co-authors make the extreme assertion: 'no one has ever developed a strategy through analytical technique. Fed useful information into the strategy-making process: yes. Extrapolated current strategies or copied those of a competitor: yes. But developed a strategy: never.'

The Descriptive Schools

Amongst the Prescriptive group of schools the *Design School* is the one most characterized by having a single person as its central actor. Among the Descriptive approaches, the *Entrepreneurial School* stands out in this way. Here the 'visionary' holds centre stage, except in this case it is through applying gifts such as intuition, judgement, wisdom, experience and insight that ideas are translated into the bones of a strategy to which others will add the flesh.

The picture of entrepreneurs leading their vision to a reality goes back as far as any of the other schools, indeed to classical times. So Schumpeter represents a relatively early champion for it, writing as he did in the 1930s, although it has its exponents lately in Drucker, Kaplan and Mintzberg himself.

The Entrepreneurial School

This school has as its central concept *vision*. The strategy formulation process is focused on the individual leader and involves intuition, judgement, wisdom, experience and insight.

The premises of this school are:

▮ Strategy exists in the mind of the leader in the form of a vision of the organization's future.

▮ Strategy formulation is only partly a conscious process.

▮ The leader promotes the vision single-mindedly and keeps close control over implementation, reformulating it as necessary.

▮ Thus the strategy is deliberate in overall vision and emergent in how its detailed implementation unfolds.

▮ The organization is similarly malleable.

▮ Entrepreneurial strategy tends to take the form of a niche, protected from forces of outright competition.

The Cognitive School

This one focuses on the mind of the strategist. The school includes work on cognitive bias, the information-processing view of strategy and the idea of strategic cognition as a process of construction.

The picture here is one of an individual thinking through what is required and what the options are, and coming to a grand design all of his/her own.

Mintzberg and his fellow critics do not afford much credence to this school but recognize it as a distinct approach to strategy formation and it is perhaps significant that they do not acknowledge brainstorming amongst a group as a sufficiently viable alternative to the individual 'mental giant'.

A more radical approach is represented by the idea of strategy as interpretation, based on cognition as construction. To proponents of this view the mind imposes some interpretation on the environment – it constructs its world.

The premises of the Cognitive School are summarized as follows:

▌ Strategy formulation is a cognitive process that takes place in the mind of the strategist.

▌ Strategies thus emerge as perspectives – in the form of concepts, maps, schemas and frames.

▌ Inputs flow through all sorts of distorting filters before they are decoded by the cognitive maps or else are merely interpretations of a world that only exists in terms of how it is perceived.

It is self-evident that the ideas of this school are less likely to find favour with practising managers than the preceding ones.

The Learning School

Proponents of this school see strategy as an emergent process. This school 'took off' with the publication, in 1980, of James Brian Quin's *Strategies for Change: Logical incrementalism.* The radical idea of this school is that the traditional image of strategy formulation was a fantasy, one that may have appealed to managers but did not correspond to what actually happens in organizations. Proponents of this approach ask how strategies actually get formed in organizations. Researchers found that in practice strategies could be traced back to a range of actions and decisions by people other than members of top management. A scientist in a laboratory might come up with a new product or a sales team's efforts could change a company's market position.

Mintzberg's own work falls into this category. He defines strategy as a pattern or consistency in action and distinguishes deliberate from emergent strategy.

The seminal work of Hamel and Prahalad (1994) fits into this school. They conceive of strategy as a collective learning process aimed at developing and exploiting 'core competences'. Their concept of 'strategic intent' is one of an approach that defines emerging market opportunities and provides a rallying cry for employees. (This concept might better fit the Entrepreneurial School, with its emphasis on visionary leadership.)

Hamel and Prahalad's other concepts are 'leverage' and 'stretch'. Stretch is to do with having high aspirations (BHAGs or big, hairy, audacious goals). Leverage is to do with various ways of making the most of available resources.

Hamel has also argued for 'revolution', the need for companies to seek to change the basis of competition in their industries.

The ideas of this school are closely allied with writings on the subject of the 'learning organization', such as Senge's *The Fifth Discipline* (1990).

The premises of the Learning School are:

▌ The complexity of the environment precludes deliberate strategy making. It must involve a process of learning over time in which formulation and implementation start to merge.

▌ There are many potential strategists in most organizations.

▌ The learning proceeds in emergent fashion as people think retrospectively and make sense of actions.

▌ The role of leadership is not to create strategy but to manage the process of strategic learning.

▌ Strategies appear first as patterns out of the past, and only later as plans for the future or as perspectives to guide overall behaviour.

The Power (or Political) School

The term 'power' is used here to refer to the exercise of influence beyond the purely economic, but including economic power used beyond accepted market-place competition. There is an important distinction to be made between 'micro power' and 'macro power'. The former relates to the exercise of power within the organization in connection with the processes of strategic management. The latter is to do with the exercise of power by the organization in its external relationships. The *Political School* focuses partly on what goes on inside the firm – on the battles that are fought internally among line managers and staff professionals for resources, status and promotion. Given the complexity of organizations and the pressures on individuals to perform, or at least to appear to do so, it is not surprising that many of the battles are fought at this level. What is surprising is that what emerges could be described as strategy. While Cyert and March recognized this in *A Behavioral Theory of the Firm* (1963), Mintzberg gives this added credibility by acknowledging the part that ploys and alliances within a firm can play in tracking its development. The importance of the exercise of micro power as a determinant of strategic direction is well illustrated by the case of Marks and Spencer in the late 1990s (see page 243).

A second subset of the Political School, the macro element concerns the use of power by the organization (rather than within it in its micro form) and often involves illegitimate means, such as a large national employer pressurizing a government for loans or preferential sourcing of state procurement orders.

Mintzberg's team deal with stakeholder analysis under the macro power heading, describing it as an attempt to cope with political forces through a rational approach. They also bring strategic alliances and strategic sourcing under this heading, introducing at this point Hamel's concept of 'collaborative advantage'.

The premises of the Power School are summed up as:

▌ Strategy formulation is shaped by power and politics. The strategies that result tend to be emergent and take the form of positions or ploys rather than perspectives.

▌ Micro power is to do with strategy making among parochial interest and shifting coalitions.

▌ Macro power is the process by which an organization seeks to promote its own interests by controlling or cooperating with other organizations.

The Cultural School

Organizational culture is defined as the shared beliefs that are reflected in traditions and habits as well as more tangible manifestations – stories, symbols, buildings, the way employees dress and address each other etc.

Pettigrew's study of ICI (1985) falls into this group, as does the work of Rhenman (1973) and Normann (1977) in Sweden. Kotter and Heskett's (1992) study of the relationship between culture and business performance also fits in here.

The premises of this school are:

▌ Strategy formulation is a process of social interaction based on the shared beliefs and values of the members of the organization.

▌ Individuals acquire these beliefs and values through a process of socialization that can be either tacit and largely non-verbal or can involve systematic indoctrination.

▌ Individuals cannot normally fully describe these beliefs and values; indeed they may be only partly conscious of them.

▌ Strategy is deliberate even though not fully consciously thought out and takes the form of a collective perspective.

▌ Culture and the ideology that goes with it do not encourage strategic change but rather the perpetuation of the existing strategy. An example of this is the way in which IBM's traditional mainframe culture stood in the way of early adoption of PCs.

The Environmental School

Writers of this genre regard the organization as relatively passive, reacting to changes in the environment. Mintzberg asserts that at least this school helps redress the balance by positioning environment alongside leadership and the organization as the three central forces shaping strategy.

The origins of this approach lie in contingency theory, which argues that there is no one best way to manage an organization – it all depends on the situation.

The premises of this school can be summed up as follows:

▌ The environment is the central actor in the decision-making process.

▌ The organization must adapt to the environment or perish.

▌ The role of leadership is to read the environment and help the organization adapt.

▌ Organizations end up clustered in distinct ecological-type niches, where they remain until conditions become too hostile.

Surprisingly, Mintzberg and his fellows do not cite the work of the Tavistock Institute as representing this group. The emphasis placed by Tavistock workers on the organization as an open system would seem to fit very well.

The Configuration School

This stands on its own, separate from the Prescriptive and Descriptive groups of theories.

The authors' ambitious claim for this school is that it 'offers the possibility of reconciliation, one way to integrate the messages of the other schools' (Mintzberg, Ahlstrand and Lampel, 1998). The school has two aspects to it. One, configuration, describes the state of the organization and its context. The other, transformation, describes the process of making strategy.

The premises are:

▌ At a given point in time an organization can be described in terms of some kind of stable configuration and structure that fits a particular context and gives rise to a particular strategy.

▌ From time to time a process of transformation to another configuration interrupts these stable periods.

▌ Over time these transformations may form a pattern or life cycle.

▌ The key to strategic management is to know when transformation is needed and to manage the process of transformation effectively.

▌ The various schools of thought on strategy represent various configurations. That is to say the process of making strategy can involve conceptual designing, planning, positioning, vision, learning etc, but each in its own time or context.

▌ Similarly, the resulting strategies can take the form of plans, perspectives, ploys, patterns or positions.

Mintzberg offers his own classification of configurations. These are, briefly:

▌ the entrepreneurial organization – informal, flexible, largely controlled by the entrepreneur;

▌ the machine organization – a well-oiled machine with a formal hierarchical structure involving line management, and a supporting set of staff functions;

▌ the professional organization – the professional workers dominate, with a small staff function, and line management is largely unnecessary or ineffective;

▌ the diversified organization – a set of relatively autonomous units joined together by a loose administrative structure based on a head office;

▌ the adhocracy – brought into being to accomplish a particular task, eg a film crew;

▌ the missionary organization – one with a strong culture and strongly held and widely shared beliefs, which, at the extreme, is a cult;

▌ the political organization – the opposite of the missionary, an organization riven by dissent and conflict.

Among the works that Mintzberg discusses under this heading the following are perhaps best known:

▌ Alfred Chandler's study of strategy and structure (1962). He identified four stages in the life cycles of companies. First comes the initial acquisition of resources, the setting up of marketing and distribution channels and securing control over supplies (vertical integration). Secondly comes the drive for the efficient use of these resources, usually through a functional organization structure. Thirdly, there is another period of growth involving new product lines and/or diversification. Finally, there is a second shift in structure to a divisionalized form.

▌ Miles and Snow's (1978) classification of configurations:
   – defenders – aiming at stability and defending a narrow range of products within a narrow market segment;
   – prospectors – searching for new product and market opportunities;
   – analyzers – seeking to minimize risk while seizing opportunities, a balanced approach;
   – reactors – inconsistent and unstable, simply reacting to the environment.

▌ Various studies of the process of organizational transformation:
   – Pettigrew's (1985) study of change in ICI;
   – studies of Jack Welch's transformation of GE by leadership, such as Tichy and Sherman (1993);
   – the work of Kotter (1995) on transformational leadership;
   – the work of Beer, Eisenstat and Spector (1990) on bottom-up transformation.

SUMMARY

Strategy is a complex process of determining the actions that need to be carried out in order to achieve the organization's purpose. It is focused on the medium- to long-term future rather than on current operations. The choice of actions will inevitably depend on how the organization defines its purpose or mission. Is it to maximize shareholder value? Is it defined in inclusive terms, taking into account the needs and concerns of stakeholders? Or is it defined in aspirational terms as in the case of Merck's 'Medicine is for the patients, not for profits'?

What is in practice achievable will to a considerable extent depend upon a whole range of factors, including:

▌ the organization's ability to identify, objectively, its own strengths and weaknesses, coupled with its resolve in strengthening its capabilities;

▌ the extent to which opportunities and threats are thrown up by changes in the business environment and the organization's ability to identify these and adapt to them in a timely way;

▌ the extent to which management is diverted from strategic decision making by short-term pressures;

▌ the ability to implement strategic change successfully.

It is generally accepted that there are two types of strategic decisions to be made (see Figure 1.1). One type, known as corporate strategy, is to do with the overall strategic purpose and direction of a company; the other, known as business or competitive strategy, is to do with the achievement of a sustainable competitive advantage in a specific market. In the multi-business company these are distinct processes, but in the single-business firm they merge into one.

Corporate strategy	Competitive strategy
Purpose or mission Shareholder value? Stakeholder interests? Aspirational?	Achieve sustainable competitive advantage by: Leveraging resources Developing capabilities
Means: Good parent Select portfolio Guard reputation	and Competing on cost, or differentiating, or occupying a niche

Figure 1.1   *Strategic management in a nutshell*

There is certainly no shortage of advice available to companies seeking to improve their strategic management processes. The prescriptions on offer vary, and over the past 50 years there have been waves of fashion in strategic thinking. In the early years there was a belief in the rationality and linearity of the process. The term 'long-range planning' was coined to describe an activity that involved large planning staffs and huge amounts of number-crunching and analytical activity, and culminated in the production of a substantial document – the strategic plan – which was out of date almost as soon as it was produced and which usually ended life in the bottom of a desk drawer.

Those who have set out to study what actually happens rather than to prescribe how it should be done have served us rather more effectively. They have shown how important are factors such as organizational politics and culture. Mintzberg, in particular, describes how strategy 'emerges' rather than being the result of a master plan. Others have stressed the importance of leadership and vision and the need for organizations continually to reinvent themselves. Thus, the key to strategic management is to know when transformation is needed and to have the will and the competence to manage the process of transformation effectively.

2

The environmental context

INTRODUCTION

In the context of strategy formulation the business environment is taken into account in two ways. First, the effectiveness of a strategy, as it is played out over time, will to a large extent depend on what is happening in the wider or *macro* environment of economic and social change, political developments and technological progress. These developments may offer new opportunities; equally they may constitute threats.

The second way in which the environment is taken into account is to build into the strategy the company's way of dealing with its immediate or *transactional* environment. This consists of its current and potential future competitors, its current and potential future customer base, its supply chain and its sources of capital. In this chapter, issues to do with the macro environment will be reviewed. The transactional environment will be considered in later chapters.

The business environment is inherently unstable, even turbulent. Recession follows boom and is in turn followed by the next upturn. Bear markets follow bull markets. Rates of inflation vary over time and between nations. Currencies fluctuate in value. New technologies displace whole industries. These kinds of instability are obviously important to take into account when formulating strategy and assessing risk. Yet these kinds of change are constant, in the sense that they occur without there being any *fundamental* shift in the nature of the business environment. From the strategic viewpoint, the really challenging issues are those that arise from such a fundamental change and it is clearly the case that that is what we are experiencing as we enter the 21st century and the era of the 'New Economy'.

THE IMPACT OF THE 'NEW ECONOMY'

From the viewpoint of business strategists the most important recent and current trends in the macro environment are those that tend to be lumped together under the heading of the 'New Economy'. The new economic era, by whatever name we call it, has been heralded for a long time; with the advent of the 21st century it has finally arrived. Its further development, however, has a long way to go.

There will always be a demand for a simple label by which to describe complex phenomena, but that should never be allowed to obscure the nature and depth of that complexity. The scope of the New Economy encompasses much more than dotcom companies and the Internet. It is not, in other words, the same as the 'e-economy' or the 'dotcom economy' although it embraces both these concepts. Clearly, the new information and communication technologies that have brought dotcom businesses into being are simultaneously restructuring global markets and whole industry sectors, challenging conventional economic thinking and redefining how business is done.

James D Wolfensohn, President of the World Bank, has emphasized the broad scope and impact of the New Economy (2001):

> The New Economy is shorthand for nothing less than a revolution in the way business works, economic wealth is generated, societies are organized, and individuals exist within them. Today's realities are telephone-based service centers in India serving US consumers, and new technologies underpinning extraordinary shifts in everything from food production to the health products addressing long standing tropical diseases. The knowledge and information revolution provides a historic opportunity, a new age with enormous potential in promoting competitiveness, new economic growth and jobs, better access to basic services, bigger impacts from education and health interventions and, most importantly, enhanced empowerment of local communities and stronger voices for poor people.

Table 2.1 summarizes the main differences between the 'Old Economy' and the 'New'.

Aspects of the new economic environment

The key elements of the new economic environment that impact on business strategy are:

Table 2.1 *Old Economy and New Economy comparisons*

	Old Economy	New Economy
Key industries	Oil, mining, steel, vehicles, railways, shipping	Computers and software, biotechnology, personal and financial services, entertainment
Key resources	Energy, labour	Information, knowledge and talent
Technology	Power trains, machine tools etc	Information technology
Product life cycles	Measured in decades	Measured in years or months
Trade pattern	International	Global
Working day	8 hours	24 hours
Communication media	Letter, telephone, fax	Mobile devices, e-mail, Internet and intranet
Organization structures	Centralized, hierarchical, functional	Devolved, flat, flexible
Workforce characteristics	Mainly male, semi-skilled or unskilled	No gender bias; high proportion of graduates

▌ the steadily increasing globalization of business;

▌ the invisibility and intangibility of an increasing proportion of economic activity;

▌ the impact on business of opportunities created by new technology such as mobile communications, the Internet, the intranet, satellite communications and the like.

Globalization

We are certainly a single global economy compared with thirty years ago, but we can say with equal certainty that we'll be even more globalized in 2050, and very much more in 2100. Globalization is not the product of a single action, like switching on a light or starting a car engine. It is a historical process that has undoubtedly speeded up enormously in the last ten years, but it is a permanent, constant transformation. It is not at all clear, therefore, at what stage we can say it has reached its final destination and can be considered complete.
(Hobsbawm, 2000)

Manufacturing operations will continue to shift from Western economies to those countries that offer access to cheaper labour. Equally, technology is allowing more and more knowledge-based work such as software creation and call centre operation to be shipped to the lowest-cost environments such as India. This will bring jobs to emerging economies but will also create severe pressures for companies in the advanced economies to move operations overseas or to outsource more activities to lower-cost environments.

In recent years globalization has accelerated as a result of the increasing adoption of free-trade policies and the deregulation of markets, policies vigorously pursued by the member countries of the Organization for Economic Co-operation and Development (OECD) through the World Trade Organization (WTO).

The OECD/WTO view is that open trade has been a driving force for global economic growth, whereas the existence of barriers to trade in the 1930s was a major factor bringing about world-wide depression. Many activists in the fields of human rights and environmental protection are profoundly sceptical about its benefits.

The 'death of distance'

'The "death of distance" that is intrinsic to information networking is among the most important forces shaping society at the beginning of the 21st century' (Cairncross, 1997). Teleworking across the time zones is steadily increasing.

The 'working day' has no meaning when communication via electronic mail, voice mail, and facsimile transmissions can be sent or received at any time of day or night. This development has very considerable implications for the design of organizations and the business processes in use.

Invisibility and intangibility

When it comes to achieving business success, the traditional factors of production – land, labour and capital – are rapidly becoming restraints rather than driving forces. Knowledge or intellectual capital, and talent, which generates new knowledge and new products, have become the key resources.

A knowledge economy

One measure of the importance of knowledge is the value of intellectual property. For example, in 1999 copyright became the USA's number one earner of foreign currency, outstripping clothes, chemicals, cars, computers and planes. The United States produced $414 billion worth of books, films, music, television programmes and other copyright products.

Knowledge, as a factor of production, has a number of distinguishing features when compared with land and capital:

- ▌ It cannot be used up. If one person or a single organization uses some land or some capital it is not possible for another person or organization to make use of the same resource. Yet in the case of knowledge any number of people can use the same piece of knowledge simultaneously without depleting it. And today, because of the existence of the World Wide Web, millions of people can have access to vast stocks of knowledge at nil or marginal cost.

- ▌ Knowledge as property is hard to protect. Patents cannot protect much of the valuable knowledge that companies possess. Much of it moves from one organization to another as people change jobs.

- ▌ Traditional accounting practices are not very much use when trying to quantify the impact of knowledge on wealth creation. Company balance sheets can give precise information about the value of a firm's capital assets and land valuations, but it is much more difficult to assess the value of a firm's stock of knowledge. The difference between the value of a company's assets and its market value gives some indication, but the stock market valuation also reflects other factors such as the value of brands and, notably in the case of dotcom companies, expectations of future earnings. It is not only difficult to quantify the value of the stock of intellectual capital, but it is even more difficult to measure how efficiently the intellectual capital is being used, despite the fact that it is the major investment expenditure of many 'New Economy' firms as well as their key resource.

Perhaps the first public acknowledgement of the key role of knowledge in wealth creation was the address given to the Annual General Meeting of the Anglo-Dutch company Unilever by the then chairman, Ernest Woodruffe, in 1972. Unilever, he said, had competitors with similar access to capital, which faced lower taxes and enjoyed government subsidies. What they lacked, however, was the

immense body of varied knowledge and commercial skills which Unilever has built up over the years.

In every aspect of the business knowledge is vital; and much of the knowledge which is important to a firm like Unilever cannot be found in books; it has to be acquired often expensively, sometimes painfully, by experience and deliberate enquiry.

Knowledge is not cheap. Around the world we spend many millions in acquiring it. But without this expenditure we could not survive against competition.

The economies of using knowledge over and over again, everywhere adapting it to local needs, are very great. Knowledge has no marginal cost. It costs no more to use it in the 70 countries in which we operate than in one. It is the principle which makes Unilever economically viable. The knowledge Unilever has is both extensive and complex. It is the source of your profits and of the main benefits Unilever brings to the peoples of the countries in which it operates.

Knowledge management is, therefore, an important strategic capability. Much of the literature that deals with this focuses on the role of information technology; but the implications for the management of people are equally important – particularly the treatment of the increasingly valuable and valued knowledge professionals. This brings into focus another important issue – the management of talent.

The role of talent in the 'New Economy'

Sooner or later all knowledge is obsolete – and today it is likely to be sooner rather than later. Talent is the only remaining scarce resource and as such the true source of competitive advantage. The nature of the typical 'New Economy' enterprise, therefore, is better described as 'talent-intensive' rather than 'knowledge-intensive' (Sadler, 1993).

The economic value of talent is illustrated dramatically by the fact (according to *Fortune* magazine) that, in 2000, the US basketball player Michael Jordan's personal economic value derived from copyrights and merchandising exceeded the gross national product of the kingdom of Jordan. Much of the talent that creates the wealth of the 'New Economy', as in Jordan's case, is not easily encapsulated by the term 'intellectual capital'. The 'knowledge-intensive industries' such as software writing, pharmaceuticals, computers and aerospace are obviously key industries in the 'New Economy'. At the same time, very rapid growth is taking place in such fields as music, the arts, sport, fashion and aesthetic design.

The term 'talent' embraces the kind of outstanding intellectual skills involved in designing a space probe or a new micro-miniature electronic circuit. It also embraces the kinds of abilities or aptitudes possessed by outstanding sports players, actors, musicians, writers, television presenters, chat-show hosts, architects and artists.

Peter Drucker (1992) has remarked that knowledge, like electricity, is a form of energy that exists only when it is being used. The same is true of talent. It follows that economic success will accrue increasingly to those companies that are most capable in identifying, educating, developing and exploiting the talents of their people. This is the true meaning of strategic human resource management.

The impact of new technology

New technology in the field of telecommunications is creating a whole new set of threats and opportunities for business organizations. In particular the watershed years bridging the 20th and the 21st centuries have seen explosive growth in a range of uses of the Internet and intranet – as an advertising medium, as a marketing tool that makes possible a greater degree of interaction between supplier and customer, as a means of communication with stakeholders and the public at large, and as a medium for learning and the integration of widely dispersed organizations.

It has resulted in large numbers of quick-off-the-mark new entrants into markets eating into the market shares of established businesses. Successful organizations now come in all shapes and sizes. A new source of competition could be a multinational corporation with huge financial resources; it could, however, be an enthusiastic young entrepreneur with an idea and a computer, who intuitively understands that it is now perfectly possible to become a one-person global enterprise. There is, in short, hardly a company in existence that is not vulnerable to the Internet's potential to diminish the significance of, for example, size, location, time, distance and physical resources.

In *The Death of Distance*, Frances Cairncross (1997) describes how, by using technology creatively, small companies can now offer services that, in the past, only large corporations could provide. The cost of starting new businesses is declining, and so more and more small companies will spring up. Many existing companies will develop into networks of independent specialists; more people will therefore work in smaller units or alone.

Moreover, the technology is moving so fast that it's all too easy to be either too early or too late. In such a world, the timing of an investment or a product launch is critical and it is how companies deal with this factor that determines who falls by the wayside and who moves through to the next round. The aim is to be ahead of one's competitors, however briefly.

As an example of the speed of change in the technology, in September 2001 Motorola unveiled a microchip that is 40 times faster than existing technology. This will enable applications such as streaming video to mobile phones. Motorola's chief technology officer claimed that the discovery had the potential to change the telecommunications and computer industries as radically as the invention of the first chips in 1958.

The old economy is not dead

To keep matters in perspective, these observations do not suggest that the economic order is being completely overturned – the 'New Economy' is an 'add-on' to the traditional economy; it does not take its place, just as the industrialized society was an add-on to the agricultural society that preceded it. The mature industries of the 'Old Economy' will continue to operate albeit in largely changed locations. The fact is that around the world the automotive industry remains the largest in terms of revenues and employment. There are more cars and aircraft being constructed than ever, more roads being built, more steel being made. The difference is that in the OECD countries these traditional industrial activities comprise an ever-shrinking share of gross domestic product (GDP) relative to the newer industries providing communication, information, entertainment and professional and personal services.

Also, these industries are mature. They are characterized by slow growth and low margins. Companies seeking faster growth and higher margins will need to look increasingly at the newer industries.

THE NEW AGENDA – SUSTAINABLE DEVELOPMENT AND CORPORATE SOCIAL RESPONSIBILITY

The future of humankind on this planet depends on the sustainability of a complex system involving three interdependent, highly fragile subsystems – the natural environment, the social/political system and the global economy. It is axiomatic that a catastrophic event in any one of these would result in severe consequences for the others. Catastrophic failure could arise, either regionally or globally, as a result of a massive environmental disaster, a major – even nuclear – war, the breakdown of law and order and social cohesion in a region such as the European Union or the meltdown of the world's financial markets.

The environmental challenge

In the final third of the 20th century public concern about the activities of business and the sustainability of contemporary patterns of economic growth centred initially on their environmental impact. Rachel Carson's *Silent Spring* (1962) sparked the 'environmental revolution'. She drew public attention to the massive destruction of wildlife caused by the use of chemical insecticides and other biocides. Organizations such as Friends of the Earth and Greenpeace were founded; support for such bodies as the World Wildlife Fund grew rapidly.

Enthusiasm for environmental conservation waxed and waned over the next 30 or so years. The first wave saw the publication of the report of the Club of Rome, *Limits to Growth* (1972), and fizzled out with the OPEC action to raise the price of oil in 1973. The ensuing world recession saw the environment relegated to the bottom of the agenda. In the following years, however, concerns were reactivated by the Union Carbide disaster in Bhopal, India, the discovery of the hole in the ozone layer in the Antarctic, Chernobyl and the pollution of the Rhine. In 1987 another influential publication helped trigger a new wave of concern. This was *Our Common Future* produced by the World Commission on Environment and Development, under the leadership of Gro Harlem Brundtland, Prime Minister of Norway. This report brought the concept of sustainable development to the attention of a world-wide audience.

A second wave of activity, from 1987 to 1990, was signalled by the adoption of policies for environmental protection by world politicians, by the emergence of a 'green' consumer movement and by public outrage at the Exxon Valdez disaster. Once again, however, economic recession pushed such matters into the background. Despite the publicity accorded the UN summit in Rio in 1992, little progress was made. The major focus of attention by activists during this period was Shell and its actions in Nigeria as well as the controversy over the Brent Spar oilrig.

The 'triple bottom line'

At the time of the Johannesburg Summit, 2002, a third wave of concern and activity is now evidently gaining strength. It is marked by a more balanced approach to sustainable development in that the *social* and *economic* dimensions of sustainability are being given equal weight alongside the environmental. An important new development is the extent to which cooperation is gradually beginning to replace conflict and hostility in the relationship between large companies and NGOs and pressure groups. Sustainable development and corporate social responsibility are now part of the board agenda in an increasing number of the world's most powerful and influential companies.

Simon Zadek (2001) sees the recent renaissance of interest in corporate social responsibility as an outcrop of the 'New Economy':

> Success in the 'New Economy' is as much about a corporation's ability to build a sense of shared values with key stakeholders as it is about the technical quality of products and services. Corporations that achieve this will extract the maximum premium for their branded, lifestyle products, get the best employees on terms that secure their committed labour to the business, and most effectively offset criticism from increasingly globalized networks of non-governmental organizations.

Why attitudes are changing

The reasons for changing attitudes to sustainable development and corporate social responsibility are to be found in a number of trends.

Increasing affluence

Firstly, the increasing affluence of Western society has generated a fundamental shift in consumers' values, away from traditional ones that support the struggle for survival in conditions of scarcity and in favour of ones that relate more to the quality of life than to material factors. A community living in conditions of poverty, with high unemployment, will welcome the setting up of a new manufacturing plant in their vicinity because they value the material prosperity and employment it will bring. They are not too concerned about the polluting smoke that comes from its chimneys, the noise from its forges or the fact that its processes are dangerous and toxic. A prosperous community, however, will oppose any development that threatens the purity of the air they breathe or the pleasant views as they take their evening strolls.

The power of global business

The second major influence is the very success achieved by many business organizations, which has made them both large and extremely powerful. Of the 100 largest economies in the world, 50 are corporations. General Motors' sales are approximately equivalent to the GDP of Denmark, and the largest 200 companies' combined sales make up approximately a quarter of the world's total economic activity. Through mergers and acquisitions their size continues to grow. Vodafone has merged with Mannesheim, SmithKline Beecham with GlaxoWellcome, AOL with Time Warner and Hewlett Packard with Compaq.

Recent riots against 'global capitalism' are an example of the growing concern about the way this immense power is wielded. In the writings of John Le Carré (2001) the international pharmaceutical industry has taken the place of Soviet bloc espionage as public enemy number one.

Critics such as David Korten (1996), Naomi Klein (2000) and Noreena Hertz (2001) point out that some of the 'anti-competitive practices' that are being removed by the World Trade Organization were put in place with the aims of protecting people's jobs and ways of life and protecting the natural environment. They argue for 'fair' trade as well as free trade. They see international competition as a major barrier to the implementation of effective measures to alleviate the world's economic, environmental or social problems, be they in advanced, developing or non-industrialized countries. Global deregulated capital flows and multinational corporations are relatively unrestricted by national boundaries. The corporations, they argue, by their ability or threat to move their investments elsewhere, force nations to compete with one another for capital, jobs (and therefore votes) and ever-scarcer natural resources.

It is pointed out that no nation is seeking unilaterally to re-regulate financial markets because such action would cause capital flight, devaluation and inflation if not outright economic collapse. Similarly, policies that address environmental or social problems requiring higher public spending or higher costs for industry are opposed on the grounds of loss of competitiveness, adverse market reaction or the threat of job losses. Global competition is also the reason why international agreements on reducing global warming emissions or other such targets are unlikely to prove successful for, to be successful, they would require far-reaching structural changes to industry across the world, changes which cannot be contemplated under present market conditions.

Furthermore, the WTO, being the one institution with supranational authority in economic matters, has the remit of preserving the free movement of capital and corporations: the very forces that serve to restrict the power of nation states. In deregulating capital markets, nations have therefore unleashed a force they can no longer unilaterally control.

Globalization, it is asserted, has given birth to the 'stateless corporation'; people and assets move and transactions take place regardless of national borders. There is little regulation and tax avoidance is rife. Governments' attitudes are influenced by the imperative need to attract inward investment and to be competitive in their export markets. National fiscal and monetary policies are subject to outside influences and pressures. Globalization of trade and finance is moving ahead much faster than any form of intergovernmental regulation and governance.

The very large corporations are *de facto* wielding political as well as economic power. Increasingly the legitimacy of this situation is being challenged and companies are realizing that to maintain a 'licence to operate' they have to do much more than simply stay within the law. The scandals associated with Enron and Andersen have contributed to the general mistrust of big business and have added weight to the arguments of those most critical of the free-market system.

Many groups and organizations are seeking to challenge the international economic system and to modify its impact on developing countries, using a range of strategies. The demonstrations in recent years against the WTO in Seattle, Prague, London and Genoa by organizations including the International Forum on Globalization brought this subject to the attention of the general public and placed it firmly on the international agenda. The United Nations agenda for the 21st century (Agenda 21) has also given rise to a great deal of thinking and local action on environmental issues, as has the publicity surrounding the Johannesburg Summit in August 2002 and its widely perceived failure.

Ambivalent attitudes to new technology

A third problem arises from the close link between business growth and technological developments. While people understand the role of technology in human progress they are also mistrustful of it. Already there is an international boycott on genetically modified foods and growing concern about the health issues associated with nuclear power and the intense use by young people of mobile telecommunications equipment.

At the same time the development of the Internet has made possible the rapid sharing of information about what companies are doing, for good or ill.

Increasing litigation

Particularly in the United States, but also elsewhere, individuals and communities are resorting to litigation in response to what are seen as damaging actions on the part of corporations. The awards made by the courts are reaching sums sufficient to threaten the financial stability of even major companies.

After several false starts, it is clear that the goal of sustainable development and the acting out of corporate social responsibility are now firmly included among the strategic issues facing companies. The terms are now embedded in the languages of politics and business and the issues are here to stay.

COMPANY STATEMENTS ON SUSTAINABILITY AND CORPORATE SOCIAL RESPONSIBILITY

BP

We welcome the opportunity which sustainable development offers to align industrial and social agendas better. We need to be part of the solution to the complex questions associated with future global energy supplies. We have no wish to be seen as the problem or even as part of the problem. We wish to be engaged on major public policy issues such as climate change, environmental protection and human rights.

Interface

What is sustainability? It's more than environmentalism. It's about living and working in ways that don't jeopardize the future of our social, economic and natural resources. In business, sustainability means managing human and natural capital with the same vigour we apply to the management of financial capital. It means widening the scope of our awareness so we can understand fully the 'true cost' of every choice we make.

Norsk Hydro

Hydro will be in the forefront in environmental care and industrial safety. The challenge we face is to find the proper balance between caring for the environment and serving human needs. Hydro's mission is to take care of the environment and the wellbeing of future generations. This will be the basis of our company policy and decision making. Hydro will demonstrate openness in environmental policy. We will develop and publicize information on all significant environmental aspects of our activities.

Novo Nordisk

Sustainable development continues to be a complex challenge – notwithstanding the difficulties there can be in defining the term and the means by which we can measure progress towards it. For how exactly can we define the 'carrying capacity of the earth', and ensure that we are not 'compromising the ability of future generations to meet their needs'?

The Turnbull recommendations

One consequence of the changes in public attitudes discussed above, together with the reaction to several corporate scandals such as Enron and Worldcom, is that company law is under review on both sides of the Atlantic.

UK companies are to have to take social, environmental and ethical matters into account when they assess business risks and report on them more fully in annual reports, following new guidance from the Turnbull committee.

In the UK, the Institute of Chartered Accountants in England and Wales set up a committee, chaired by Nigel Turnbull, and asked it to come up with ways of implementing the Stock Exchange's Combined Code of the Committee on Corporate Governance, which was published in June 1999. The committee is seen as the last piece in a jigsaw of corporate governance codes and recommendations drawn up by committees chaired by Sir Adrian Cadbury, Sir Ronald Hampel and Sir Richard Greenbury.

The committee's report on internal control proposed that company board members should formally consider all relevant risks, not just the narrow financial ones, that face their organizations, and that audit committees should be asked to carry out a 'wider review of internal control' that includes 'reputational and business probity issues' and matters such as 'safety and environmental issues'.

These recommendations represent a compromise position between the two extremes of full corporate disclosure of risks on the one hand, and, on the other, merely printing a few vague lines in an annual report.

The Turnbull committee's final report was endorsed by the Stock Exchange, which has written to company secretaries and finance directors of all UK listed companies telling them they will have to implement the Turnbull committee's recommendations.

TWO KINDS OF PRESSURE

Business leaders are under pressure from two quite different sources. On the one hand there are the competitive pressures of the marketplace, coupled with pressures from shareholders and their representatives. On the other hand there are the pressures from governments, intergovernmental bodies, NGOs and other pressure groups calling for greater corporate social responsibility.

It is evident that, for most businesses, the competitive environment in which they operate has become tougher in the last decade or so as the New Economy has developed. There are several reasons for this. The deregulation of international trade coupled with increasing numbers of global corporations has meant that companies' home markets, which were once relatively protected, are now opened up to new sources of competition. Whereas 10 years ago Tesco could concentrate on competing with Sainsbury for market leadership in the UK supermarket business, today it faces competition from Wal-Mart.

Technological change has broken down many of the traditional demarcations between industries, so that banks find themselves competing with organizations as diverse as Marks and Spencer or General Motors in the field of credit finance. The Internet has provided new channels of distribution and entrepreneurs have in many cases been quicker off the mark than established businesses to exploit these. The rise of Amazon.com is an obvious example.

The emphasis on shareholder value and on short-term gains in share prices in the financial markets has added greatly to these pressures.

Whereas in the past fund managers and analysts were content to leave it to managers to decide where to invest surplus capital, the prevailing view is that the market knows best and the expectation is that managers should focus on the core business and return any surplus cash to shareholders. This has the effect of increasing the pressure on managers as it makes the short-term performance of the business much more apparent.

At the same time companies are being subjected to pressures of a quite different kind. These are ones that result from changing social values and consequential changes in expectations on the part of society. The most public expressions of these pressures have taken the form of mass demonstrations in several cities throughout the world. The violence accompanying these has been rightly condemned, but there is growing acceptance that the issues raised by the great majority of peaceful protestors are important and worthy of serious consideration.

Books such as Naomi Klein's *No Logo* (2000) and Noreena Hertz's *The Silent Take-over* (2001) have become international best-sellers, exerting a powerful influence on people's attitudes to business.

Western free-market capitalism is evidently under attack. If it is to survive it is vitally important that business organizations, including the financial institutions, should come to terms with these pressures for the adoption of a wider set of goals beyond shareholder value and that they should produce a balanced response to the expectations of the various groups of stakeholders and the public.

An important consideration is that a financially sound, prosperous and growing business is better able to afford to respond to these pressures than one that is struggling to survive. In this important sense, therefore, it can be argued that a company's first responsibility to society is to be financially viable, to use the resources, material and human, that it takes from society so as to create wealth, rather than destroy it. Nor should it be overlooked that the goods and services supplied by a company, together with the employment it creates, constitute its major contribution to society as well as being the source of its profits. Given, however, that society increasingly expects much more from the business enterprise than shareholder value, value for customers, jobs, and fair dealing with suppliers, the practical problem for managers is how to meet these additional demands and yet remain competitive in a world of intensifying competition.

Faced with such an array of demands the harassed company director might ask 'What business are we in? Are we here to make a profit and thereby create value for our shareholders or are we now part of the social services?' He or she might point out that were the business to attempt to meet all these expectations fully the consequence might well be to go out of business. Nevertheless the fact remains that these issues are more and more becoming subject to legal sanctions with the result that there is no option but to meet them. The regulations on such matters as health and safety of consumers and employees, waste disposal, discrimination on ethnic or gender grounds, the selling of insurance policies and other financial instruments are growing all the time. During the period of the first New Labour administration in the UK (1997–2001) additional regulations affecting business included the adoption of European Union directives on working time, data protection and pollution, minimum wage legislation, the introduction of stakeholder pensions, the Disability Discrimination Act, the Part-time Workers Directive and others. The arguments for self-regulation are strongly made by business spokespersons, but in the absence of a really effective and concerted response in favour of effective self-regulation by the great majority of companies the trend to increased legislation will continue.

Even in cases where there is the will to translate the fine words about social responsibility into action there are some formidable practical difficulties. Until relatively recently the task of management was less complex. The clear aim was to make a profit; this was achieved by the exercise of commercial judgement, organizing ability and people management skills. In making decisions the manager had to observe a few simple rules of the game. Today it is not just that the rules of the game have become much more complex: it is a whole new game demanding different skills, particularly leadership skills, and such a range of issues to be taken into consideration that, increasingly, the 'stoppages' take up more time and energy than the 'play'. The decision maker is faced with a whole series of regulations and a wide range of representations from consumer groups, pressure groups to do with the environment, media attention, government agencies etc. The decision-making process involves genuine dilemmas where it is far from clear where the best course of action lies. This was famously so in the case of Shell and the problem of the disposal of the Brent Spar oil platform.

The key role of leadership

Meeting the changing expectations of society will call for radical changes in attitudes and behaviour on the part of boards of directors of businesses large and small and the investment community. Companies will need to win the cooperation of all their stakeholders in this process.

A MORI poll conducted in 1998 put the statement 'Industry and commerce do not pay enough attention to their social responsibilities' to a range of respondents. Fewer than 40 per cent of 'captains of industry' agreed with this statement compared with nearly 70 per cent of the general public. The degree of complacency shown by business leaders may have diminished since 1998, but clearly there is a huge perception gap to be closed.

Business leaders like Lord Browne of BP who are genuinely trying to resolve the real dilemmas involved in working towards sustainability sometimes feel aggrieved at being personally attacked by activists and feel that their attackers fail to make any distinction between those business leaders who are really concerned about these important issues and those who are not. There is some justification for these feelings.

ANTICIPATING ENVIRONMENTAL CHANGE

Scenario planning

Scenario planning is a recognized technique for dealing with an uncertain and rapidly changing environment and was pioneered by Shell. It is of most value to companies with long lead times for investment and which need to consider how robust their investment strategies will be under a range of future environmental conditions.

Each 'scenario' is an internally consistent picture of a possible future. It is usual to cover a range of situations in terms of favourability – an optimistic scenario, a pessimistic one and one in between. Probabilities of occurrence can be assigned to each of these. The usefulness of the technique is limited in three main ways. First, the number of possible futures is very large and it is only possible to consider a very small proportion of them. Secondly, it is often the most significant events that are least likely to be built into scenarios simply because they are unpredicted. The sudden collapse of the Soviet bloc is one such example. Thirdly, the value of a scenario is a function of the variables that are included within it and it is not always the case that all the future relevant variables are identified.

Contingency planning

Scenarios that give rise to possible damaging combinations of events will call for plans to be made to cope with these events should they occur. For example, a scenario giving a high degree of probability of a particular country descending into political anarchy would necessitate the creation of a contingency plan for closing the business and evacuating all expatriate employees from that territory. Most large businesses now have 'disaster' contingency plans to deal with the impact of terrorist activity.

SUMMARY

As with any other massive wave of socio-economic change, the 'New Economy' will bring problems as well as benefits. In the words of James D Wolfensohn, the President of the World Bank, (2001):

The New Economy has the potential to unleash extraordinary development benefits and real social and environmental gains, but to achieve such gains requires participation and intervention at the local, national and global level. The New Economy will most effectively deliver a positive balance of benefits and costs if we ensure that societies are fully able to take advantage of the arising opportunities by encouraging socially and environmentally responsible business conduct. This can often best be achieved through partnerships that bring together, and create synergies in, the competencies of civil society and labor organizations, businesses, governments and international bodies.

The economic structure of the developed nations now straddles three stages of economic growth—agricultural, industrial and post-industrial. In terms of share of employment and gross domestic product, the post-industrial sector, comprising mainly services of various kinds, is by far the largest. There is a partial correlation, but not a perfect one, between this classification and the distinction between the so-called 'Old Economy' and 'New Economy' in that a great deal of manufacturing and agriculture is 'Old Economy' and much of the services sector is 'New Economy'. Increasingly, however, these distinctions become blurred as new technologies, from satellite communications and computer simulation to genetic engineering, are brought to bear in traditional industries. The conclusion is that every business, no matter in what industry sector it may be, will increasingly need to come to terms with the new technologies and learn how to manage knowledge and talent and deploy other 'New Economy' capabilities.

At the same time those responsible for strategy formulation cannot escape the requirement to build social and environmental outcomes as well as economic ones into their companies' explicit goals. The twin pressures of growing governmental regulation and public demonstration are unlikely to diminish in the foreseeable future. This means, in effect, that strategy formulation today is a radically different process calling for quite different types of analysis than those that have become part of the conventional wisdom or the strategy consultants' toolkit. The number of companies struggling to develop a coherent and pragmatic policy for corporate social responsibility bears witness to this.

Corporate strategy

INTRODUCTION

Part 2 will be concerned with the formulation and implementation of strategy in the multi-business company at the level of the head office – in other words with *corporate* strategy rather than *business* or *competitive* strategy. In practice, of course, multi-business companies vary greatly in size and complexity. At one extreme can be found giant global enterprises like General Motors, while on a much smaller scale the regional construction firm with two divisions, one building speculative housing and one working on contracts to local authorities and similar clients, is also a multi-business organization. In principle, the same issues apply. It is the role of the head office or parent company to determine the overall purpose or mission of the organization and its strategic goals. It is the task of the subsidiary to build and maintain a competitive advantage in the market in which it operates such that it can achieve a superior return on invested capital.

The issues to be covered in this part are:

▌ defining the corporation's mission and purpose;

▌ the role of the parent company:
  - adding value;
  - strategies and styles;
  - sustaining competitiveness;
  - structure and culture;
  - reputation and brand identity;

▌ building the portfolio:
  - industry analysis;
  - diversification;
  - vertical integration;

▌ strategic options:
  - acquisitions or organic growth;
  - outsourcing;
  - strategic alliances;
  - partnership sourcing;

▌ functional strategies:
  - manufacturing;
  - marketing;
  - human resources.

3

Clarification of purpose or mission – the starting point for strategic management

INTRODUCTION

Fundamental to the process of giving coherence and direction to the actions and decisions of an organization is the defining of the organization's purpose. Looking at how companies define their purposes (or neglect to do so), they fall into four groups:

■ companies that focus exclusively on the creation of shareholder value;

■ companies that define purpose in terms of meeting the needs and expectations of all stakeholders – employees, customers, suppliers and the community as well as investors;

■ companies that define purpose in terms of aspirations or values;

■ companies that simply carry out their activities without attempting to offer a formal definition of purpose (many, if not most, small enterprises and family businesses fall into this category).

SHAREHOLDER VALUE

For many business organizations the definition of purpose is starkly simple – it is the maximization of shareholder value. Alan Kennedy's book *The End of Shareholder Value* (2000) chronicles the rise of the idea that this is the purpose of business. According to Kennedy, shareholder value had its origins in the observations of a number of academic accountants who saw that they could better predict stock market price levels by discounting future cash-flow streams rather than looking at traditional measures of performance such as earnings per share. US investment bankers took up this idea in the late 1970s and early 1980s. The insights given by the new methodology were used to buy companies whose stocks appeared to be undervalued. These companies, once acquired, were then 'restructured' to release hidden reserves of value before being sold on to new owners. This created a need for a defence against corporate raiding of this kind and boards began to pay closer attention to shareholder value. Companies began to realign executive compensation to place more emphasis on stock options. Driven by these incentives, directors of companies set about restructuring their companies to cut out underperforming divisions, cutting costs, closing older plants, moving production to emerging economies and outsourcing much non-core activity. The results were seen in significant increases in company performance and a related surge in stock market prices.

In Kennedy's view, things then started to go wrong. The means to an end became an end in itself. By the end of the 1990s shareholder value was becoming counterproductive. Directors saw that they could become seriously rich just by pushing their company's stock to new heights. The result was extreme short-termism. The interests of stakeholders other than investors were increasingly disregarded. Long-serving employees were laid off or forced into early retirement, suppliers were squeezed until they went out of business, and customers' needs were neglected. Now, he argues, stakeholders are forming into pressure groups such as consumer associations and associations of pension funds and beginning to fight back. Thus the title of his book, which implies that the era of obsessive concern with shareholder value is now coming to an end. The evidence he produces in support of this argument is somewhat weak and most experts would feel that the obituary notice is premature.

Kennedy charts the growth of the obsession with shareholder value in the USA, starting with GE under Jack Welch. He concludes that the companies that have followed Welch's example have mortgaged their futures in return for a higher stock market price in the present.

The most compelling argument for putting shareholders' interests first is that they are the business's owners, and as such are free to do with it as they wish provided they stay within the law. At one time this may have been so, but today, in the case of the vast majority of firms of significant size, the 'owners', both individuals and institutions, are better described as 'investors'. They are free to move their capital to where it will achieve the greatest short-term gain. By no stretch of imagination do they see themselves as owners.

The stock market is mostly a secondary market. If A buys B's shares none of the money goes to the company. Businesses get most of their new money from retained earnings or bank loans. There is no sense of ownership in the secondary market. If dissatisfied, shareholders leave rather than try to change things. Yet these secondary shareholders have the right to sell the business over the heads of its workers.

Philip Goldenberg (1997) states the legal position as follows: 'Directors' duties are owed to their company, not to any third party group.' In discharging their duty to the company they must have regard to the interests of shareholders (if the company is solvent – if it is insolvent, then creditors take the place of shareholders for this purpose):

> This obligation to have regard to the interests of shareholders is not related to the actual shareholders at any given moment in time, but to the general body of shareholders from time to time (one may alterna- tively, as I have said earlier, express this as that it is to the actual body of shareholders but in their capacity as continuing shareholders). Accordingly, the duty of directors is to maximise the company's value on a sustainable basis. There is nothing in law to prevent directors from having regard to the interests of third parties with whom the company has a relationship (sometimes called stakeholders) – employees, customers, suppliers, financiers and the community generally – if they judge, reasonably and in good faith that to do so is conducive to the success of the company. Indeed, for directors not to give appropriate weight to all their company's key relationships may well inhibit them in the proper discharge of their duty.

Argenti (1996) argues that a company can only operate successfully if it has one clear overriding purpose, ie creating shareholder value. However, he falls into a trap of his own making when he states: 'Companies are there for the shareholders, just as a school is for the children, a hospital for its patients, a trade union for its members and the AA for its motorists.'

What if the school and the hospital are in the private sector? Does a hospital in the NHS exist for its patients, while one in the private sector exists solely for its shareholders? If Argenti, having suffered a heart attack, found himself being carried into a hospital with a banner above the door stating 'Our sole concern is to create value for our shareholders' his heart condition might take a turn for the worst. And now that Centrica owns the AA does it suddenly no longer exist for the benefit of motorists? This is not the message contained in its promotional literature.

THE STAKEHOLDER APPROACH

An early instance of a business leader applying the stakeholder approach to the definition of company purpose is a speech given in 1951 by Frank Abrams, then Chairman of Standard Oil of New Jersey, in which he said 'The job of management is to maintain an equitable and working balance among the claims of the variously directly interested groups – stockholders, employees, customers and the public at large.'

In the 1960s the Stanford Research Institute in the United States and the Swedish management theorist Eric Rhenman fostered the approach. Enthusiasm for it grew as business leaders saw that the success of the Japanese management system owed much to stakeholder ideas.

One of the strongest critics of the stakeholder approach is Sternberg (1999). She argues that 'Stakeholder theory is the doctrine that businesses should be run not for the benefit of their owners, but for the benefit of all their stakeholders.' Some advocates may make such an assertion, but there is no generally accepted body of theory in which it can be found, still less is there anything that would justify the term 'doctrine'. The stakeholder approach argues rather that companies should be run to create wealth in ways that are sustainable and that to do this means, *inter alia*, taking into account all the relationships of mutual dependence that are involved in its activities.

John Plender (1997) points out that in the stakeholder or inclusive model of corporate governance managers are seen as trustees of the wealth inherited from the past, with an obligation to preserve and enhance that wealth in the long-term interest of the company, so as to ensure its sustainability. He points out that one result of the so-called shareholder value model of business strategy is the tendency to maintain or improve dividend levels almost regardless of the company's performance with the result that income on equity shares has become increasingly fixed rather than residual. Thus investors are having it both ways – the benefit of a low-risk fixed return as well as enjoying the lion's share of profit growth. Plender points out that this results in more pressure during economic downturns to cut spending on such things as research and development, investment and training and is a major factor in the popularity of downsizing.

Who the stakeholders are depends on the nature and purpose of the organization. Most companies have four 'active' or transactional stakeholders because they operate in the three market-places (for capital, labour and goods and services) and enjoy services supplied by the local community. But many privately owned companies have no investor stakeholders; and regulated companies might regard the regulator as a stakeholder. Some companies, particularly those that have embraced ideas of corporate social responsibility (CSR), employ wider definitions of stakeholders. For example, the Co-operative Bank includes past and future generations.

There is some evidence to the fact that the stakeholder approach is related to above-average business performance.

Research by Waddock and Graves (1997) looks at the link between stakeholder relations, quality of management and financial performance. Their analysis of the *Fortune* 500 Reputation Survey results shows that building positive stakeholder relationships is associated with other positive corporate characteristics. Solid financial performance goes along with good treatment of stakeholders, such as employees, customers and communities. They also found that companies that treat their stakeholders well are also rated by their peers as having superior management.

Professors Kotter and Heskett (1992) of the Harvard Business School carried out another research project that relates the stakeholder approach to sustained business performance. They studied 207 firms drawn from 22 different industries. Using a simple questionnaire they constructed a 'Culture Strength Index' for each company. The questionnaire, which was addressed to top management, invited them to rate the firms in their own industry on the degree to which they believed that their managers had been influenced by having a strong corporate culture – for example, to what extent did they speak of their company's distinctive style or way of doing things, to what extent were the values explicit and to what extent had the firms been managed according to long-standing policies and practices, not just those of the current CEO?

They then calculated measures of economic performance for these companies, using three methods:

▌ average yearly increase in net income;

▌ average yearly return on investment;

▌ average yearly increase in share price.

There was a slight tendency for firms with strong cultures to have outperformed those with weak cultures over the previous decade.

Twenty-two companies from 10 different industries were then selected for further study. All had strong cultures. They included such firms as Hewlett Packard, American Airlines, Wal-Mart, Pepsi Co, Xerox, Texaco and Citicorp. Comparing them on an industry basis, industry experts were invited to rate all 22 companies on how much value they placed on leadership and on stakeholder relations, ie relationships with customers, employees and shareholders. Twelve were classified as placing strong emphasis on relations with stakeholders, while 10 were judged as paying little attention to stakeholder relations.

Finally, the researchers compared the performance of the 12 companies that placed strong emphasis on stakeholder relations with the performance of the group of companies, 10 in number, that did not.

The top 12 increased their net incomes three times more than the 10 poor performers; their share price rose between 400 and 500 per cent between 1977 and 1988, compared with 100 per cent for the 10. The 12 achieved a return on invested capital of 11.3 per cent compared with 7.73 per cent for the 10.

UK company law

The UK's Company Law Steering Group issued a consultative document, *Modern Company Law for a Competitive Economy*, in February 1999. In this, two options were set out – the Enlightened Shareholder Value option and the Pluralist alternative. Under the Pluralist scheme the rights of the various stakeholders would in some way become legally enforceable. Under the Enlightened Shareholder Value approach much more discretion would be left to boards to decide how to fulfil their obligations.

The Centre for Tomorrow's Company, in giving evidence to the steering group, argued for this latter approach. The following points were made:

I The law should be clarified so that directors were clear that their duty was to the company.

I Directors should continue to be legally accountable to shareholders for the performance of that duty.

I The law should be clarified so that directors were left in no doubt that not only were they permitted to have regard to the interests of other key stakeholders, but that they were very unlikely to be able to do their duty by the company unless they showed such regard.

▮ While boards thereby retained the freedom to exercise their wider accountability to stakeholders in their own way, the framework governing measurement and reporting of their performance should be strengthened to reinforce the 'culture of challenge'.

▮ Companies seeking to take over other companies should be required to make clear the likely social, ethical and environmental impacts, and the board of the target company should be permitted to take account of these consequences in deciding whether to recommend such a bid.

▮ The legal and regulatory framework should encourage companies to set out their purpose and vision, their values, their success model and their key relationships.

ASPIRATIONAL PURPOSE

According to Andrew Campbell of the Ashridge Strategic Management Centre, purpose is something independent of both shareholder value thinking and stakeholder thinking. It should come first. Once a purpose has been chosen, it then has implications for each stakeholder. If there are shareholders, their returns will be affected by the purpose chosen.

The point is often made that if a company declares the creation of shareholder value as its purpose then this is hardly likely to be inspiring and motivational for the shop floor or graduate entrants. But even a statement of purpose that is about meeting the needs of all the stakeholders is unlikely to call forth exceptional commitment and effort. For this to happen the purpose needs to be inspiring or challenging, seen as worth while, as serving society in some higher way than the material interests of the stakeholders. It also needs to be capable of being clearly articulated in very few words and sufficiently tangible and quantifiable that the extent of its achievement is capable of verification by measurement.

I want to discuss why a company exists in the first place... I think many people assume, wrongly, that a company exists simply to make money. While this is an important result of a company's existence, we have to go deeper and find the real reasons for our being... We inevitably come to the conclusion that a group of people get together and exist as an institution that we call a company so that they are able to accomplish

something collectively that they could not accomplish separately – they make a contribution to society.
(Dave Packard, Hewlett Packard)

Hamel and Prahalad (1994) put the case for what they term 'strategic intent'– the 'enticing spectacle of a new destination or at least new routes to existing destinations'. Strategic intent should identify a goal that is capable of energizing and commanding the allegiance of the entire workforce. Examples include Apple's quest to create the first really user-friendly computer and British Airways' intent to become the 'World's favourite airline'.

In 1983, Colin Marshall became chief executive of British Airways, at a time when it was loss-making, unloved by the travelling public and suffering from low staff morale. He set this as the objective and, given the state of the company's reputation at the time, this was indeed a 'new destination'. The objective was brief, clear, capable of measurement and made no reference to shareholders or profits. The equally brief but powerful value statement 'Putting people first' supported it. The goal was both tangible and verifiable in that there are various annual surveys that indicate the popularity of the world's major airlines. The result was one of the most remarkable turnarounds, in both profitability and reputation, in the history of UK industry.

By the autumn of 1985, BA was able to tell its staff that it had been named airline of the year for the second year running by the magazine *Executive Travel*. At the time, Marshall said: 'A corporate mission is much more than good intentions and fine ideas. It represents the framework for the entire business, the values that drive the company and the belief that the company has in itself and what it can achieve.'

Some companies remain true to the ideas about purpose and values first set out by a visionary leader from the past – usually the company's founder. One such example is Ove Arup. The company that bears his name states its objectives as follows: 'Our objective is to help our clients meet their business needs by adding value through technical excellence, efficient organisation and personal service. The breadth and depth of our technical skills are applied to projects throughout the world, large and small, simple and complex. We seek to continuously improve our products and services and, by these measures, we add value to our clients' projects and achieve quality that they can rely upon.'

The US pharmaceutical company Merck provides another example. George C Merck, son of the company's founder, defined its purpose as: 'to provide society with superior products and services. We are in the business of preserving and improving human life. All of our actions must be measured by our success in achieving this goal. We expect profits from work that satisfies customer needs and that benefits humanity.'

Interface, the world's largest manufacturer of commercial floor coverings, has a long-standing commitment not only to becoming fully sustainable but also to becoming a 'restorative' company, ie one that enhances the environment rather than depletes it:

> World-wide, all of us at Interface have a common goal: create zero waste. For the last five years, we've been working hard to get there. We call our effort QUEST. It's an acronym that stands for Quality Utilising Employee Suggestions and Teamwork. Through QUEST teams around the world, we're re-examining our sources of waste and creating ways to reduce and finally eliminate them. We're redesigning and rethinking products so that we can deliver more with less. We're reengineering production processes to reduce resource consumption. If part of a process or product doesn't add value, we eliminate it. And that philosophy goes beyond manufacturing. Our aim is zero waste in every discipline, from accounting to sales to human resources. We've come a long way already, eliminating more than $90 million in waste since 1994.

SUMMARY

In the past, the purpose of business was taken for granted and seldom debated. In the 1960s the chairman of Unilever was asked to address members of a senior executive development course on the subject of Unilever's objectives. He stood up and said 'Unilever's objective is to make profits. Are there any questions?' Few chairmen of major companies would be so blunt today, but many would cite the creation of shareholder value as the sole purpose of the enterprise. The choice of a purpose reflects the organization's values, and an exclusive focus on the bottom line reflects materialistic and economic values. By contrast the adoption of a wider purpose, one that embraces benefits to humankind and obligations to stakeholders, reflects a set of humanitarian values and a desire to be of service to the community. Such a purpose both gives greater legitimacy to the corporation in the eyes of the public and makes it more attractive to potential employees who would like to feel they are making a contribution to society over and above making the shareholders richer.

4

The role of the parent company

INTRODUCTION

In carrying out its task the head office must normally perform certain basic minimum functions in addition to the definition of purpose and setting of strategic goals. These include fulfilling legal and statutory requirements and basic corporate governance functions, such as publishing annual reports, submitting tax returns and ensuring conformity with health and safety regulations. It must determine an organization structure for the group as a whole, appoint the most senior executives, raise capital, deal with investor relations, and establish and operate control processes to guard against fraud and ensure compliance with company policy. The parent company will also usually allocate resources between its divisions or subsidiaries and set performance targets – both financial and non-financial (for example in relation to percentage of on-time deliveries). Beyond this there are other functions or services that it may choose to carry out – such as the operation of a group pension scheme or a central service such as IT. There are very many decisions of this kind to be made and many of them are strategically important. The key issues are discussed in what follows.

ADDING VALUE

What have GE, Hanson, Unilever, ABB, Canon and Grand Metropolitan in common? According to the research team of the

Ashridge Strategic Management Centre (Goold, Campbell and Alexander, 1994) they were all 'good parents' in the mid-1990s, which means that they managed their relationships with subsidiary companies in ways that added significant value beyond the cost of maintaining their respective head offices.

Goold and his colleagues begin by reminding us that the justification for multi-business companies is under scrutiny. Value gaps between stock market valuation and the break-up value of large groups have attracted predators; many examples now exist of companies flourishing following management buy-outs from parent groups; and there is a long list of failed acquisitions. They assert that the large majority of multi-business companies do not add value, they destroy it, and they do so because they lack an appropriate corporate strategy.

They argue, however, that companies should not merely aim to add value – they should seek to achieve 'parenting advantage', aiming to be the best possible parent for a range of businesses.

The extent to which this aim is achieved will reflect the degree to which there is a good fit between the characteristics of the parent company and those of the subsidiary. Goold and his team state that the characteristics of the parent that should fit the subsidiary's profile fall into five groups:

▌ First there are 'mental maps' – defined as the rules of thumb and mental models used by managers to interpret information.

▌ Secondly there is a wide range of structures, systems and processes.

▌ The third group consists of the central functions and services.

▌ Skills and people make up the fourth group.

▌ Finally, there are the 'decentralization contracts', which define the issues that will be influenced by the centre and those that will be delegated.

Value, in their view, is created when these characteristics are well suited to the needs of the subsidiary. Surprisingly they do not include compatibility of corporate culture in the list – a factor that research has shown to be important in relation to the success or failure of mergers and acquisitions.

Successful parents focus on the opportunities for value creation that exist in their subsidiaries. They have considerable insight into how to exploit these opportunities, they bring their own distinctive parenting characteristics to bear, they clearly see the critical success factors of the businesses and they have an equally clear view of their own 'heartland', ie the type of business to which they are particularly capable of adding value.

Good parents add value in four principal ways. The one that has most influence on performance in the opinion of Goold and his colleagues is 'stand-alone influence' – appointing divisional chief executives, influencing management development and succession planning, approving budgets, strategic plans and capital expenditure.

The others are:

▌ creating linkages (the well-known synergy effect);

▌ providing central functions and services;

▌ selecting the portfolio.

The thesis is tightly argued and well supported by examples illustrating best practice. Ideally these would be balanced by equally well-documented cases of bad parents that destroy value but for obvious reasons these are absent. The authors acknowledge that their central concept of parenting advantage is not capable of precise measurement but argue that it is no less powerful for that.

The issues raised by this work have very important implications for strategic management. Despite some notable exceptions and some well-publicized slimming-down exercises our industrial and commercial landscape is still populated by some sizeable head offices that consume considerable amounts of cash, lock up assets in property and hoard some of the most talented personnel. Investors are right to challenge such companies to justify this use of scarce resources.

PARENTING STYLES

Goold and his colleagues in their earlier work discerned some broad patterns in the parenting process that they term 'parenting styles' (Goold and Campbell, 1987). They distinguish three such styles: the strategic planning style, the strategic control style and the financial control style.

The strategic planning style

Parent companies using this style are closely involved with their subsidiaries in the formulation of strategy. They provide an overarching clear sense of direction and expect their different businesses to reach agreement with head office on major issues. This approach of necessity involves having sizeable planning staff groups at the centre backed by powerful functional groups in areas such as marketing or human resources. The control process is such that operating plans or budgets are seen as the detailed quantification of the first year of a strategic plan. Monitoring of performance on a monthly basis is treated with relatively low priority compared with ensuring that the business is pursuing the agreed strategy. Managers are encouraged to identify with the corporation as a whole rather than the particular subsidiary they belong to and rewards are based on overall corporate performance as well as on the performance of their subsidiary. In their initial studies Goold and Campbell identified several UK companies using this style, including BP, BOC, Cadbury Schweppes and Lex Service Group, but in later work they reported that they found that apart from Shell relatively few successful companies in the West were following this approach and that some, such as BP and IBM, had practised it in the past but had moved away from it. They found this style to be the most practised among Japanese companies, citing Canon as an outstanding example.

Businesses suited to this style typically face large, high-risk investments in assets, technologies or market development that are critical to their longer-term futures. They operate in rapidly changing, fast growing or fiercely competitive industries where there is a need to focus on the long-term sustainability of a competitive position rather than current performance.

The strategic control style

Companies using this style decentralize strategy formulation to subsidiaries but retain a role in checking and assessing what is proposed. This is a more 'bottom-up' approach but the centre may offer suggestions and will approve only those proposals that meet certain strategic and financial criteria. Head office staff are primarily concerned with carrying out head office functions (financial control, secretariat, legal etc) but may include some central service departments whose services are available to subsidiaries – often on a voluntary basis. The strategic management, planning and budgeting and capital allocation processes are designed so as to test the assumptions behind the business units' proposals.

Parent companies with this style do place great importance on the achievement of financial objectives but also emphasize explicit strategic targets or milestones that are measurable. Managers are expected to identify closely with their business and are rewarded largely on the performance of that business rather than that of the corporation as a whole. In the UK the research team identified ICI, Courtaulds and Vickers as users of this approach to strategy. They also found that it was significantly the most popular style – in a survey of UK companies, well over half identified themselves as strategic control users. Other examples of its champions were 3M, ABB, Emerson, GE, Grand Metropolitan, RTZ and Unilever. Goold and Campbell point out, however, that use of this style is no guarantee of success. Of five such companies in their original study, two (Plessey and Imperial Group) have been acquired by other companies, two have split up (ICI and Courtaulds) and one (Vickers) has undergone considerable portfolio restructuring.

This style, which holds a balance between the extreme positions of the other two, is compatible with a wide range of types of business.

The financial control style

Companies with this style strongly favour decentralization and structure their businesses as stand-alone units with full responsibility for their own strategies and plans. The role of the centre is to set the financial targets that must be met; there are no excuses for failure. Hence the numbers employed at head office are small. In many cases there is no formal strategic planning process. Instead there are annual budgets, financial targets and thorough processes for the approval of capital expenditure, involving considerable emphasis on speed of payback. Managers' careers and bonuses depend on their ability to meet the financial objectives. These companies are often active acquirers, looking for underperforming businesses likely to benefit from more stringent financial control systems. UK companies with this style included BTR, Hanson, GEC and Tarmac; it is uncommon on the Continent and almost unknown in Japan.

This style is suited to businesses that are underperforming, giving scope for improved financial performance. It is also appropriate for companies in mature industries and a stable competitive environment that are being managed for strong cash generation, and for businesses aiming for a rapid short-term turnaround in profitability.

In more recent work (Goold and Campbell, 2002), the Ashridge team have looked again at the sharing of roles and responsibilities between parent companies and operating units in highly complex businesses and reached the conclusion that in such businesses the distinction between parent company and business unit becomes blurred and that in consequence the emphasis on the 'added-value' role of the parent is less relevant.

SUSTAINING COMPETITIVENESS

As well as adding value the parent company is charged with the task of maintaining the existence of the business, which in turn means maintaining its competitiveness and its value in the eyes of investors.

The achievement of economic sustainability is not necessarily something that can be guaranteed by even the highest quality of management. New technologies or prolonged and deep recessions can destroy whole industries, let alone individual companies. Nevertheless, investment analysts will want to be assured that a company in which they are considering investing has in place strategies to sustain its competitiveness. These will include the provision of adequate financial reserves, adequate investment in modern plant and equipment, for which figures are normally readily available, and adequate investment in human capital and intellectual capital, where figures are still relatively rare. Other factors to be taken into consideration are the company's reputation with the public at large, the level of satisfaction and loyalty of its customers, the quality and reliability of its suppliers and the robustness of its processes and systems.

It cannot be stressed too strongly that a very weak indicator of economic sustainability is the company's current and recent level of profitability. Mark Goyder, of the Centre for Tomorrow's Company, writing to *The Times*, points out that in an article about Marks and Spencer the company was described as 'having destroyed most shareholder value in the past three years'. He suggests that the real story was that, although the price of the company's shares fell heavily during that period, shareholder value was in fact being destroyed in earlier years while the company's profits were still buoyant. 'Creation and destruction of shareholder value are the result of how a company is led, how it innovates, what commercial decisions it makes and how well it listens to and learns from its customers, employees and suppliers.'

Companies that are built to last

An important piece of research by Stanford University Business School (Collins and Porras, 1995) throws some light on the question of what policies and practices contribute to the achievement of a sustainable business.

This is a study of some large US companies that have been more or less consistently successful over 50 years or more, and have become the leaders in their industries. Characteristics of these companies are compared with those of other companies that have been less successful but that, nevertheless, have also lasted well and have generally outperformed the stock market – the silver and bronze medallists as distinct from the gold medallists.

The two groups of companies are:

Leading companies	Also-rans
3M	Norton
American Express	Wells Fargo
Boeing	McDonnell Douglas
Citicorp	Chase Manhattan
Ford	GM
GE	Westinghouse
Hewlett Packard	Texas Instruments
IBM	Burroughs
Johnson & Johnson	Bristol-Myers-Squibb
Marriott	Howard Johnson
Merck	Pfizer
Motorola	Zenith
Nordstrom	Melville
Philip Morris	RJR Nabisco
Procter and Gamble	Colgate
Sony	Kenwood
Wal-Mart	Ames
Walt Disney	Columbia

The cumulative stock market returns of $1 invested in the leading companies on 1 January 1926 would have produced $6,356 by 1 December 1990, compared with $955 from an equal investment in the comparison companies and $415 in the general stock market.

How the companies differ

The leading companies and the others are compared on 21 character-istics. The results of this comparison are shown in Table 4.1.

Table 4.1 *Characteristics of companies that are built to last*

	Characteristics	Leading Companies	Others
		Number of High Scores	
1.	Employees feel they belong to an elite	15	2
2.	Having a mission statement	14	1
3.	Historical continuity of company values	13	0
4.	Actions consistent with stated values	13	0
5.	Continuity of management	16	5
6.	Indoctrination of recruits in the values	12	1
7.	Willingness to take big risks	13	3
8.	No 'saviour' CEO from outside	13	3
9.	Investment in people	10	0
10.	Mechanisms acting as early warnings	10	0
11.	Use of highly challenging goals	13	4
12.	Early adoption of new ideas	9	1
13.	People either fit well or not at all	8	0
14.	Purposeful progress and evolution	8	1
15.	Succession planning	7	0
16.	Autonomous operational units	8	2
17.	Management development	7	1
18.	Objectives beyond profit	7	1
19.	Investment for the long term	6	0
20.	Historical pattern of setting stretching targets	5	0
21.	Use of other mechanisms to influence behaviour	4	0

The best of the best

Some of the leading companies scored significantly higher on the criteria than the others. On this basis the companies in the United States that best serve as models for those chief executives who are concerned about sustained growth and profitability over the long run are:

▌ Merck, Hewlett Packard and Procter and Gamble (10 Highs);

▌ Motorola and Marriott (9 Highs);

▌ 3M, Boeing, GE, Nordstrom, Sony and Wal-Mart (8 Highs).

Good to great

More recently Collins and his research team studied the financial records of 1,435 firms that belonged to the *Fortune* 500 from 1965 to

1995. They searched for firms that had produced mediocre (or worse) returns for 15 years and then had outperformed the market by a factor of three times or more for 15 years. They found only 11 such companies and labelled them 'good to great'. This elite group consisted of Abbott Laboratories, Circuit City, Fannie Mae, Gillette, Kimberly-Clark, Kroger, Nucor, Philip Morris, Pitney Bowes, Walgreens, and Wells Fargo. Collins's team then identified two comparison groups: a direct comparison group of companies in the same industries that had not improved their performance, and another group that had produced superior returns for a while but had been unable to sustain that improvement. Collins and his team then studied the differences among the groups.

They found that good-to-great companies had leaders who combined a self-effacing humility with a fierce professional will to succeed rather than larger-than-life celebrity leaders, a feature of the comparison groups. In the good-to-great companies, these leaders first assembled a team of disciplined people and then, through disciplined thought and action, decided what should be done (as well as what they should stop doing) and how to do it (or stop it). 'Who' came before 'what' or 'how'. The good-to-great group did not spend more time strategizing than did the others (all the firms had well-defined strategies), and they paid scant attention to managing change, motivating people or creating alignment. With the right people, these issues seemed just to melt away.

A central finding of the study is that the good-to-great firms disciplined their thought with what Collins calls a Hedgehog Concept, named after writings by the Greek poet Archilochus about the hedgehog, who knows one big thing (as opposed to the fox, who knows many small things). A Hedgehog Concept is a deep understanding that flows from the intersection of three circles:

1. what you can (and cannot) be the best in the world at;

2. what drives your economic engine;

3. what you care passionately about.

Collins suggests that this understanding is not a one-time achievement, but an evolving product of an iterative process best conducted in leadership councils of the right people, who engage in dialogue and debate guided by the three factors.

Is sustainable industry leadership unachievable?

Creative Destruction (2001), by consultants Richard N Foster and Sarah Kaplan, casts new light on the organizational environments that produce superior performance. The subtitle of the book, *Why companies that are built to last underperform the market – and how to successfully transform them*, summarizes their message. They used a custom-built database to track 1,008 companies in 15 industries from 1962 to 1998 and showed that long-lived corporations typically underperform market averages as represented by the S&P 500. Thus the notion of excellence, of a corporation surviving indefinitely while producing superior returns, is largely mythical. It is the new entrants into an industry that produce superior returns and then usually go through an ageing process accompanied by declining performance.

The authors suggest that creative destruction is necessary within corporations if they are to mimic the scale and pace of change of a market-place. They cite the venture-capital firm Kleiner Perkins Caufield & Byers and buy-out specialists Kohlberg Kravis Roberts & Co as examples of organizations that create, operate and trade in ways that encourage creative destruction. The example of the process within a single firm is drawn from the authors' work with Johnson & Johnson, where they ran a series of corporate dialogues that resemble the councils espoused by Jim Collins in *Good to Great (2001a)*.

Harvard Business School professor Clayton M Christensen, in *The Innovator's Dilemma: When new technologies cause great firms to fail* (1997), has examined in detail why organizations seem incapable of reinventing themselves. He was fascinated by the experience of the computer disk-drive industry, where the leaders in one generation of drives seemed incapable of staying atop the market in the next generation. Smaller entrants who attacked from 'underneath', using what Christensen called 'disruptive technology', displaced the older players. Christensen has since regretted using the term and now prefers to talk about 'disruptive business models', for often the new technology was not radically different from the old. Rather, the differences lay in the resources, processes and values required to exploit the new technology. Thus Christensen has outlined what is effectively a corporate process of maturation and ageing whereby the strengths and relationships developed to exploit one situation turn out to be weaknesses and constraints in other contexts. Capability and disability are two sides of the same coin, and one is replaced by the other as contexts change.

These findings appear to contradict those of Collins and Porras, but the difference is explicable by the fact that companies like 3M,

Hewlett Packard and Johnson & Johnson may be among a minority that are capable of reinventing themselves from time to time.

STRATEGY AND ORGANIZATION AT CORPORATE LEVEL

Strategy and structure

In theory there should be a good fit between an organization's strategy and the organization structure through which that strategy is to be implemented.

An organization structure can be designed to achieve a number of outcomes, some of which may be in conflict. The principal ones are the following (Sadler, 2001):

▌ *Control*. Achieving a high level of control over the activities of members of the organization and the related costs will be a primary objective of organization design in companies that aim to be competitive through being the lowest-cost producer. A relatively steep hierarchy accompanied by narrow spans of control will ensure close conformity with company policies and processes.

▌ *Connections*. Providing appropriate interfaces with key players in the organization's transactional environment, such as customers, suppliers, joint venture partners, fund managers and planning authorities.

▌ *Creativity and innovation*. This objective – to create an environment in which innovation can flourish – is the prime function of organization design in companies with an essentially creative task, such as advertising agencies, design consultants and architectural partnerships.

▌ *Commitment*. The commitment of the workforce is vitally important to all organizations and is considerably influenced by organization design. Small rather than large organizational units with clearly defined tasks and self-managed teams are key elements in encouraging commitment.

▌ *Coordination*. Where there is a requirement for different units or divisions of the company to work closely together provision must be made for this in the design of the structure. This usually involves cross-boundary project teams of various kinds.

▌ *Competence and capability*. The design of the organization can either facilitate or obstruct the sharing and transfer of best practice and the processes of organizational learning and knowledge management.

Chandler (1962) was an early student of the relationship between strategy and structure. He traced the development of the multi-business company from its emergence in the years before the Second World War. Companies like General Motors, Du Pont and Standard Oil became too large and complex to be capable of being managed with a monolithic functional structure. They were producing an ever-widening range of products and serving a range of markets at home and, increasingly, overseas. They sought salvation in decentralization and divorced the ongoing task of coping with a competitive environment in a specific product/market from the issues of overall strategy and resource allocation. The popularity of divisional structures rose rapidly in the post-war period, becoming the norm for large companies by the 1970s.

Divisionalization

Divisionalization can take a number of different forms. The divisions may be based primarily on products. Examples range from the case of diversification – for example Hanson – where the products are unrelated to cases where the products are part of a connected family of products. An example of the latter would be an oil company where all the products, such as petroleum spirit, propane gas and chemicals of various kinds all derive from the dominant product, oil. As we saw earlier, companies with divisions based on unrelated products tend to use a financial control style of parenting whereas ones with divisions based on a group of related products mainly use a strategic planning approach.

Another basis for divisionalization is to differentiate between markets served. A common example is to have separate divisions or subsidiaries serving the corporate and consumer markets, as in the case of automotive distributors who make the distinction between fleet sale to companies and showroom-based sale to the public. Pharmaceutical companies have separate divisions serving the distinct markets of over-the-counter sales to the public, sales of ethical products to the medical profession and sales to health services. This approach is strategically appropriate in cases where there are wide differences in the requirements of different market segments or where the distribution channels for different segments are distinct.

A third possible basis for divisionalization is on a geographical basis – either regional divisions within a country or separate country-based divisions or subsidiaries in the case of an international business. This form of divisionalization is aligned with strategic goals in cases where local tastes, climatic differences or regulatory factors call for varied approaches to competing in different countries or regions of a country.

Very large, complex, international businesses have to deal with a range of products, serving a number of distinct markets or market segments in a very large number of different companies. To meet the demands of this complexity calls for extremely complex, even Byzantine, structures. In many cases companies seek to resolve some of the complexity by adopting a matrix structure. This involves a dual reporting arrangement. The example in Figure 4.1 is of a company in the computer industry that produces hardware, software and consumable supplies. It operates in three main geographical regions. In any one location local executives would report to the head of the product division on some issues, such as pricing, promotion and distribution policies, and to the regional vice president on other matters, such as human resources management. Matrix structures can cause confusion and many companies have abandoned the attempt to achieve coordination in this way.

Corporate culture

Organization design is not just about getting the structure right. It also involves issues to do with culture. Corporate culture is an elusive

	HARDWARE	SOFTWARE	SUPPLIES
EUROPE			
AMERICAS			
FAR EAST			

Figure 4.1   *A typical matrix organization structure*

concept, difficult of definition. It is an amalgam of traditions inherited from the past, shared values and beliefs, a common mindset, characteristic behaviours ('the way we do things round here') and symbols such as splendid corporate head offices. Organizations vary according to whether or not they are seen as having a strong corporate culture. Companies with notably strong cultures include IBM, Hewlett Packard, and Procter and Gamble in the United States and Shell and Marks and Spencer in the UK. Kotter and Heskett (1992) argue that having a strong culture can be both a strength and a weakness in that a strong culture may inhibit an organization's ability to change in line with important changes in its competitive environment. This was certainly a factor in Marks and Spencer's fall from grace in the late 1990s. They suggest that culture needs to be strategically appropriate with the implication that it should be kept constantly under review. When a company with pride in its traditions and a strong culture merges with another major enterprise an important issue is cultural compatibility. There is evidence that many acquisitions and mergers fail because of failure to take this factor into account. It will be interesting to see what will be the outcome, in terms of its impact on culture, of the acquisition of Compaq by Hewlett Packard – an acquisition that was strongly opposed by the Hewlett and Packard families, largely on the grounds of cultural incompatibility.

The difficult process of identifying the culture of a company and changing it is treated in Chapter 13.

REPUTATION, IMAGE AND BRAND IDENTITY

A fourth major strategic role for the parent company is the building and maintenance of a favourable reputation with the company's various stakeholders and a strong brand identity.

> All organisations have licences to operate. Not in the formal sense of pieces of paper or certificates, although these are issued in certain cases (such as the airline industry or the operator of the National Lottery), but in the informal sense of whether people are willing to accept and deal with the organisation. Anyone who chooses to deal with an organisation is, in effect, implicitly granting that organisation a licence to operate, just as anyone who elects not to deal with a particular organisation is denying that organisation's licence to operate. At a practical level this means that all organisations are granted licences to operate by several different parties (regulators, employees, customers, suppliers),

and that each of these parties can seek to revoke the organisation's
licence to operate at any time.
(Neely, 1998)

In the past there was a more tolerant attitude to corporate behaviour, or
at least there were lower expectations that companies would or should
behave ethically. As long as companies made the products people
wanted and provided jobs, people were prepared to overlook their
shortcomings. This is no longer the case. Better-educated, more-
affluent, better-informed citizens are much more concerned that
corporate excesses should be checked and indeed punished.

The fact that increasing numbers of people have access to the
Internet makes companies more vulnerable if their actions do not meet
public expectations. Large global companies have attracted around
them a whole array of Web sites devoted to exposing every failing.
Investigative journalism and TV programmes like the BBC's
Watchdog add to the flow of exposure of cases of wrongdoing or sharp
practice.

Svendsen (1998) argues that companies are starting to recognize
that in a networked world their reputations depend on communicating
openly, behaving ethically and developing credible relationships with
their stakeholders and particularly with the communities in which
they operate.

As an indication of the growing importance of perceptions of
corporate social responsibility as a shaper of reputations, a recent
survey of 26,000 consumers conducted by Harris Interactive Inc
included 'social responsibility' as one of six main categories used to
gauge the reputations of well-known companies. An article in the *Wall
Street Journal* (7 February 2001) reported on the survey and noted that
Daimler-Chrysler, Home Depot, and Johnson & Johnson ranked
highest in perceived social responsibility.

The survey report pointed out that if companies were to behave
more like responsible citizens they would avoid the embarrassment of
running an expensive advertisement at the same time as receiving
some adverse publicity due to some irresponsible act. As advertising
professionals, the report's authors knew that this was a frequent occurrence; they called it 'Combined Inactivity', the paid-for publicity
being cancelled out by the negative impact of the company's actions.

Research by Columbia University indicates that about one-third of
shareholder value in many sectors of industry is accounted for by
company reputation. A study by Ernst & Young estimates that the
intangible assets of skills, knowledge, relationships and reputation

account for two-thirds of market valuation for companies focused on knowledge creation.

Volvo spent years building a reputation for making safe cars – not fast cars or sexy cars, but cars that gave their owners a feeling of security for themselves and their families. Yet in May 2001 the company suffered a great deal of negative publicity and the threat of prosecution for manslaughter, having been accused of failing to disclose a potential fault in nearly 20,000 cars that could cause partial brake failure. It was alleged that two children were killed by one car as the driver frantically stamped on a brake pedal that failed to respond. Documents obtained as a result of a raid on a Volvo dealership showed that the company became aware of the fault in 1997 and alerted dealers, but did not recall the vehicles that potentially had the problem, merely recommending that rectification be carried out during routine servicing. The company admitted the problem was unlikely to have been rectified on every car and that failure to disclose it may have been a 'misjudgement'.

This is an example of how a company's reputation ties in with its business success model. Volvo's share of the passenger car market rests largely on its niche position as the manufacturer that puts safety first. Anything that damages the company's reputation on safety issues strikes directly at the basis of its market share and ability to command a premium price.

A company's reputation is an important factor in enabling it to recruit and retain highly talented people. *Fortune* magazine has established that the single most reliable predictor of overall excellence in a company is its ability to attract and retain talented employees.

In recent years there have been several instances of companies suffering significant costs and other adverse consequences following damage to their reputations.

SHELL

The most well known case in recent years is that of Shell. The reputation of this highly respected Anglo-Dutch company took a bad knock in the mid-1990s over two issues – the scrapping of the

Brent Spar oil platform and its involvement with the military regime in Nigeria.

In 1995 Ken Saro-Wiwa, a writer and opponent of the regime in power, together with eight colleagues, was tried and executed. They were accused of conspiring to murder several people killed in political disturbances in Ogonland in the previous year. These disturbances involved clashes between minority groups and the government and between the groups and Shell over alleged environmental despoliation of their region and over the distribution of government oil revenues. The convictions were the outcome of a trial that independent observers considered unfair. In spite of appeals from other countries, including UK Prime Minister John Major and Nelson Mandela, the executions went ahead. Protests against Shell broke out all over the world. In the short term the impact on Shell's business was relatively slight, in that at the end of the year its share price and profits stood at record levels. Nevertheless the impact was profound. The image of the company had been tarnished. Individual senior executives felt branded. The company's confidence in its scenario planning techniques was badly dented – it had failed to anticipate or deal adequately with the situation. The lessons were quickly learnt and Shell produced its first Social Report in 1998. This was despite the fact that in 1997 John Jennings, the retiring chairman, had stated that the board could not accept the demands of activists that the company should produce one.

TEXACO

A reputational issue of a quite different kind hit another oil company – Texaco – at about the same time. In 1994 six black employees filed a race discrimination lawsuit against the company. In 1996 their lawyers released to the *New York Times* a tape of Texaco executives allegedly making racist remarks and conspiring to conceal company documents. This aroused huge media interest and generated a public outcry. The company's new CEO, Peter Bjur, wisely chose not to go into denial, but instead announced that the company would derive benefit from the affair by making the achievement of diversity a competitive advantage. He negotiated a settlement of the lawsuit for $115 million, a one-off salary increase and an investment of $30 million in programmes to improve the company's racial climate. In the end the company came out well, largely due to Bjur's open style and personal involvement.

NIKE

The third high-profile case in the 1990s was that of Nike. In 1996 there were demonstrations by activists at the opening of the company's San Francisco store on the grounds that the company's products were produced under sweatshop conditions. At first the company's response was defensive. It argued that a poorly paying job was better than no job; that the issue of low wages in developing countries was not something any one company could do anything about and that protests should be directed to the UN; and that in any case Nike was dealing with the problem.

Following world-wide concern over its activities, the Nike board changed its approach. First it stopped the use of the hazardous chemical toluene. Also it began supporting research initiatives and conferences on international manufacturing practices and instituted some independent monitoring of its production sites. The Nike case led to the setting up of an independent monitoring service, the Apparel Industry Partnership and the Apparel, Footwear and Retailing Working Group of the NGO Business and Social Responsibility.

The lessons

When major issues of this kind arise, company responses fall into the following broad categories:

▌ *Denial*. These companies treat the issue as a matter for the public relations function to handle, comforting themselves with the belief that sooner or later media attention will switch to other issues and other companies. Top management keeps a low profile and refuses requests to meet the media.

▌ *Defence*. These companies take the issue seriously but attempt to defend and justify the company's position. Top management becomes involved. Lawsuits are defended.

▌ *Initial defence followed by acceptance of the need to change*. In such cases it becomes clear to top management in the course of conducting a defence that the weight of public opinion is over-whelmingly strong. Also it is sometimes the case that as top managers are briefed they come to appreciate the full extent of the impact of the company's activities.

▐ *Openness, dialogue and jointly developed action programmes*. In these cases top management gives clear leadership. Once rare, this response is becoming more common and will one day become the norm. More and more companies, before responding to an issue, take advice not from the traditional PR agency but from one of the many specialist consultancy firms that have sprung up in the field of social responsibility.

Ideally, of course, companies should not be in the position of being taken by surprise when an issue surfaces in the public domain. The strategic planning process should involve scanning the horizon for such potential problems, asking such questions as 'What could happen that could seriously damage our reputation?' or 'What could happen that could put us out of business?' Even more important is 'What could happen that could implicate this company and its officers in the death and serious injury of human beings?' In India the legacy of the Union Carbide disaster at Bhopal still lingers on.

Corporate governance, company reputation and executive remuneration

The compensation gap between top managers and rank-and-file employees has been growing rapidly in recent years – most noticeably in the United States, but also in the UK and other European countries.

In the United States, from 1965 to 1980 the indices of pay growth for CEOs and rank-and-file workers grew at about the same rate, thus maintaining a pay differential that had existed since the end of World War II. The gap then started widening and then explosively so. A sense of outrage has been growing and epithets such as 'obscene' or 'shameful' are frequently heard. A company can make the case for the level of compensation it provides for its CEO, citing the levels paid in comparable companies and the need to be competitive to retain top executive talent. But such arguments count for little when the public and employees make the comparison that matters to them – comparing the CEO's salary with their own. The sense that something is wrong has been aggravated by evidence that there is a lack of correlation between high levels of pay and company performance. Institutional investors on both sides of the Atlantic are using their clout to press for reform.

At the other extreme there have been cases of companies setting an example of moderation. Few would go along with the formula adopted at one time by Ben and Jerry's ratio of 5 to 1 between the highest- and lowest-paid workers. Peter Drucker has suggested 20 to 1, an approach adopted by companies such as Herman Miller. In companies like Intel, Monsanto or BP it is more like several hundred to 1, once options and bonuses are taken into account.

There is now considerable investor pressure for greater moderation in the allocation of executive options and for stronger links between remuneration and performance. Companies are urged to establish their own ratio of CEO pay to shop-floor pay, to explain the rationale for it to shareholders and to justify further any drift from this ratio subsequently.

A report to the International Corporate Governance Network by its subcommittee on executive remuneration recommended the following:

▌ Transparency. Salary, incentives and all other payments and benefits for directors should be published.

▌ Remuneration committees should publish the expected outcomes of the remuneration structures.

▌ Options should be issued at regular intervals rather than in one large batch.

▌ The true cost of options should be shown as a charge on the revenue account.

▌ The remuneration report should be a separate voting item at every AGM.

▌ Remuneration committees should control the appointment of remuneration consultants.

▌ Companies should not make loans to their directors.

▌ Cash transaction bonuses on the completion of acquisitions or mergers should not be payable.

▌ Fund managers should increase the resources allocated to the analysis of remuneration structures.

Brand identity

The dangers of tampering with brand identity can be illustrated by the example of BP. In July 2000 BP spent £135 million in a complete corporate rebranding operation. Out went the shield logo that had symbolized the company for over 70 years and in its place came a yellow, green and white sunburst with the slogan 'Beyond Petroleum'. According to an article in the *Independent* (19 April 2001) this has met with a mixed reaction. At first it was welcomed by environmental NGOs who interpreted it to mean that BP, looking to the future and concerned about climate change, was envisaging its own future in leading the development of alternative forms of energy. BP did not actually state this at the time, but nor did it go out of its way to refute it. Moreover the reputation of its CEO Lord Browne as a person deeply concerned for the environment gave credence to this interpretation. In the intervening months BP has pursued its oil exploration programme as vigorously as ever, however, and, according to the *Independent*, the BP Press Office now says that the words 'Beyond Petroleum' mean only supplying natural gas as well as oil and putting groceries in petrol station shops.

This illustrates the dangers in this field of creating an impression of a gap between corporate statements of policy and intent and what actually happens. BP is today the target of much hostile comment from activists and it is probable that the strength of their attacks has been heightened by the fact that false hopes have been raised.

SUMMARY

In the case of the multi-business company substantial costs are incurred at the centre in the form of employment costs, consultancy and professional services and the costs of premises. To justify these costs the head office must add more in terms of value to its subsidiaries or divisions than the sum of such central costs. In many cases it is clear that this is not so.

In practice there are two extreme approaches to the management of the multi-business company. At one extreme (the strategic planning style) the company will have a large head office with many central services and a substantial strategic planning staff. Some years ago, when ICI epitomized this approach, there was a huge number of staff employed at its London headquarters in Millbank House. In the divisions the burden of this central cost was reflected in the fact that it was known as Millstone House.

The other extreme is classically represented in the UK by the former Hanson conglomerate, characterized by a slim head office engaged in building the portfolio of businesses and subjecting them to a tight discipline of financial control. This formula appeared to work very well for a time, but as growth and earnings per share fell away the company was split up.

Today, most companies have adopted an approach somewhere between these two extremes.

It does seem to be the case that there is, in any case, no such thing as a formula for success that will guarantee sustained competitiveness over time. Although the classic research project Built to Last provides evidence to show that over more than 50 years certain US companies have consistently been the leaders in their industries, these may well be the exceptions and even in these cases the survival of the companies concerned has not always looked secure, as was famously the case with Ford in the early 1980s.

What is clear is that the sustainability of the large multi-business company is conditional upon the success of its management in continuously adapting its structure and culture to the changing business environment, guarding its reputation and building the strength of its brand or brands. Among the cases at the end of the book, that of Tesco has been included to illustrate how this process has been carried out with considerable success by a UK supermarket, while the tragic case of Marks and Spencer serves as an object lesson of what can happen as a result of complacency, arrogance and short-term thinking.

5

Building the portfolio (1): analyzing industry and competition

INTRODUCTION

Before starting a new business or making an acquisition in a new industry, it is essential to know something about the industry that is being entered. In particular, it is important to know about the attractiveness of the industry being entered in terms of its profit potential and how competitive advantage is obtained. Industry analysis is concerned with these two issues.

ANALYZING INDUSTRY ATTRACTIVENESS

For an industry to be economically viable, the basic condition is that it must add value: the product it produces must have a value to customers which is greater than the cost of production. If the industry is viable, then the next issue is *who gets the surplus*. This depends on the dynamics of competition in the industry, which in turn depends on the structure of the industry. Consider the production of bread. Customers may be willing to pay £2 for a loaf of bread. If bread is supplied by a monopolist, then that monopolist may be able to charge a full £2 a loaf, and full surplus value is earned in profits by the monopolist. But suppose there are many bakeries competing. The price will tend to fall towards the cost of production (say, 60p), and the surplus is received by consumers. However, the story is not as simple as that. There will be a chain of suppliers: the farmer who grows the wheat, the miller who makes the flour, the baker who produces the bread, the retailer who sells it. The distribution of the surplus between these firms depends on their relative bargaining power.

To analyze systematically the structural features of an industry which determine the intensity of competition and the level of industry profit, Michael Porter's well-known 'five forces of competition' model can be used (see Figure 5.1).

The Porter framework identifies five sets of competitive forces. The profitability of the industry depends on the aggregate impact of these five forces – although in practice it may take only one or two of them to produce intensively competitive circumstances within an industry and to result in marginal profitability. Each of the competitive forces will be considered in turn.

Threat of substitutes

The availability of substitutes is a major factor influencing customers' willingness to pay a premium price for a product. This price sensitivity on the part of customers is indicated by the *price elasticity of demand* for the product. If there are close substitutes available, there is a limit to the price that customers are willing to pay; demand is *elastic* with respect to price, ie the customer will respond to a higher price by switching to a substitute product. Soft drink manufacturers can easily

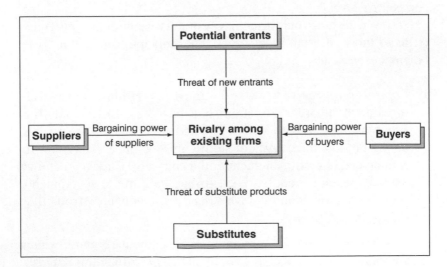

Figure 5.1   *The five forces model of competition*

use either cane sugar, beet sugar or corn syrup in their manufacturing processes – as a result the demand for corn syrup tends to be price elastic. Conversely, there are no viable substitutes for centre court seats at Wimbledon, thus the price for these is *inelastic*.

The extent to which the threat of substitutes constrains industry pricing depends on three factors:

▌ the extent to which substitute products are available;

▌ the relative price/performance characteristics of the alternatives;

▌ costs which customers face in switching between substitutes.

Threat of entry

The potential for new entrants into an industry acts as a direct constraint on the profit margins that established firms can earn. Consider the taxi market in London. An office with a telephone, a radio, a car and a driver are all that is required to set up in the minicab business. With cellular telephones, even the office can be dispensed with. During periods of prosperity when demand for taxis is expanding new firms enter; then in recessions taxi businesses disappear. A similar phenomenon occurs in many service businesses: for example the proliferation of estate agents during any property boom. Any industry that is earning a return on capital in excess of the cost of that capital will tend to attract firms from outside the industry. Unless the entry of new firms is barred, the rate of profit must fall to a competitive level.

However, in most industries new entrants cannot enter on equal terms to those of established firms. The principal sources of these *barriers to entry* are:

1. *Capital requirements*. Many industries require substantial investment in order to establish a business. British Satellite Broadcasting and Sky TV each invested over £500 million pounds during the first three years of setting up satellite TV services. In commercial aircraft manufacture, the entry costs are so great that the only recent entrant has been Airbus Industrie, a government-sponsored joint venture involving five companies from five European countries.

2. *Economies of scale*. In some industries, particularly those which are capital intensive or research intensive, efficiency requires production on a very large scale. In the motor industry the impor-

tance of scale has resulted in the elimination of most smaller players in the volume car business.

3. *Absolute cost advantages*. Irrespective of scale economies, established firms may have a cost advantage over new entrants. This may result from tying up low cost sources of raw materials, or from cost efficiencies arising from economies of learning.

4. *Product differentiation*. In an industry in which products are differentiated, established firms possess an advantage over new entrants by virtue of brand recognition and customer loyalty. The appeal and familiarity of the Coca-Cola and Pepsi-Cola brand names make it difficult for any entrant into cola soft drinks to obtain a significant market share.

5. *Access to channels of distribution*. Product differentiation barriers relate to the preferences of established products. However, for consumer goods manufacturers the biggest barrier may be distributors' preferences for established firms' products. Limited capacity in distribution channels (eg shelf space), risk aversion and the fixed costs associated with carrying an additional product result in distributors' reluctance to carry a new manufacturer's product.

6. *Supplier qualification*. It is not only the manufacturers of consumer goods which have problems in gaining market access. The diffusion of quality management programmes in industry has meant that increasingly suppliers of components must achieve certified supplier status in order to gain access to larger customers. This compels prospective suppliers not only to meet or exceed the standards set down by customers, but to assume the costs of the certification procedures.

7. *Government and legal barriers*. There are many potential regulatory barriers ranging from public licences to patents, copyrights and trade secrets. Industries subject to heavy government involvement through regulation, procurement and environmental and safety standards can have stringent and expensive barriers to entry.

8. *Retaliation*. The effectiveness of these barriers to entry in excluding potential entrants depends on the entrants' expectations of possible retaliation by established firms. Retaliation against a new entrant may take the form of aggressive price cutting, increased advertising or a variety of legal moves.

How these barriers to entry can be overcome depends on the would-be entrants' resources. Barriers which keep new firms out of an industry may be ineffective against established firms. Within the European Community, many new entrants to national markets are established firms from other countries taking advantage of the removal of regulatory barriers. Thus while lack of capital, expertise or reputation may make entry into insurance very difficult for new firms, in Germany, Britain and Spain there has been considerable activity by firms expanding between countries. Similarly, barriers to entry into international air transport tend to be high. Yet the financial resources and market visibility of Richard Branson's Virgin Group facilitated Virgin Atlantic's successful entry into this industry.

Rivalry among existing firms

For most industries, the main determinant of the overall state of competition and the general level of profitability is competition between the firms within the industry. Some of the main factors determining the nature and intensity of competition between established firms are:

1. **Seller concentration**. Seller concentration refers to the number of competitors in an industry and their relative sizes. The simplest situation is one of a monopolistic firm, such as Xerox in the copier business during the 1970s – a stand-alone giant. Here one company dictates price and there is no competition. Two or three companies in a market may be a small enough number for co-ordinated pricing behaviour with minimal price competition. As any air traveller knows, the greater the number of airlines which fly a particular route, the more likely there is to be aggressive competition over fares.

2. **Diversity of competitors**. The propensity of firms to engage in aggressive price competition also depends on their characteristics. The more alike firms are in their goals, strategies and cost structures, the more likely their interests are to converge, and the probability of 'peaceful co-existence' increases. In the once sedate world of British stockbroking, the acquisition of British brokerage houses by banks, insurance companies and by American, Japanese and European companies has done much to increase the intensity of competition.

3. **Product differentiation**. In a commodity business, products are largely undifferentiated, and customers tend to buy on the basis of

price alone. In such circumstances price is the main competitive weapon, and price competition seriously damages margins. Where products are highly differentiated, as in the case of books, perfumes, and management consulting services, price is only one variable influencing customer choice, and competition is likely to occur primarily based on quality, product design, advertising and promotion. Such competition may well be intense, but at the same time non-price competition may permit profit margins to remain at healthy levels.

4. *Excess capacity and exit barriers*. The propensity of firms within an industry to resort to aggressive price competition depends largely on the balance between capacity and output. Decreased market demand or overinvestment in production capability can lead to overcapacity. In the service industry, inaccurate forecasts of demand often cause excess capacity. Consider the capacity management problems associated with correctly scheduling staff in the restaurant and hotel businesses or increasing facility utilization during times of lower demand.

   The presence of unused capacity encourages firms to compete for additional business in order to spread fixed costs over a greater sales volume. As long as a lower price continues to cover variable costs, the firm is economically justified in continuing to produce. However, profits are compromised under these conditions. Impeding the firm's exit from the industry under such circumstances may be various 'barriers to exit'. Where resources are durable and specialized, as in the case of the steel industry for example, or where employees are entitled to job protection, barriers to exit may be substantial.

5. *Cost conditions*. Suppose that excess capacity exists within an industry – how severe will price competition be? Much depends on the structure of costs. Take as an example the airline business. Once flight schedules have been set, almost all costs are fixed. Hence if airlines have excess capacity on a particular route, they will be willing to fill empty seats at any price which covers the small variable costs of extra fuel, ticketing and customer service. In high fixed cost businesses such as airlines, steel, petrochemicals and theme parks, periodic excess capacity tends to be associated with heavy discounting and industry-wide losses.

6. *Market growth rates*. Where markets are mature a company can only achieve growth by making inroads into the market shares of competitors. This situation also tends to lead to intense competition.

Bargaining power of buyers

Buyers are customers who may be distributors, consumers or other manufacturing or service organizations. There are two primary factors that are important in determining the strength of buying power:

1. *Buyers' price sensitivity*. Buyers are most sensitive to the price of items for which the costs are a relatively large proportion of the buyer's total costs. Where a product or service does not involve a large expenditure, the buyer will not think it worthwhile to devote time to searching alternatives or engaging in bargaining. The 20 per cent return on sales earned by Devro, the Scottish manufacturer of synthetic sausage skins, may reflect this factor. (See 'A leaner business that has more bite', *Financial Times*, 16 April 1993, p33.) Substitution enters the picture again here: buyers are able and want to switch to another product if there is little product differentiation. Also strong competition between buyers compels them to seek assiduously the lowest possible prices from sellers. Last, but not least, is quality and its relationship to price sensitivity. Over the last few years, there has been an increased emphasis on product quality. It is widely agreed that customers are willing to pay a premium price for quality. Whereas some buyers may be less concerned about price, others may continue to compete for low prices in an effort to realize higher margins on quality products.

2. *Relative bargaining power*. In the last resort, bargaining power depends on the extent of the threat and each party's willingness to refuse to do business with the other party. The balance of power between the two parties depends on the credibility and effectiveness with which each makes this threat. Key issues are the relative costs which each party sustains as a result of the transaction not being consummated, and the expertise of each party in leveraging its position through negotiating skills. Three factors are likely to be important in determining the bargaining power of buyers relative to that of sellers:

▌ **Size and concentration**. The smaller the number of buyers, the less easy it is for a supplier to find alternative customers if one is lost. The bigger the customer's purchases, the greater the damage from losing that customer. The larger the size of the buyer relative to the supplier, then the better able the buyer is to withstand any financial losses arising from failure to reach agreement.

▌ **Vertical integration**. Firms that are able to integrate vertically enjoy increased bargaining power as buyers. The introduction by supermarkets of 'own brand' products has done much to undermine the bargaining power of food manufacturers.

▌ **Buyers' information**. The better informed buyers are about suppliers and their products, prices and costs, the better able they are to effectively bargain over prices and terms.

Bargaining power of suppliers

The balance of power between suppliers and firms within the industry depends on the same factors that determine the balance of power between firms in the industry and buyers – we are simply shifting the focus of attention upstream. Suppliers are powerful to the extent that they are large and concentrated, and they supply an input for which there is no alternative and where switching costs are high for the firms in the industry. Powerful suppliers include vital component suppliers (such as Intel in relation to the computer industry), suppliers of professional services (such as auditing firms), and some trade unions, especially those which supply workers with unique skills.

A growing trend is for buyer/supplier relationships to be seen as a basis for collaboration. Known as 'partnership sourcing', this trend is discussed in Chapter 8.

THE APPLICATION OF INDUSTRY ANALYSIS: FORECASTING PROFITABILITY

Different industries have achieved very different levels of profitability. Some, such as pharmaceuticals and tobacco, have earned attractive returns with average return on capital significantly above the cost of capital. Other industries such as minerals, steel, nonferrous metal processing and shipbuilding have earned returns well below these industries' cost of capital. In yet other industries, such as construction and airlines, returns have been highly cyclical. In consequence, marginally efficient firms get squeezed out during periods of recession.

By analyzing the structural factors which drive the various competitive forces, it is possible to understand and explain why some industries earn consistently high profits, others consistently low profits, and others follow a highly cyclical pattern.

However, there is little value in explaining past profitability. The real value of industry analysis is its ability to *predict* industry profitability in the future. When starting up a new business, or diversifying from one industry into another, a crucial issue is whether the new industry offers a benign or a hostile environment for earning profits. There are three stages in predicting industry profitability:

1. **Explaining past profit performance**. By analyzing the structural factors which have driven competition and industry profitability in the past, it is possible to explain why profitability has been high, low or average, and identify those structural factors which have been most influential.

2. **Identifying structural change**. The second stage is to predict how the industry structure will change in the future. This requires the principal trends in the industry structure to be identified. Is the industry becoming more or less concentrated? Is capacity growing faster than demand, and if so how much excess capacity is likely? Is new technology causing substitute products to appear? How is the balance of power shifting in relation to suppliers and buyers? What is happening to entry barriers?

3. **Analyzing** how the changes in industry structure will influence competition and profitability in the future.

Systematic analysis of industry attractiveness is important for all types of business. It is just as important for an entrepreneurial start-up as it is for Hanson in deciding whether to enter the coal mining industry. Industries dominated by small businesses are particularly likely to have environments which are not conducive to profitability. For example, a travel agency considering opening up a new branch in a new location should analyze the attractiveness of that local market in terms of:

▌ the number of competitors;

▌ the extent to which they offer differentiated services;

▌ their service capacity relative to market demand;

▌ the power of local property landlords;

▌ the power of corporate customers to demand discounts;

▌ the likelihood of additional entrants.

Very often this structural analysis will not come up with clear answers. For many industries, some trends are likely to be favourable to future profitability, others will be unfavourable, and determining the net impact will be difficult. However, simply undertaking the analysis is conducive to a deeper understanding of the industry environment, and carrying out a 'first-cut' analysis of industry structure will reveal areas where further research will prove useful.

CHANGING INDUSTRY STRUCTURE

By understanding how industry structure affects competition and profitability, it is also possible to identify how a firm can influence the industry structure in order to improve the balance of competitive forces, and so enhance industry profitability. Firstly, mergers represent a particularly direct and effective way of eliminating competition. For precisely this reason antitrust laws exist to prevent and control mergers which lead to a monopoly. Secondly, the bargaining power of suppliers and buyers may be counteracted by various mechanisms. During the 1960s, for example, British food processing companies were instrumental in encouraging US can making companies to enter the UK market to counter the supplier power of the Metal Box Company. Thirdly, entry barriers can be erected by a variety of mechanisms. Brewing and oil companies have built barriers to their industries by forward integration into retailing. As a result of their control over pubs and petrol stations, it has been difficult for new entrants to establish distribution outlets.

In many heavy manufacturing industries some of the most intractable structural problems have arisen from excess capacity. A critical factor in restructuring the depressed European petrochemicals industry has been the facilitation of capacity adjustment by companies swapping assets to achieve greater consolidation within individual market segments.

MARKET SEGMENTATION

One of the greatest difficulties of industry analysis is defining the industry itself. An industry is a group of firms supplying a particular market. But where should the market boundaries be drawn? Are Sega and Nintendo competing within the video games industry, the home computer industry, or the home entertainment industry? These problems of definition are eased by the ability to segment industries into more narrowly defined groupings. Thus the car market is typically segmented into a number of product categories: luxury cars, sports cars, family cars, people carriers, passenger vans, small cars and so on. It is also possible to segment the industry geographically: into major regions (North America, Western Europe, Eastern Europe, Far East, etc), or even more finely into individual countries (Britain, France, Germany, Spain). Consumer markets are generally segmented in terms of age, sex, social class, stage in life cycle, lifestyle and interests. Industrial markets are segmented according to such criteria as size of firm, volume of transactions, distribution channel, quality and service requirements, and public versus private sector. Figure 5.2 shows a segmentation of the restaurant industry in a medium-sized town.

The principal stages of industry segmentation analysis are as follows:

1. Identify segmentation variables in terms of product types, customer types, distribution channels, alternative technologies and so on.

	Type of cuisine					
	Hamburger	Fish	French	Italian	Chinese	Indian
Up-market waiter service		Seafood restaurants	French restaurants	Italian restaurants	Chinese gourmet restaurants	
Medium-priced waiter service	American-style cafés and diners		French bistro-style cafés	Pasta restaurants	Chinese restaurants	Indian restaurants
Fast food and take-away	McDonald's, Burger King etc	Fish and chip shops		Pizza parlours	Chinese take-away	Indian take-away

(left axis label: Type of restaurant)

empty segment ▨

Figure 5.2   *Segmentation of the restaurant industry in a medium-sized British town*

2. Combine correlated variables and eliminate variables which are strategically less important in order to distinguish the key segmentation variables which divide the industry.

3. Analyze the attractiveness of the different segments using Porter's five forces of competition framework. When analyzing entry, note that barriers to entry relate not only to entry from *outside* the industry, but also to entry from different segments *within* the industry. Barriers between industry segments are referred to as *barriers to mobility.*

4. Examine linkages between segments which might make it attractive to be in multiple segments rather than being concentrated in an individual segment. For example, in the world car industry the specialist manufacturers of luxury and sports cars have found it increasingly difficult to compete because the large-scale manufacturers which straddle multiple segments are capable of spreading their R&D, manufacturing, marketing and dealership costs across a wider model range.

The segmentation of the restaurant industry shown in Figure 5.2 is likely to be a useful stage in analyzing competitive positioning for a new entrant. An important issue for someone starting a new restaurant is the level of competition within individual industry segments. If a town with a population of 100,000 is already served by five up-market French restaurants, this might imply market saturation and stiff competition. Market segments in which there are no firms operating are particularly attractive. In the case of the restaurant industry, does this imply an unexploited opportunity, or an absence of market demand?

SUMMARY

At any one point in time industries vary in their attractiveness; also the attractiveness of any particular industry to an investor will vary over time, owing to such things as the state of the economy, government regulation and market conditions. It is important to gain understanding of the reasons why profitability may be above or below average. Five factors tend to determine this:

▌ barriers to entry;

▌ the possibility of substitution;

▌ power of suppliers;

▌ power of buyers;

▌ intensity of competition.

Industry analysis should focus on the future rather than the past or the present and attempt to predict how the above variables might change.

A passive approach may leave a company victim to changes in industry structure that have a damaging effect on its fortunes. Companies should try to be proactive and alter industry structure in their favour – for example by making a strategic acquisition or forming a strategic alliance.

It is also important to segment an industry and look to see which segments are the most attractive.

6

Building the portfolio (2): vertical integration

INTRODUCTION

Vertical integration is a firm's ownership of vertically related activities. Vertical integration can occur in two directions:

▌ *Backward integration* where the firm takes ownership and control of producing its own inputs (eg the Body Shop's production of many of its own toiletries and cosmetics);

▌ *Forward integration* where the firm takes ownership and control of its own customers (eg Coca-Cola acquiring many of its local bottlers within the US).

Vertical integration may also be *full integration* or *tapered integration*:

▌ *Full integration* exists between two stages of production, A and B, when all stage A's production is sold internally, and all stage B's requirements are obtained internally. Thus at most integrated steel plants, all pig iron production goes into steel making and none is purchased from outside.

▌ *Tapered integration* exists when stages A and B are not internally self-sufficient. Thus car manufacturers have traditionally been partially backward integrated into components – for example, most of General Motors' spark plugs, instruments and ignition equipment are supplied externally, but a portion of many of these items is produced by its AC-Delco division. Tapered integration is also typical of the oil industry. 'Crude rich' companies (such as Statoil) are net sellers of crude oil, 'crude poor' companies such as Exxon have to supplement their own production with purchases of crude to keep their refineries supplied.

In some industries companies are highly vertically integrated. The major oil companies own and control their operations from exploring for new oilfields, down to retailing petrol at company-owned filling stations. In other industries there is little vertical integration. In constructing buildings, separate companies are involved in design (architects), the supply of building materials, general contracting, specialist contracting (scaffolding, electricians, plumbers) and in several other activities. Even within the same industry, companies can vary greatly in the extent of their vertical integration. In plain paper copiers, Xerox has traditionally been highly vertically integrated, developing most technology in-house, manufacturing most of its own components, and supplying its copiers through its own sales and service organization. Most of the companies which challenged Xerox in this market were much less vertically integrated. Canon, Kodak, Oki and Sharp have relied more on licensing technology, they bought in most components and used independent dealers for sales and service. Which is best: to make or to buy, to sell to independent distributors or to own in-house distribution channels?

COSTS OF USING THE MARKET

For many types of transaction, markets are highly efficient and there is no advantage from vertical integration. Where inputs are supplied by competitive conditions, where information is readily available, and where switching costs are low, the transactions costs associated with dealing across the market are low. This is especially the case for commodities. Few flour milling companies own wheat farms. This is because these items are standardized and supplied through highly efficient commodity markets.

For some types of transaction, these conditions are not present. Consider a tree plantation and a sawmill. Transport costs mean that the sawmill must be built in close proximity to the tree plantation. But if the trees and the sawmill are owned by separate companies, several problems arise in negotiating market contracts:

1. The *small numbers problem*. If there is one forest owner and one sawmill owner, one is a monopoly supplier, the other a monopoly buyer. Price depends on bargaining power and negotiating ability, and there is no obvious equilibrium. This situation is likely to encourage unproductive investments whose primary aim is to improve the bargaining power of one party relative to the other.

2. Where *transaction-specific investments* must be made (eg in building a sawmill in a remote location, by the forest company growing trees) the risks associated with the relationship may act as a deterrent to investment. Polaroid Corporation's in-house manufacture of film for its instant cameras reflects (among other factors) the difficulty which the company would have in encouraging film manufacturers to invest in facilities dedicated to the production of Polaroid film.

3. *Limited information and the risk of opportunism* can also encourage vertical integration. If the quality of the wood can only be detected after sawing the trees, there may be incentives for the tree grower to grow poor quality trees and for the sawmill owner to misrepresent the quality of the sawn wood. If there is vertical integration, corporate head office can give precise instructions to each division about specifications and required quality levels.

4. *Taxes and regulations on market transactions*. If a government imposes taxes or other regulations on an intermediate market, this can provide an incentive for a company to vertically integrate. If sales of logs are subject to some form of 'environmental protection tax', forest owners will forward integrate in order to avoid the tax. OPEC quotas on sales of crude oil have encouraged the national companies in member countries to forward integrate into refining and petrochemicals as a means of 'cheating' on their quotas.

5. *Contracting costs arising from uncertainty*. As noted above, spot contracts for commodity items involve low contract costs. However, in supplying logs to a sawmill, a long-term contract would probably be desirable. How can the contract be framed to take account of changing circumstances? Prices need to include some provision for inflation, provision needs to be made for the changing quantities demanded by the sawmill and changing availability of trees, the circumstances of *force majeure* must be specified, and so on. Not only does this increase the initial costs of the contract, it may also give rise to continuing costs of contract enforcement and interpretation and lead to opportunism.

These transaction costs of using the market provide incentives for vertical integration, but any decisions on vertical integration must take account of the costs associated with internalizing transactions. Managing an extended vertical scope within a company involves difficult problems:

1. *Achieving scale efficiency*. One of the risks of vertical integration is that optimal scale can vary substantially between different stages of production. Vertical integration may therefore result in sub-optimal scale and high costs in certain activities. In car manufacture, an assembly plant can be fairly efficient at 200,000 units a year; efficiency in engine manufacture requires a scale of production in excess of one million units a year; while efficiency in new product development requires even larger volumes. As a result, Rover Cars became less and less vertically integrated to the point where it is primarily an assembly operation, buying in most components and sub-assemblies and relying increasingly on Honda for technology and design.

2. *Managing strategically different businesses*. One of the main sources of administrative costs in internalizing vertically related businesses arises from co-ordinating businesses which, in strategic terms, are very different. By strategically different we mean businesses where the basis of competitive advantage differs because the industry environments are very different, and the resources and capabilities required for success are also different. For example, why is it that vertical integration between manufacturing and retailing companies is so rare? It would appear that manufacturing and retailing are quite different types of business. Success in manufacturing requires manufacturing capabilities, technological strengths, and competence in product development. Retailing requires rapid adjustment to consumer demand and competition, astute buying practices, and constant attentiveness to the store's image and managing the relationship with the customer. Managing across such different businesses is a difficult challenge for top management, not just in terms of the knowledge and insight required, but also in designing corporate systems which are appropriate to both.

3. *Flexibility*. Both vertical integration and market transactions can claim advantages with regard to different types of flexibility. As noted above, where co-ordinated investments are required managerial control can offer advantages over arm's-length arrange-

ments between separate firms. However, where the required flexibility is responsiveness to uncertain demand, then there may be advantages in market transactions. The lack of vertical integration in the construction industry reflects, in part, the need for flexibility in adjusting both to a cyclical pattern of demand and to the different requirements of each project. A vertically integrated construction company would encompass design and engineering capabilities, general building contracting, and the provision of specialist services such as steel fixing, plumbing, air conditioning, electrical work and joinery. Such vertical integration would mean greater difficulty in adjusting both to expansion and contraction in orders, and to meet the particular needs of different types of project.

4. *Compounding risk*. To the extent that vertical integration ties a company to its internal suppliers, it compounds risk since problems at any one stage of production threaten production and profitability at all other stages. In the manufacturing of sports shoes, the reliance of Nike and Reebok on contracts with independent manufacturing companies in Asia and elsewhere reduced Nike's exposure to exchange rate, political and quality risks.

Table 6.1 summarizes the factors which are important in determining the merits of vertical integration compared to market transactions.

LONG-TERM CONTRACTS AND 'QUASI-VERTICAL INTEGRATION'

So far, vertical integration has been contrasted with market transactions where these have been interpreted mainly as spot contracts. However, spot contracts are not the only or even the most common type of market transaction between companies. The supply of components and raw materials to manufacturing firms usually involves a long-term relationship between the supplier and the manufacturer – although not necessarily with a written long-term contract. Similarly, most supply relationships between manufacturers, distributors and retailers are long term. In some cases these relationships are formulated into written contracts which specify the nature and responsibilities of the agency, distributor or dealership relationship.

The important feature of such longer-term vertical relationships between independent firms is that they can avoid some of the transaction

Table 6.1   *Vertical integration versus market transactions: a review of the relevant considerations*

Issue	Implication for vertical integration
How many firms are there in the vertically related activity?	The fewer the companies the greater the attraction of vertical integration.
Do transaction-specific investments need to be made by either party?	The greater the requirements for specific investments, the more attractive vertical integration is.
Does limited availability of information provide opportunities to the contracting firm to behave opportunistically (ie cheat)?	The greater the difficulty of specifying and monitoring contracts, the greater the advantages of vertical integration.
Are market transactions subject to taxes and regulations?	Vertical integration is attractive if it can circumvent taxes and regulations.
How much uncertainty exists about the circumstances prevailing over the period of the contract?	Uncertainty raises the costs of writing and monitoring contracts, and provides opportunities for cheating, therefore increasing the attractiveness of vertical integration.
Are the two stages similar in terms of the optimal scale of operations?	The greater the dissimilarity in scale, the more difficult vertical integration is.
How strategically similar are the different stages in terms of key success factors and the resources and capabilities require for success?	The greater the strategic dissimilarity, the more difficult vertical integration is.
How uncertain is market demand?	The greater the demand uncertainty, the more costly vertical integration is.
Does vertical integration increase risk by requiring heavy investment in multiple stages and compounding otherwise independent risk factors?	The heavier the investment requirements and the greater the independent risks at each stage, the more risky vertical integration is.

costs associated with market transactions without the need for full vertical integration. Where the vertical relationships are especially close and long term they have been referred to as *'quasi-vertical integration'* or *'value-adding partnerships'*. An example of one type of relationship – franchising – is given here. Other types of long-term relationship will be discussed in Chapter 8.

The franchise system of McDonald's Restaurants

A franchise agreement is a contract between a franchiser, who owns a brand name and has developed a system for supplying a product or service, and a franchisee, who purchases the right to use that brand name and business system at a specified location. The purpose of the franchise is to offer the co-ordination advantages of vertical integration, while maintaining the flexibility advantages associated with independent contracting companies. Many of the transaction costs associated with market exchanges are avoided by a contract which is long term, comprehensive and supported by a close relationship between franchiser and franchisee. The reputation that McDonald's has established through many thousands of franchise agreements over a long period gives the new franchisee trust in the relationship, and also provides a disincentive for McDonald's to engage in opportunistic behaviour. Co-operation is also fostered through a comprehensive training programme for franchisees in which McDonald's instils its philosophy and values in the new franchisee. At the same time, because the franchise relationship is between separate firms it avoids several of the problems of vertical integration. Franchisees bring their own capital, hence reducing financial requirements and risk for the franchiser. McDonald's Restaurants Inc and the individual franchised restaurant are very different businesses. In terms of scale, one is global, the other local. In terms of strategy, McDonald's is involved in managing a complex system requiring elaborate management information systems, new product development, and highly sophisticated marketing. The individual restaurant is involved in flipping burgers, serving milkshakes, avoiding waste and keeping the premises clean. The franchise system in which the franchisee works for profit provides direct incentives for increasing revenue and reducing costs.

SUMMARY

Vertical integration is of two kinds – forward integration where a manufacturing or raw materials company moves closer to the ultimate customer, or backward integration where a retailer acquires manufacturing resources or a manufacturer acquires components suppliers or raw materials sources. Companies adopt vertical integration strategies for a variety of reasons. They may want to alter industry structure so as to improve their own competitive position; they may want to secure strategically important sources of supply or equally important channels of distribution. Some industries such as oil companies tend to be vertically integrated while in others such as construction it is unusual. There are, however, differences within industries. In retailing, for example, companies such as Laura Ashley, Body Shop and Clark's Shoes are largely vertically integrated, while others in the same fields of clothing and footwear industry such as Nike are not.

Vertical integration pays off in cases where transaction costs involved in using the market are significant.

Vertical integration creates problems as well as bringing potential advantages. For example, it involves managing different kinds of business, such as manufacturing and retail, a challenge not always successfully overcome. Also vertically integrated firms can lack flexibility and, because they tend to use transfer pricing, they can lose touch with market conditions.

7

Building the portfolio (3): diversification

INTRODUCTION

One course of action open to companies looking to grow is to diversify, ie move into industries using different technologies or serving different markets. Where the technologies or markets involved are very diverse this is known as unrelated diversification and the marketing group is commonly described as a conglomerate. Where there are evident synergies between the technologies or markets concerned, this is known as related diversification. Both kinds will be considered in this chapter.

CONGLOMERATE OR UNRELATED DIVERSIFICATION

The five principal arguments that have been proposed to justify unrelated diversification are discussed below.

Risk reduction

By spreading investments across several industries a firm is subject to less risk: cash flow is more stable over time. But does pooling risk in this way increase shareholder wealth through increasing the stock market value of the company? Modern finance theory suggests that it does not. So long as shareholders have the opportunity of holding diversified portfolios, they can create their own diversification. Moreover, such portfolio diversification by investors is likely to be less costly than business diversification by firms. An individual investor's transaction costs (brokers' commissions and other costs) in building a diversified portfolio are low. Corporate acquisitions, on the other hand, are expensive. Not only do buyers incur heavy fees to investment banks and public relations consultants, the acquisition price they pay to gain control of target companies is typically 20 to 40 per cent above the prevailing stock market value of the company.

Economies in corporate services

Even where there are no operational linkages between businesses, there may be opportunities for cost savings through pooling common services with the diversified company. Such common corporate services including legal services, public relations, treasury, internal audit and investor relations. Acquisitions are usually followed by a merger of corporate functions and the sale of the acquired company's head office.

Economizing on transaction costs

Within the diversified company, individual businesses tend to be independent profit centres which compete for investment funds allocated by the corporate headquarters. Hence they have been likened to internal capital markets where the primary functions of the corporate headquarters are to monitor financial performance, to allocate investment funds and to make acquisitions and divestments. Headquarters exerts financial discipline by rewarding successful divisions and their managers, while subjecting unsuccessful divisions to low capital allocation, low managerial remuneration and ultimate divestment.

Compared with independent specialist firms seeking investment funds through the external capital market, diversified companies' internal capital markets offer certain advantages. First, internal capital markets may avoid some of the transaction costs of external capital markets: both equity finance and debt finance are costly in terms of fees, top management time, and other costs of using the market. Second, external capital markets have limited information on the performance and prospects of independent companies. In contrast, a corporate headquarters within a diversified business has highly detailed information on its member divisions and can be much more astute than external investors and lenders in assessing future returns on new investment in different businesses. In addition, the top management is capable of imposing sanctions after poor financial performance more quickly and effectively than the board of directors or shareholders of an independent, specialist company.

The capital allocation advantage of a diversified company over groups of specialized companies also exists in relation to the labour market – particularly that for managers. As companies grow and change they require new and different managers. Hiring new managers externally is fraught with difficulty. Information on past performance is poor and it is difficult to predict performance in a new situation. Recruiting for senior management positions can incur costs which amount to one year's salary. In a diversified company, the corporate personnel function can build up profound knowledge of the abilities of individual managers and their effectiveness in different types of situation. Large diversified companies tend to have corporate management development units whose task is to identify and nurture managerial talent and plan the careers of high-potential managers.

Not only can diversified companies operate internal labour markets which are more efficient than external labour markets, the greater range of opportunities that a large diversified company can offer compared with a small specialized company may result in diversified companies attracting a higher quality of employee. Large diversified companies can offer greater job security and a wider range of opportunities.

Exploiting inefficiencies in the market's valuation of companies

Diversified companies are characterized by the active way in which they deal in assets. The most prominent strategic role of their top managers tends to be making acquisitions and divestments. If they are to create value in trading assets through 'buying cheap and selling dear' their top managers must possess better knowledge than the market. Even if the stock market is inefficient, in the sense that securities prices do not accurately and fully reflect all available information, and if certain investors possess superior knowledge, intuition or forecasting abilities, this does not provide a rationale for acquiring companies. George Soros has made some strikingly accurate judgements on the direction of market movements. During 1993 he was one of the most prominent of the 'gold bulls'; his belief led him to acquire a large shareholding in Newmont Mining, North America's largest gold producer, but provided no incentive for him to acquire the whole company or even to request a seat on the board. Superior market knowledge or understanding is most effectively exploited through the securities markets; it does not require managerial control of the companies involved. In order to justify the acquisition premium paid in a takeover bid, the acquiring company's ability to create value must depend on its achieving managerial control. For example, if creating value requires a break-up of the company or some other form of restructuring, this would require the exercise of managerial control.

The problem of managerial motives

The above arguments point to profit advantages associated with diversified companies. However, another possibility is that diversification is motivated more by the interests of top managers than by the interests of shareholders. The evidence of company case studies, interviews with managers and quantitative research lends support to this view. The lack of effective shareholder control over companies has permitted influential chief executives to run large companies as their personal fiefdoms. The behaviour of Russ Johnson at RJR Nabisco (prior to the buy-out in 1990), Tiny Rowland at Lonrho, the late Robert Maxwell at Pergamon Press, Maxwell Communication and Mirror Group Newspapers, and Harold Geneen at ITT all point to the propensity for diversification to be used as a means to build corporate empires which satisfy the chief executive's ego rather than create value for shareholders.

HANSON

In 1964 Hanson Trust was created by James Hanson and Gordon White. Hanson PLC went on to become one of the world's biggest diversified companies with annual profits of more than £1.5 billion and a strategy of growth through acquisition.

In the 1970s and 80s Lords Hanson and White turned Hanson into a multinational concern with interests across the world ranging from chemical factories in the United States to electricity supply in the UK and gold mines in Australia. Hanson produced cigarettes and batteries, timber and toys, golf clubs and jacuzzis, cod liver oil capsules and cranes, cement and bricks. It was the classic conglomerate and was, for some considerable time, conspicuously successful, a success that was reflected in its share price. Its approach was to seek out underperforming companies with significant market share in mature industries and by stripping out costs and improving management disciplines to bring about step changes in profitability.

By the mid-1990s the climate in which Hanson operated began to change as investors began to look beyond the traditional big conglomerate to companies focused on single sectors. The reasons for this were mixed. Partly it was simply that conglomerates were going out of fashion following some spectacular failures. Partly it was down to the fact that Hanson was finding it increasingly difficult to find companies that fitted its formula and thus to maintain its growth. Also, once the companies in the Hanson empire had received their turnround treatment there was little further scope for internal improvement in efficiencies. The share price went into steep decline and in January 1996 the decision to demerge the business into four separate companies was taken. Imperial Tobacco, The Energy Group and the US chemicals business, Millennium, subsequently became quoted companies in their own right. Hanson's strategy was to change from a diversified industrial conglomerate into a focused heavy building materials business. The major building materials companies remaining within Hanson were ARC, Hanson Brick and Cornerstone.

Lord Hanson stepped down as chairman in December 1997. He was succeeded by Christopher Collins.

From 1997 to 2000 the Hanson board undertook the substantial changes required to deliver the new strategy. The remaining non-core businesses were sold. Considerable sums were spent on acquisitions to build up the existing businesses and capital investment on plant upgrades was stepped up to improve efficiency and reduce costs.

Early in 1999, to highlight the fact that Hanson was now a unified company, the names of all the operating companies were changed to Hanson. ARC became Hanson Quarry Products Europe; Cornerstone became Hanson Building Materials America, and Hanson Brick became Hanson Bricks Europe. The company's business in South-East Asia became Hanson Pacific.

Acquisitions continued, particularly in the United States, and the company was developed into a global player with the acquisition in May 2000 of the Australian construction materials business Pioneer International.

In January 2002 Hanson created an integrated building materials business in Europe by combining its quarry products and bricks operations into a new division called Hanson Building Materials Europe.

Today, Hanson is one of the world's leading building materials companies and is the largest producer of aggregates and the third largest producer of ready-mixed concrete in the world with over 31,000 employees and operations in 19 countries across four continents.

In 1997, when the decision to demerge was taken the company's share price stood at 298.5p. By 1999 it had risen to 618p. Since then it has suffered from the general stock market decline, but at time of writing (October 2002) was at a respectable price of 498p.

One consequence of growth-motivated diversification mergers has been opportunities for releasing shareholder value through breaking up diversified companies. The leveraged buy-out of RJR Nabisco organized by Kohlberg, Kravis and Roberts was the biggest example of a more general phenomenon where companies have been acquired with a view to divesting diversified activities. The success of these efforts in boosting the market valuation of the companies involved has encouraged many companies to divest earlier acquisitions to boost their share price. In the oil industry, for example, virtually all the diversification of the late 1970s and early 1980s has been undone as companies have returned to being simply oil and gas companies. Thus British Petroleum sold its Scicon computer software and services subsidiary, its 40 per cent stake in Mercury Communications, its minerals and coal subsidiaries, and most of its nutrition business.

THE CASE FOR RELATED DIVERSIFICATION

Michael Porter (1980) suggests three 'essential tests' which need to be met in determining whether diversification is likely to create value for shareholders:

▋ *Industry attractiveness* – is the industry to be entered structurally attractive, or capable of being made attractive?

▋ *Cost of entry* – is the cost of entering the industry sufficiently low that it does not offset all the advantages of being in the industry?

▋ *Competitive advantage* – is the competitiveness of the new business enhanced by its link with the existing business, or alternatively, does the existing business benefit from its link with the diversified business?

The first condition can be met by unrelated diversification. For a company in an unattractively structured industry – such as steel, agriculture or foundries – entry into pharmaceuticals, biotechnology or management consulting may offer more attractive investment opportunities. The problem, however, is that the second test tends to counteract the first. The primary reason for some industries offering above average returns is that they are protected from new competition by barriers to entry. As a start-up pharmaceutical company, it is highly unlikely that a new entrant would earn a return on capital that is anything like that of GSK or Pfizer. To avoid barriers to entry created by patents, scale economies and product differentiation, it is always possible to acquire an established company. But given that the market price of the company will fully reflect its profit prospects, the acquisition price will result in the diversifying firm paying a premium to enter the industry. The perceived attractiveness of the stockbroking business during the 1980s both in Britain and the United States resulted in buyers paying acquisition prices which doomed them to low returns for the foreseeable future.

Hence diversification yielding shareholder value almost always requires *synergy*: some relationship between the core and the diversified business which results in the creation of competitive advantage. Synergy is present when there are *economies of scope* in the supply of different products. Economies of scope are cost reductions resulting from different products being produced within the same company rather than by specialist companies. Economies of scope require the presence of a common input which is 'lumpy', ie not divisible into small units.

According to the types of resource being shared, quite different patterns of diversification strategy can be noticed.

Sharing physical assets

The most obvious examples of economies of scope are sharing capital assets such as production plant, distribution facilities, communication networks, and the like. For example:

▌ Diversification in financial services has been partly motivated by companies' desire to exploit economies of scope by selling a range of financial products through a common distribution channel. Thus British banks lumbered with huge and increasingly costly networks of retail branches have diversified into insurance and stockbroking.

▌ Food processing companies have become increasingly diversified
as they have sought to exploit economies of scope in their distribution and marketing systems. Philip Morris's willingness to pay
50 per cent above stock market value to acquire Kraft in 1988
reflected the economies which it perceived in sharing distribution,
marketing and purchasing between Kraft and its other food
subsidiary, General Foods.

▌ The recent burst of mergers and joint ventures between telecom-
munication and cable TV companies has been motivated by the
desire to spread the huge costs of installing fibre-optic cable
networks across telephone, TV and information services.

Sharing intangible resources and transferring capabilities

Economies of scope are also possible from sharing intangible
resources (such as brands and company reputation) and transferring
organizational capabilities across different businesses. The primary
organizational differences between this form of synergy and sharing
physical resources is that sharing intangible resources and capabilities
requires little or no integration at the operational level – simple
transfer is enough. Consider the following examples:

▌ ***Brands***. In a number of consumer goods industries the ability to
extend brand equity into related markets has provided a rationale
for diversification, for example Gillette's diversification from
razor blades into men's toiletries, Mars' diversification from
confectionery into ice-cream, and American Express's introduction of a wide range of financial products and travel services
under the 'American Express' trademark. The most direct indication of the economies of scope available from branding is in
advertising. Companies such as Sony, IBM and Black and Decker,
whose brand names span a number of products, are able to spread
the costs of their brand advertising over a broader sales base than
more specialist companies.

▌ ***Reputation***. When reputation is attached to a company rather than
to a brand name, a similar transfer of competitive advantage may
be possible. Marks and Spencer's reputation for quality and fair
dealing facilitated its entry into the retailing of processed foods
and financial services. The competitive advantage associated with
reputation may extend beyond customer goodwill. Marks and
Spencer's advantage in food retailing was also a result of its repu-

tation for fair, supportive supplier relations which gave it an advantage when obtaining supply agreements with food manufacturing companies.

▌ *Technology*. Technical knowledge is frequently able to be applied in different ways. Honda's design and manufacturing knowledge in four-stroke engines facilitated its diversification from motorcycles to cars, generators, lawn mowers and marine engines. At Hewlett-Packard, expertise in electronics and a strong culture of innovation have taken the company into calculators, personal computers, printers and a range of other products. General Motors' acquisitions of Hughes Aircraft and EDS were perceived as a way of acquiring necessary technological and information processing skills.

▌ *Marketing capabilities*. In addition to opportunities for transferring brand names, companies may also be able to transfer marketing capabilities in terms of brand management, new product introduction, market research and channel management skills. Philip Morris's diversification from tobacco to beer (Miller), soft drinks (Seven Up) and processed foods (Kraft and General Foods) has been based on its strengths in brand management, market segmentation and international marketing. Diageo's acquisition of Distillers was based on the belief that the transfer of marketing capabilities between the two companies would enhance the competitive advantage of both.

▌ *Operational capabilities*. Manufacturing capabilities may also be transferable to industries where process technology is similar. The tendency for chemical companies to be diversified across a broad range of chemical products reflects in part the similarity of production technologies within the sector and the need for similar types of operational capabilities. Harley-Davidson's diversification into defence contracting and camper trucks was partly motivated by its belief in its ability to transfer its expertise in small volume, high quality, highly flexible manufacturing from motorcycles to these other products. Canon's diversification from cameras into copiers, printers and facsimile machines has been assisted by its skills in manufacturing precision engineered products.

Sharing general management skills

The sources of synergy that have been discussed so far have implied some relationship between the different businesses within the firm. If resources and capabilities are to be shared or transferred, then some technical or market linkage is normally required between the businesses. However, the capabilities which are transferred within the diversified company may not be merely functional capabilities, they may also be general management capabilities. For the corporate headquarters to infuse general management capabilities into subsidiary companies does not necessarily require there to be any technical or customer linkages between the businesses – the businesses must simply possess certain managerial similarities. Although the individual businesses of a highly diversified company may be unrelated in terms of markets and technologies, they do bear certain managerial similarities. For example, Hanson's businesses tended to be in mature, low-technology sectors where international competition is not a dominant strategic influence. United Technologies tends to be in technology and engineering-intensive industries, Trafalgar House is within mature, capital-intensive sectors. The value added by corporate management in these companies tends to be through the application of common systems of financial control and asset management, as was the case with Hanson, the strategic management of businesses subject to rapid technological change (United Technologies), and the ability to acquire assets at low cost and make astute investment decisions where projects are large and long term (Trafalgar House).

DIVERSIFICATION AND SYNERGY

There is little doubt that important benefits are to be obtained from sharing facilities and transferring reputation, knowledge and capabilities. The critical issue which arises is identical to that discussed in relation to vertical integration: if there are benefits to co-operation and integration, is common ownership necessary to achieve it? During the discussion of vertical integration it was noted that independent companies are capable of forming close, vertical relationships which permit intimate collaboration. Similarly with diversification; can sharing facilities, and transferring brand names, technology and capabilities not be achieved through collaboration by separate companies?

This argument comes down to one of the transaction costs of using the market versus the administrative costs of co-ordination within the diversified corporation. In the case of a transferable brand name, transfer to another product may be achieved by diversification or by licensing the use of the brand to another company. Couture fashion houses such as Christian Dior, Gucci and Calvin Klein license their brand names to suppliers of perfumes, clothing, jewellery and clothing accessories in preference to diversifying internally. The Walt Disney Company exploits the Walt Disney name and the use of its characters (Mickey Mouse, Donald Duck, and so on) both through internal diversification into videos, theme parks and educational materials, and through licensing to toy and clothing manufacturers and to comic publishers. The choice of diversification or licensing depends on the costs associated with negotiating and enforcing licensing contracts and the effectiveness of these contracts in exploiting the full value of the Disney name and characters, compared with the costs and returns from entering and managing a different type of business.

The efficiency of the market as a means of transfer depends very much on a company's ability to establish clear ownership rights in the resource or capability. If a technology can be patented, then a firm can sell its patent rights – many biotechnology companies specialize in R&D and leave commercialization to other companies. Similarly, the developers of the Dolby sound reduction systems and the Wankel rotary engine chose to market their patents rather than engage directly in the manufacture of audio systems and motor vehicles. On the other hand, EMI's doubts about the effectiveness of patent protection on its CAT scanner encouraged its diversification into medical electronics during the early 1970s. Organizational capabilities which are applicable in different areas of business are much more difficult to exploit across markets. Philip Morris could in principle exploit its marketing capabilities by establishing a consulting subsidiary to provide marketing management advice, but in practice the direct application of its marketing management capabilities through diversification into related businesses is likely to yield much greater returns.

DIVERSIFICATION AND PERFORMANCE

The rationale which a company offers for diversification is typically impeccably argued. Diversification through acquisition is normally justified on the basis of cost savings from eliminating duplication in corporate services, the integration of related facilities, the transfer of know-how and other capabilities, and the infusion of efficiency and dynamism from the managerially stronger to the managerially weaker company.

The evidence of experience tells a different story. Despite several decades of observation and research the picture remains murky. From the mass of inconsistent and inconclusive results the following generalizations may be drawn:

1. There is no basis for concluding that diversification is generally conducive to profitability and the creation of shareholder wealth.

2. The principal beneficiaries of diversification appear to be the shareholders of acquired companies (who benefit from the acquisition premium paid for their shares), and top managers who receive both psychological and financial benefit from increases in company size.

3. On balance, the weight of evidence points towards diversification having a negative effect on profitability and shareholder wealth.

Among the recent evidence on the success of diversification, the following findings are worthy of note:

▍ Among UK industrial companies it was found that profitability was positively associated with diversity up to a point, but from then on increased levels of industrial diversity were associated with lower levels of profitability (Grant, Jammine and Thomas, 1988).

▍ Among leading US corporations, 60 per cent of acquisitions which took the companies into entirely new fields were subsequently divested (Porter, 1987).

▍ The stock market's verdict on diversification is indicated, first, by the tendency for takeover announcements to lead to a fall in the buyer's share price and second, by the 'conglomerate discount' phenomenon – diversified companies tend to be valued at a lower price-earnings ratio than specialized companies.

The trend towards 'refocusing' has already been noted, when companies have attempted to create shareholder value by shedding their diversified businesses. A central feature of the 'downsizing' that has accompanied the restructuring among large US and European companies has been the divestment of the peripheral businesses acquired during the previous two decades in order to concentrate on core businesses. Splitting Courtaulds into a fibre company and a textiles company was the forerunner of a much bigger wave of divestments and flotations. Among the most notable was ICI's spin-off of its pharmaceutical interests into Zeneca plc. In many instances, companies have discovered that collaborative arrangements with other companies can yield most of the advantages of related diversification without the risks or the managerial complexities. In financial services, collaboration between banks, insurance companies and stockbrokers can yield many of the advantages of 'one-stop shopping' without merger.

MANAGING THE DIVERSIFIED CORPORATION

Why is it that diversification has proved such a disappointing, profitless experience for so many companies? In most cases it appears that the potential does exist for sharing facilities and transferring resources and capabilities between businesses. The problems occur in managing these complexities. The presence of economies of scope and transaction costs in collaborating across markets are fairly easy to identify. Often more difficult to predict are the management difficulties involved in exploiting linkages. Managing the diversified corporation involves issues of organizational structure and defining the role of the corporate headquarters in terms of strategy formulation, resource allocation and provision of corporate services. Let us consider how these management issues can be resolved.

Organizational structure

The dominant organizational form for the diversified corporation is the multidivisional structure – also known as the *'M-form'*. The organizational principle of the M-form is that operational management is decentralized to each business division, while the corporate head office is responsible for overall control, inter-divisional co-ordination, and the management of corporate issues. Beyond this principle, diversified companies display a wide range of organizational forms. In most diversified companies there is a corporate headquarters, at the next level are divisions (or 'groups' or 'sectors') which bring together strategically similar businesses, and within the divisions are the primary profit centres which may be operating companies or *strategic business units (SBUs)*. Figures 7.1 and 7.2 show the organizational structures of two diversified companies.

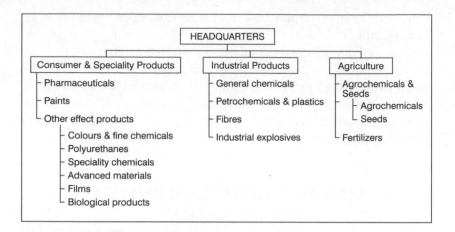

Figure 7.1   *ICI plc: group structure (prior to Zeneca spin-off)*

The M-form has developed out of two organizational types: the traditional, functionally structured company, and the holding company. The two pioneers of the M-form, DuPont and General Motors, are examples of each type of evolution.

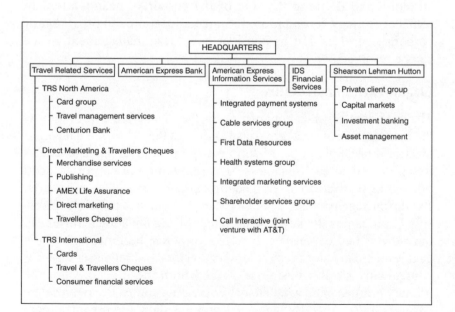

Figure 7.2   *American Express Company, Inc: group structure*

▌ *DuPont*'s adoption of the multidivisional form resulted from the increasing difficulties of co-ordinating product diversification within a functionally structured company. Because there was little need for operational co-ordination across the major product sectors, reorganization around product divisions enabled co-ordination between marketing, manufacturing and product development to occur at a lower level in the organization, thereby reducing the information and decision-making burden on headquarters and permitting corporate headquarters to focus on strategic issues.

▌ *General Motors* developed as a *holding company*, a company formed from acquisition where the subsidiaries retained their identity and operational freedom, and the parent company's control was achieved through being the largest shareholder. For General Motors, and other holding companies since, the disadvantage of this structure is that it does not facilitate the exploitation of synergies within the group. Hence General Motors's solution was to merge the various subsidiary companies into 14 product divisions – some responsible for particular product types (GM Truck Division, Samson Tractor Division, Inter-Company Parts Division, etc), others responsible for particular models (Chevrolet Division, Buick Division, Cadillac Division, etc).

By the mid-1960s, the M-form based on product-based divisions was the dominant organizational form for large diversified companies in all industrialized countries. Since that time, the M-form has continued to spread. During the 1970s and 1980s, many multinational companies (including Philips and ICI) replaced organizational structures based on geographical divisions by product-based multidivisional structures.

How activities are divided between corporate and divisional levels depends, in part, on the closeness of relationships between the divisions. In cases where the businesses are unrelated the headquarters is usually small, reflecting the fact that there is so little in common between the divisions that there is little scope for centralizing common activities. Where diversification is related, then there is likely to be more scope for centralizing activities such as engineering, information systems, research, market analysis and strategic planning.

PORTFOLIO PLANNING MODELS

Portfolio planning models are a set of techniques to provide guidelines to corporate management about resource allocation and strategy formulation among the different businesses within a diversified corporation. Although a variety of techniques have been developed, they share a common framework. The essence of that framework is to assess business units in relation to two criteria:

▌ the attractiveness of the market;

▌ the competitive advantage of the business.

The most widely used variants are the McKinsey/General Electric portfolio analysis matrix and the Boston Consulting Group's growth-share matrix (see Figure 7.3).

The McKinsey/GE matrix assesses industry attractiveness in terms of several factors including market size, market growth rate, industry profitability, cyclicality and ability to raise prices. Competitive advantage ('business unit position') is assessed in terms of market share, competitive position relative to competitors, and relative profitability.

The BCG matrix uses univariate measures of both industry attractiveness and competitive advantage. Industry attractiveness is measured by the growth rate of market demand. Competitive advantage is measured by relative market share (the market share of the business unit relative to the market share of the largest competitor).

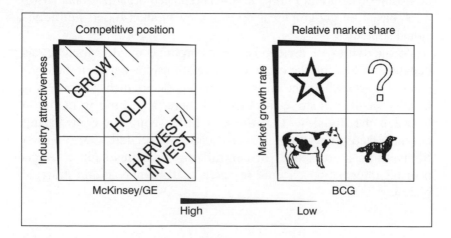

Figure 7.3   *The McKinsey/GE and BCG portfolio planning matrices*

Once the business units of the company have been positioned within the matrix, both approaches yield similar implications for strategy. Those businesses which score high on both industry attractiveness and competitive position (the 'stars' in the BCG matrix) are those which offer the best long-term profit prospects and are the businesses which should be the primary targets for corporate investment. Businesses which score low both on industry attractiveness and competitive advantage (the 'dogs' in the BCG matrix) offer poor profit prospects and are primary candidates for divestment.

The BCG analysis puts special emphasis on the cash flow implications of the different quadrants.

Market growth is associated with negative cash flow due to investment requirements, while relative market share is associated with positive cash flow – profits from competitive advantage. Hence strong businesses in low growth industries tend to earn a substantial cash surplus ('cash cows') which can be used to invest in growth businesses.

Portfolio planning matrices may have value in initiating discussion on corporate strategy and resource allocation within the diversified firm. However, it is difficult to justify the use of these matrices except as superficial, first-cut analyses. The shortcomings of these techniques include:

▮ The *criteria*. In the case of the BCG matrix, there is very little theoretical or empirical support for the notion that the profit prospects of a business are determined by two variables: market growth and relative market share. Although the McKinsey matrix is somewhat more sophisticated, it too suffers from the broadness and naïvety of the assumptions which it implicitly involves.

▮ *Measuring the criteria*. Even if the criteria did possess some validity, there are huge problems of measurement. In the BCG matrix the definition of the market is critical to both variables. For example, what is the market in the case of the Morgan car company? Is it the global sports car market, in which case Morgan has a negligible share? Or is it a much narrower segment of cars hand-built by craftspeople, in which case it has a significant share?

▮ The *implicit assumption* is that every business is independent. If the competitiveness of one business depends on synergies with other businesses, then the techniques which view the diversified company as a portfolio of independent businesses are simply not valid.

SUMMARY

Among the different areas of strategic management, diversification stands out as the most fraught with danger and most closely associated with failure. Why have diversification strategies so frequently performed poorly? Two problems are paramount. First, diversification strategies have often been driven more by managerial than shareholder interests. Diversification has permitted growth and, for many companies, greater earnings stability. However, neither of these achievements creates value for shareholders. The 'back to basics' movement of the past ten years and the divestment of so many diversified businesses by large corporations are primarily the result of the increased priority which companies accord to shareholder interests. Second, diversification strategies have typically been based on inadequate analysis. In particular, the benefits of synergy have been overestimated and the organizational problems of exploiting these synergies and managing increased complexity have been underestimated.

In appraising diversification opportunities, the analysis points to the merits of applying the following guidelines.

Define carefully the goals of diversification

To avoid the conflict between managerial and shareholder goals it is important that managers carefully analyze the reasons for diversification. If diversification is motivated by unattractive investment opportunities within the firm's core business, managers need to be clear about whether diversification will yield returns to shareholders in excess of simply returning cash flows directly to them in the form of higher dividends.

Apply Porter's 'Essential Tests'

If diversification is pursued in order to create shareholder value, then Porter's tests provide an excellent screen for determining the diversification's potential to increase profitability. The first test, *industry attractiveness*, needs to be considered jointly with the second test, *cost of entry*. There is little point in entering an industry where average profitability is high if the cost of entry negates those profitability advantages. The third test, *competitive advantage*, is the critical one. As the entry of many commercial banks into stockbroking and investment banking has shown, it is possible to lose large sums of money by investing in what appears to be an attractive industry. Conversely, as Hanson proved, it is possible to diversify into mature, low growth industries such as building materials, typewriters and tobacco and make very healthy profits.

The competitive advantage test: appraising synergy

If two businesses A and B are brought under common ownership, through what mechanisms is the competitive position of either A or B enhanced? The analysis suggested several opportunities for synergy:

▌ cost economies for shared activities;

▌ the transfer of intangible resources (such as brand names and technology) and organizational capabilities;

▌ access to superior general management skills.

It was also suggested that there may be benefits from diversification even when it involves completely unrelated businesses. Such unrelated diversification may lead to efficiencies when the internal markets for capital and labour within the conglomerate company are more efficient than the external markets for these resources.

Diversification versus contracts or strategic alliances

In order to determine whether exploiting synergy requires the company to diversify, it is vital that top management considers whether synergistic linkages can be exploited by contracts or alliances with other companies which avoid the capital costs of diversification while preserving greater flexibility. Harley-Davidson derives a large proportion of its profits from the use of the Harley-Davidson name and insignia on motorcycle accessories, T-shirts, jackets, key rings and toys. While Harley-Davidson could diversify into the manufacture of these items, it can exploit its brand name more easily with very low investment costs by licensing agreements.

Recognizing the managerial costs of diversification

Diversification decisions must consider both benefits and costs. There is a danger that companies appraise the potential benefits of synergy and avoidance of transaction costs, but ignore the managerial costs associated with the multibusiness corporation. The diversified company is more complex than the specialized company – top management must allocate resources between divisions, oversee business strategy formulation, and monitor divisional performance. This requires a different set of top management capabilities from those required in the specialist company. Post-mortems of failed diversification strategies have given rise to two types of comments from the managers involved:

▌ We never knew what we were getting into – it was only afterwards that we realized that the new business was very different from our main business.

▌ It was a terrible diversion of top management time. We couldn't concentrate on making money in our core business because the problems with our diversified businesses ate up management time and energy.

8

Strategic options

Strategic options are defined as key decisions or choices between alternative courses of action that are irreversible in the short run and have important implications for the competitiveness of the enterprise. This chapter offers brief reviews of some of the more important ones.

MERGERS AND ACQUISITIONS VERSUS ORGANIC GROWTH

There have been waves of fashion in mergers and acquisitions, including a trend for diversification in the 1960s and 1970s and leveraged buy-outs fuelled by high-risk, high-yield debt in the 1980s. By 2000, however, the frequency of these types of transactions had greatly declined. In the first nine months of that year they accounted for less than 2 per cent of all acquisitions in the United States, down from a high of 34 per cent in 1988.

The late 1990s saw both an increase in mergers and acquisitions generally and a growing emphasis on providing a strategic rationale. Some were designed to improve competitive positioning, as in Hewlett Packard's acquisition of Compaq, Pfizer's takeover of pharmaceuticals competitor Warner-Lambert and GlaxoWellcome's merger with SmithKline Beecham. Others involved acquirers moving into highly related businesses.

Some other deals were intended to redefine a business model – for instance, AOL's merger with Time Warner, completed in January 2001.

It remains to be seen how well these more recent mergers work out and to what extent the strategic rationale stands the test of time.

Examples of failure to realize expected dividends are not hard to find. For example, Credit Suisse Group, the world's 11th-largest financial-services group paid $2 billion in 1997 to acquire Winterthur, a European insurance underwriter, in a deal it said would yield synergies of more than $300 million a year. Now, mounting losses at Winterthur have forced Credit Suisse to inject $1.3 billion of fresh capital into the insurer to strengthen its weakening balance sheet. More recently, Munich-based insurance company Allianz, the world's second-largest insurer, shocked investors in July 2002 when it announced that it would fail to meet its $3 billion profit target for 2002 after reporting a loss of $350 million in the second quarter – mainly because of problems at its Dresdner Bank unit. Allianz paid $20 billion in 2001 for Dresdner in the hopes of cutting costs and generating new business worth $880 million a year, once integration was completed.

Photon magazine (September 2002) describes AOL's acquisition two years ago of Time Warner as 'one of the great train wrecks in corporate history'. The article goes on to assert that 'morale among the 18,000 employees is awful'. Employee stock options are 'worthless' and the company is 'riven into various fiefdoms'. Subscriber growth in the past two years has slowed – AOL added only 492,000 new members in the second quarter compared with 1.3 million a year earlier. The online advertising market is down. In the second quarter of 2002 revenue from advertising and online commerce at AOL totalled $412 million, down 42 per cent from the first quarter. Advertising revenue accounted for $342 million of that $412 million, and about two-thirds of that came from contracts entered into in the previous year. Revenue from new advertising contracts amounted to only $122 million, or just 5 per cent of the unit's overall revenue of $2.27 billion.

Finally, at time of writing, the company faces an accounting investigation. Both the Securities and Exchange Commission and the Department of Justice have widened inquiries into AOL's book-keeping in the period leading up to the 2000 deal with Time Warner. As long as the investigations continue investors are unlikely to buy back into a stock that recently dipped below $10 per share (compared with $72 when the merger was announced in January 2000).

Research findings

Several important pieces of research show that 50–75 per cent of acquisitions actually destroy shareholder value instead of achieving cost and/or revenue benefits. For example, Bekier, Bogardus and Oldham (2001) quote a Southern Methodist University (SMU) study of 193 mergers, worth $100 million or more, from 1990 to 1997, which found that revenue growth was not achieved in the great majority of cases. Measured against industry peers, only 36 per cent of the targets maintained their revenue growth in the first quarter after the merger announcement. By the third quarter, only 11 per cent had avoided a slowdown; the median shortfall was 12 per cent.

A deeper investigation showed that the acquired companies' continuing underperformance explained only half of the slowdown, the rest being due to unsettled customers and distracted staff.

Further research sampled more than 160 acquisitions by 157 publicly listed companies across 11 industry sectors in 1995 and 1996. Only 12 per cent of these companies managed to accelerate their growth significantly over the next three years. Overall, the acquirers' organic growth rates were four percentage points lower than those of their industry peers; 42 per cent of the acquirers actually lost ground.

These results were constant across different sectors and size groups and, on average, experienced acquirers didn't have better success than companies new to the activity.

Bekier and his colleagues argue that it is revenue that determines the success or failure of a merger, not cost reduction. Revenue affects the bottom line more significantly: 'Beating target revenue-growth rates by 2 to 3 percent can offset a 50 percent failure on costs.' In addition, up to 40 per cent of mergers fail to capture the identified cost savings. The market punishes such failure – failing to meet an earnings target by only 5 per cent can result in a 15 per cent decline in share price. The temptation is then to make either excessively deep cuts or cuts in inappropriate places, thus depressing future earnings by creating a state of corporate anorexia in which 'muscle' is being lost, not just fat.

Finally, they argue, companies that actively pursue growth in their mergers generate a positive attitude that makes merger objectives (including cost cutting) easier to achieve.

An emphasis on growth is far better for motivating talented employees – on either side of a merger – than cost cutting could ever be. Given the impact of revenue, it is surprising that so few acquiring companies treat it as rigorously as costs. Companies that do reap real benefit from mergers look after their existing customers and revenue. They also target and retain their revenue-generating talent – especially the people who handle relations with customers.

Successful acquirers also build into their acquisition processes three complementary strengths for achieving success. First, cost disciplines are firmly established at every level, an approach that allows senior management to focus on revenue. Second, successful acquirers recognize that successful mergers lead to a virtuous cycle of better deals and better results, so these companies create a process for handling mergers that improves with experience. Thirdly, they move quickly to instil a performance culture geared for growth, using such means as entrepreneurial, well-mentored teams with ambitious targets and incentives.

The authors conclude that success is determined above all by the ability to protect revenue and to generate growth just after a merger. Those acquirers that get the balance wrong, for example by rushing headlong into cost savings, may soon see their peers outstrip them in growth.

Main causes of failure

Based on experience, four senior officers of Bain consultants (Gadiesh *et al*, 2001) have identified five root causes of failure and have set out some 'golden rules' to guide managers to success.

The reasons for failure are: poor strategic rationale, overpayment for the acquisition, inadequate integration planning and execution, a void in executive leadership, and severe cultural mismatch.

The strategic case
Of the five, getting the strategic rationale right is vitally important. Being clear on the nature of the strategic case is critical for both pre-merger and post-merger activities. Indeed, failure to do so can trigger the four other causes of failure.

There are six key rationales for pursuing mergers:

1. *Active investing*. Leveraged buy-out companies and private equity firms engage in 'active investing' – acquiring a company, stripping out costs and running it more efficiently and profitably.

2. *Growing scale*. Mergers most often aim to grow scale, which does not mean simply getting larger. Rather, success requires gaining scale in specific elements of a business and using these elements to become more competitive overall. For instance, if materials cost drives profit, then purchasing scale will be key. If customer acquisition is more important, then channel scale will be critical. For example, the increasing globalization of the pharmaceuticals

industry led to the mergers of Pfizer with Warner-Lambert, and of SmithKline Beecham with GlaxoWellcome. Research and development costs can be spread across the entire global market.

3. *Expanding into related businesses*. This can mean expanding business to new locations, new products, higher growth markets or new customers. But most importantly, the additions should be closely related to a company's existing business. This rationale lay behind merger activity in the 1990s by Emerson, GE, and Reuters. When Travellers Group acquired Citicorp, the merger gave the two companies a complete range of financial-services products to cross-sell to their combined customers across a broad range of global markets. UK examples include the acquisition of building societies by banks.

4. *Broadening scope*. In such cases the acquirer buys specific expertise to extend its existing technology or product lines, seeing organic growth as too slow or too expensive.

5. *Redefining business*. Mergers and acquisitions can redefine a business. This is an appropriate strategic rationale when an organization's capabilities and resources become uncompetitive very suddenly, owing to, for example, a major technological change or a shift in consumer behaviour.

6. *Redefining industry*. On rare occasions a bold, strategic acquisition can redefine an entire industry, changing the boundaries of competition and forcing rivals to re-evaluate their business models. Some analysts believed GE's attempted acquisition of Honeywell would have fundamentally altered relationships in the aircraft industry, among operators, maintenance providers, leasing companies, manufacturers and parts suppliers.

Overpayment
A classic case can be seen in the series of acquisitions by Marconi at the peak of the late 90s technology boom, leading to its debt mountain and the destruction of shareholder value on a massive scale.

Integration
Success depends on identifying very early the key people to lead the organization, and removing the people likely to block the process. During the early stage, a sense of urgency is essential. Merging companies need frequent, two-way communication with employees and affected communities to air concerns and alleviate anxiety.

Success is also linked to the speed with which a merger is effected. In the BP and Amoco merger, chief executive John Browne moved at a fast pace. Working out of a 'war room' in London with an around-the-clock integration team, Browne filled all the senior management jobs and completed most of the cuts in the first 100 days of the merger.

In a merger aimed at expanding into adjacent markets, customers or product segments, the integration effort needs to focus on defining the new entity's value proposition to customers and determining how to bring it to market.

Executive leadership and communication

In the excitement of being involved in huge financial transactions and conscious of the need for confidentiality in the early stages, it is easy to overlook the importance of full and clear communication. A communication and leadership 'vacuum', however, is guaranteed to bring about a high level of unrest and damaging uncertainty among customers and employees alike.

Severe cultural mismatch

Few business marriages are made in heaven. Cultural compatibility between the partners is very important and often conspicuously lacking. Rentokil's acquisition of BET is a case in point. Year after year for 17 years Rentokil's earnings per share never failed to rise by less than 20 per cent. Its share price moved consistently higher. Its culture was one of an aggressive, dynamic business driven by a strong focus on shareholder value, led by a colourful personality, Sir Clive Thompson. BET by contrast was a less efficient, more paternalistic company with a more conservative, traditional culture. Results started to disappoint and the share price slumped.

THE ICL/NOKIA DATA MERGER – BRINGING TWO CULTURES TOGETHER

International Computers Limited (ICL) was established in 1968. In 1984 the company merged with STC, a UK electronics and communications business, and in 1990 STC sold 80 per cent of ICL to the Japanese firm Fujitsu. This was seen as a positive step by all stakeholders, and the firm soon fell into line with Fujitsu's view of a family of strategic alliances and of being a company with respect for local cultures and methods.

ICL, however, had too many country units operating below critical mass. If a viable target could be identified, ICL was interested in a merger with another company in the computer industry.

In 1991 Nokia was the second-largest publicly owned company in Finland. Its subsidiary Nokia Data had been founded in 1970 and made a name for itself with a range of stylish PCs in the 1980s. In 1991, however, the Nokia Group decided that it needed to reduce its portfolio and look for a partner in the computer business.

When Nokia and ICL met to consider joining forces in March 1991 there were strong arguments in favour of a merger. Nokia Data would treble the size of ICL's operations in Europe and was a key player in the rapidly growing PC market. The style of negotiations was open and friendly. Given the circumstances, it was obvious that both sides needed to trust each other in order to achieve mutual benefit.

It took a mere seven weeks to agree to proceed with the merger. In this time financial assessments and product plans were undertaken as well as audits and staff assessments.

On 28 May 1991 announcements were made about the merger simultaneously in London and Helsinki. It was decided that Nokia Data's PC business would be retained intact and ICL's PC operations rolled into it. Futhermore, the idea of using external consultants in the process was abandoned in favour of involving the whole of the ICL Europe HQ top management for the integration.

As in any merger activity, fears existed on both sides. These included a fear that key personnel might leave and take key staff with them. Another key concern was that top customers would defect in an environment of uncertainty. These fears were a big challenge for the integration team.

The integration team consisted of functional 'Siamese twins'. In other words the ICL logistics manager worked with the Nokia logistics manager and the pair would conduct interviews together and reach joint conclusions on a proposed organizational structure and the processes and people needed to make it a reality. The team also made visits to key customers in order to reassure them about the future.

The integration team initiated three key activities:

▌ fast development of the PC product line – the team quickly initiated the development of a new range of hardware and software;
▌ signing and branding – it was decided that the ICL name would be used throughout;

▌ reducing HQ – numbers at headquarters were reduced from 400 to around 130.

Cultural issues

In Nokia, as part of the integration process, a comparison was made on 23 parameters of organizational culture. Nokia had a simple values booklet emphasizing speed and fun, whereas ICL's 'ICL Way', based on Hewlett Packard's 'HP Way', was longer, more far-reaching and more complex. Also, Nokia put its trust in local managers to make good business, and any training was largely up to them, yet ICL had long since believed that a formal programme of management education was a vital part of making strategy happen.

Many mergers fail because of cultural mismatches and conflict. Left to lawyers and accountants, many human issues crucial to long-term success can be overlooked or even ignored. Therefore Nokia and ICL managers were asked what they wanted to see changed and their responses carefully compared. The results led to the opportunity for the synergistic emergence of a viable cultural combination.

The new management teams set about local integration and decided to appoint full-time local integration managers to coordinate various activities. Problems encountered included the Spanish unit becoming disillusioned with ICL 'interference' and the smaller ICL units of Finland and Germany complaining that they were being persecuted and betrayed. However, the majority of activities progressed smoothly.

For 95 per cent of ex-employees of Nokia Data and ICL the world looked much the same at the beginning of 1992 as it had a year earlier. They most probably had the same boss and the same colleagues. This was good in the sense that the key aim of integration – keeping the businesses outward-facing and not distracting people with too much change – had been achieved. It was bad in the sense that most did not yet feel part of one 'complete' company. The 1992 range of PCs had a successful launch, and the president sent out a 'Statement of Direction' with which to unite staff behind a common vision. The statement included lines such as 'we will not impose processes on you – you select the ones which you believe will help your business'.

Other initiatives included a promotional programme that covered a mobile show and a conference in Venice for executives of the new firm. All this helped to make staff feel part of the new ICL by the end of 1992.

In a 1993 New Year presentation, the president announced that ICL had made a profit in 1992 and that a record number of PCs had been sold. He also stated that the integration was complete.

With integration over, the firm pressed ahead with executive workshops and thinking through the strategic directions needed to win. All the senior leaders in Europe worked together on this for the first time, and shared the outcome with enthusiasm. Soon, individual country units began to take up many of ICL's training courses and by mid-1993, two years after the announcement of the merger, a new ICL could be discerned that was a true merger of cultures.

The interfaces between two corporate cultures, each spread across several national cultures, are complex and need to be understood in order to achieve a successful merger. One of the most important messages the company learnt was the benefit of giving time for merging to occur, even though some essential business decisions were made pretty quickly. Another valuable lesson learnt was the important role that shared learning can play in building shared visions and values. None of the other factors in a merger appear to be as important as the people and customers who come as part of the deal. Keeping and growing these assets must in the end remain the ultimate mark of success.

(Source: Mayo and Hadaway, 2001)

OUTSOURCING

The practice of outsourcing has developed rapidly in recent years and has moved on from involving relatively peripheral activities such as catering and security as more and more companies have come to appreciate the role it can play in strategy. Today outsourcing embraces design, manufacturing, distribution, information systems and human resource management. It is not always the case, however, that firms begin outsourcing for genuine strategic reasons; in many instances the motivation is around short-term cost saving.

The strategic aspect of outsourcing is closely related to the core competence concept of Hamel and Prahalad (see Chapter 10). They argue that the main source of competitive advantage is the existence of a set of core skills and abilities that enable the company to adapt quickly to changing market needs. Non-core activities or competences can, it is argued, be outsourced to advantage, leaving the company to focus even more strongly on the development of its core competences. This begs the question of the extent to which a company can be sure that it has correctly identified its core competences. Among the key questions to be answered are: (1) Can we achieve pre-eminence in this activity? (2) Do our customers see this pre-eminence as adding value to the product or service we supply? Canon, Honda and Nortel are frequently quoted as exemplars of answering these questions successfully.

McIvor (2001) has listed several problems that result in firms failing to gain full strategic value from outsourcing:

▋ Not having developed a formal process for evaluating the costs and benefits of outsourcing.

▋ Not integrating outsourcing into the strategy formulation process, leading to a piecemeal approach.

▋ Failure to investigate thoroughly all the cost implications.

▋ Not taking workforce reactions into account, particularly in cases where transfers of employees to the outsource contractor are involved. For example, if the outsourcing company has a defined benefit pension scheme and the contractor does not there can be strong resistance to the process.

▋ Mistaking core activities for cost centres and, having outsourced them, losing control of key activities.

STRATEGIC ALLIANCES

A strategic alliance is an agreement between two or more companies to share knowledge or resources to their mutual benefit.

Strategic alliances can be as simple as two companies sharing technological or marketing resources, or be highly complex involving several companies and international in reach. Alliances are becoming an attractive strategy for the future as opposed to simply 'going it alone' or making acquisitions. The attractiveness of joint ventures reflects a number of factors, including the reduction of risk, increasing global competition and improvements in communications technology.

There are two main types of alliance: intra-industry and inter-industry.

Intra-industry alliances can be used to protect the home market or to exploit a global one better. For example, the three main US carmakers entered into an alliance to develop a new battery for an electric car. If successful, the battery alliance could help fight off foreign competition. Also, the computer chip manufacturer Intel and the NMB Semiconductor Company of Japan enjoyed a good working relationship for many years. Intel helped build a semiconductor foundry in Japan, which provided NMB with access to Intel's world-wide sales network, and Intel in turn gained the benefit of an assured source of high-quality chips.

Inter-industry alliances can be used to pool expertise and create synergy. For example, the alliance between chemical giant DuPont and pharmaceutical giant Merck existed to combine DuPont's R&D ability with Merck's capital and market rights. Some of the main reasons why companies form alliances are:

▌ to avoid barriers to entry;

▌ to create synergy by pooling resources and sharing expertise;

▌ to reduce/share risk;

▌ to gain access to new markets;

▌ to source raw materials;

▌ to undertake development projects that are too big for a single company to fund. A lesson that companies everywhere are learning is that no one company is big and strong enough to do everything on its own. For example, computing giant IBM teamed up with a Japanese firm in order to develop LCD screens.

Technology transfer alliances are concerned with the process by which new ideas developed in one organization can be applied within another. For example, a firm can team up with another firm in the private sector, with a university or with a government laboratory to transfer technology.

Multi-division companies from Japan, the USA and Europe are joining forces to create multiple strategic alliances. Referred to as the 'octopus strategy' by the Nomura Research Institute of Japan, such alliances can bring alliance members into close contact with each other on particular projects, yet they can still be in direct competition with each other on other projects. This kind of alliance can help to diversify risk on particularly large projects, but at the same time cause coordination problems if the alliance spans continents.

As time progresses, the circumstances of alliances may change. Difficulties can arise when one party realizes it no longer needs the skills or knowledge of the other. Also, developments in technology may mean that company A no longer needs company B's expertise. Cultural differences can also lead to problems – especially between Asian and Western companies. For instance, Japanese companies have, in the past, tended to put employee interests ahead of those of shareholders. Linked to this are problems of language. Three main barriers to successful alliances can be summarized as follows:

▮ a failure to understand and adapt to a new style of management – one that involves negotiation, persuasion and patience and negates the use of position power;

▮ failure to understand cultural differences leading at the least to misunderstandings and in some cases damaging relationships;

▮ lack of commitment to succeed, often the result of attitudes of mind that favour competing rather than collaborating.

Government, industry and education all must play a role in the transformations necessary for alliances to prosper. For example, governments must reassess tax and antitrust laws to facilitate global cooperative ventures, and business schools need to help prepare managers with the necessary competences including foreign languages, understanding of cultural differences, managing culturally diverse teams and team-building skills.

A model for a successful strategic alliance

There are four critical issues in determining the model for success of a strategic alliance:

▮ *Goal compatibility*. Without this, alliance partners may pull in different directions.

▮ *Synergy*. One is strong where the other is weak. This is the major reason for and the advantage of the alliance. The partnership must be more efficient and effective than if each alliance partner was performing the similar tasks individually.

▮ *Adding value*. There must be a clear understanding of the value each partner will bring to the alliance and, equally important, of the value each one will derive.

▮ *Balancing contributions*. This is needed in order to avoid one partner dominating the alliance or one partner feeling it is being exploited.

Alliance building is now seen to be fundamental to the strategic thrust of large companies – from technology and product development strategies to the strategic role of manufacturing and marketing. Many trends point towards cooperation as a fundamental growing force in business.

The trend toward strategic alliances is clear, and not just a passing fad. In the light of increased internationalization of markets, organizations, in the process of strategy formulation, need to be looking at each other more as potential allies rather than adversaries.

PARTNERSHIP SOURCING

Partnership sourcing is defined as the process of building long-term, mutually beneficial relationships between customers and suppliers. It is a commitment regardless of size – based on trust and clear, mutually agreed objectives to strive for world-class capability and competitiveness. As an element in competitive strategy it is developed and implemented in the expectation of tangible and sustainable benefits. But there are also boundaries and limitations that management must acknowledge, recognize and work to eliminate. When partnerships work, there are clear benefits. Stock is reduced, lead times are shortened and there is greater flexibility to respond to company needs, administration costs are lower and cash flow improves. The quality of information is also improved, which means better long-term planning. And better information flow between customers and suppliers that have access to each other's technical resources leads to innovation and technological advancement. In addition there is also often a reduction in shortages of key supplies.

Partnership sourcing will have an impact on how the purchasing function thinks about the following key supply issues:

▮ *Cost versus price*. Lowest-tender contracts are not accepted merely because of low price. Service, quality, reliability and innovation have a greater bearing on supplier selection.

▮ *Long term versus short term*. Partnership sourcing focuses on the long term, with collaboration occurring at the earliest conceptual stage of design, or the earliest requirement for goods and services.

▮ *Quality controls versus quality checks*. The emphasis is on getting it right the first time.

▮ *Single sourcing versus multiple sourcing*. In most cases, reducing the number of suppliers occurs as a matter of course with the focus turning to quality partners.

▮ *Adversarial approach versus collaboration*. This is often the most difficult adjustment for purchasing officers to make – particularly those in large powerful businesses who have been accustomed to bullying small suppliers in the past.

Both parties have to feel the relationship is on a sound footing and that it will continue for the foreseeable future. They must also be able to discuss problems frankly and constructively. A disagreement should not signify the end of a relationship, but the beginning of its improvement.

For a partnership to work there must be a genuine commitment from the top of both organizations and a clear understanding by both parties of what is expected in principle and in detail. Both parties will need to have capable people involved who are sufficiently trained to carry out their jobs effectively and have enough patience to tackle obstacles and teething problems. There must be open communication between both parties, including full information concerning suppliers' costs and margins.

Preparation and planning are essential and a system to measure progress and clearly defined targets should be established at the beginning. There will also have to be a mechanism to implement change throughout the supply chain and at the customer/supplier interfaces.

Internally, the process should begin with the following:

▮ Decide which suppliers qualify as partners.

▮ Start with strategic suppliers and/or customers.

▮ Set clear, simple and easily achievable targets.

▮ Create a mechanism for driving partnership sourcing forward.

Externally the important steps are:

▮ Improve the detail and quality of information that you share with suppliers.

▋ Carefully select those suppliers with which partnerships are to be established.

▋ Publicize partnership sourcing to all significant suppliers.

Although the case for partnership sourcing is persuasive, getting there will not be easy. Among the obstacles and problems that need to be overcome, the following are the most common:

▋ *Impatience*. Partnerships take time to develop properly – often years, not weeks.

▋ *Arrogance* on the part of large companies. It is sometimes hard for proud industrial giants to acknowledge that their own internal systems and procedures need improving and that they might be able to learn from smaller partners.

▋ *Complacency*. The smooth working of the partnership should never be taken for granted. Continuous measurement and performance assessment is crucial for both parties.

▋ *Overdependency*. For the purchasing company, partnership sourcing means fewer suppliers; for the supplier, bigger orders. Openness and dependency are implied in partnership sourcing, but involve evident risks to both partners.

Types of relationship

Sinclair, Hunter and Beaumont (1996) classify relationships in the supply chain as follows:

▋ *The demands model*. The customer expects the supplier to meet specifications for a limited range of products and to meet schedules, but does not engage in joint development or long-term supply agreements.

▋ *The audits model*. Verification moves from an *ex post* to an *ex ante* approach. The supplier will be checked out, including on-site assessment, audit of quality control processes, perhaps budgets and strategies, prior to the awarding of long-term contracts. At this stage, however, joint activity remains minimal.

▋ *The supplier development model*. As well as a deeper audit this approach may include open-book arrangements, joint product and/or process development and joint training.

■ *Partnership*. Support becomes more of a two-way process, there is greater joint development activity, the expected time horizon is relatively unlimited and some form of governance structure may be formed.

Questionnaires were sent to 600 firms randomly selected from the *Sells Product and Services Directory*, and 190 usable forms were returned. Of these, 88 per cent said they had suppliers with whom they had an especially close alliance or partnership. In most cases this was true of only a small minority of their active suppliers. Most companies were aiming to reduce the number of suppliers.

Initial selection of suppliers was based on:

BS 5750 or ISO 9000 certification	67%
Audits	37%
Site visits	45%
Quality of labour force	10%
Supplier self-assessment	26%
Trial order	48%

Methods for ensuring compliance were:

Regular meetings with senior management	34%
Quality audits	42%
Spot-checks on production	17%
Training for supplier management	4%
Training for supplier workforce	0.5%
Joint problem solving	63%

Types of assistance given:

Technical advice	76%
Joint problem solving	87%
Advice on management processes	29%

Advice on HR management:

Training	9%
Communication	27%
Teamworking	18%
Other HR	7%

IKEA's success in furniture retailing has been attributed to its ability to build and maintain strong relationships with customers and suppliers. For example, IKEA emphasizes finding and training the right suppliers, commits to long-term relationships and helps suppliers improve their products by leasing them equipment, providing technical assistance and helping source raw materials.

SUMMARY

Boards of directors are faced with a range of strategic choices – decisions that, on the one hand, are of strategic importance to the company's medium- to long-term success and that, on the other hand, once made are not easily reversible. These decisions include:

▌ making an acquisition;

▌ forming a joint venture;

▌ outsourcing one or more activities;

▌ entering into long-term supply arrangements or contracts.

It is important that these decisions are taken following thorough analysis of their strategic relevance and not, as is often the case, on grounds of short-term cost saving or because the practices concerned are fashionable. Failure to exercise sound judgement in such matters can have grave consequences and may imperil the survival of the business, as was the case with regard to Marconi's acquisition/divestment strategy. It is also important that a thorough risk analysis be carried out before commitments are entered into.

Where the chosen path does not lead to the expected successful outcome the reasons may lie in the manner of execution rather than in the original decision to proceed. So-called 'soft' factors can be very important. These include: (1) the ability of leaders to make the issues clear, to mobilize enthusiasm and to provide reassurance to those who feel threatened; and (2) the importance of taking corporate culture into account.

All such strategic choices involve companies working together in one way or another. It follows that success ultimately depends on mutual trust and the perception of mutual benefit. Hence, perhaps the greatest obstacle to the achievement of a successful outcome is the macho, adversarial culture that characterizes much of industry.

9

Functional strategies

MANUFACTURING STRATEGY

Since the 1970s, spurred on by the example of Japan, US and UK companies have attempted to achieve world-class standards of manufacturing excellence. Faced with increased global competition and faster technological changes, companies in a variety of industries had to re-evaluate their manufacturing strategies and practices. In many companies, new manufacturing strategic directions were developed and new manufacturing practices were adopted. In 1990 a team from the Massachusetts Institute of Technology published the results of a study of the global automotive industry (Womack, Jones and Roos, 1990). They contrasted the traditional mass production techniques of manufacturing pioneered by General Motors and Ford with more recently developed methods used by Japanese companies such as Toyota, Nissan and Honda. These methods have become known as 'lean production', reflecting the fact that they use fewer people, less inventory, less investment in plant and equipment, less space and less time for new product development. The MIT report showed that Japanese firms produced more cars, at lower cost, with fewer employees, using less factory space than their Western rivals. Since then the adoption of lean manufacturing techniques has become an integral part of manufacturing strategy in most companies, although its implementation has not always proceeded smoothly.

Globalization has expanded market opportunities, but at the same time it has increased competition and its threats. It has increased the emphasis on technological developments and innovations. To gain a competitive advantage, many companies have focused on improvements in product or process technologies, or both. The rate of technological developments has increased exponentially, particularly in high-tech industries such as electronics, computers, biotechnology and telecommunications.

In the personal computer industry, product life cycles have decreased from years to months. As a result, companies are facing an increasingly fast-changing market with a window of opportunity that is smaller and moving very rapidly. To succeed in this environment, manufacturers have to be quick in designing and producing products – and do it at low cost with high quality. Four competitive priorities – cost, quality, time and flexibility – have emerged as critical factors for success. These competitive priorities have enhanced the strategic role of the manufacturing function in the organization, because achievement of these priorities is highly influenced by its performance.

Whereas in the past manufacturing was somewhat taken for granted, today it is more often considered a strategic asset that has a major impact on achievement of competitive priorities. Thus, the importance of manufacturing management has been rediscovered, and creating manufacturing excellence has become a strategic goal of many organizations. Adopting manufacturing excellence practices requires a major overhaul of manufacturing systems and operations and typically brings major changes to the structure and processes that subsequently lead to significant modification of organizational, behavioural and cultural aspects of the organization. Creating such major changes demands constant attention from top management.

Total quality

Whereas the productivity and cost effectiveness of the Japanese approach to mass production reflected pioneering work by Toyota, the quality of Japanese products was revolutionized by techniques introduced into Japan by US consultants, notably Dr Edwards Deming. In 1980 US industrialists studying the Japanese approach to quality discovered to their surprise that Japan's leading quality award was named after Deming, a US statistician who was by then 80 years of age. He had worked with Japanese companies in the 1950s to help them achieve a much-needed quality revolution. Deming advocated a mix of statistical quality techniques and the adoption of a total quality philosophy. Xerox was one of the first Western companies to adopt the approach and its Japanese subsidiary won the Deming prize in 1980. Total quality involves the combination of a range of techniques and approaches including the adoption of a business success model, the application of statistical quality control, certification by the International Standards Organization, commitment to zero defects, benchmarking, the setting up of quality teams at shop-floor level, appropriate measurement systems based on customer definitions of quality and the securing of the full cooperation of suppliers. ABB, for example, distributes a brochure to its suppliers, 'ABB and its expectations of the relationship', that lists its expectations as error-free quality and delivery, compressed cycle times, reasonable prices, innovative engineering capability and a share of total cost improvements.

In both the United States and Europe annual awards for quality were established. The Malcolm Baldrige Award for Quality was first awarded in 1988. Its first winner was Motorola. In Europe Xerox's UK subsidiary Rank Xerox won the Award of the European Foundation for Quality.

The EFQM model

In Europe many manufacturing companies have adopted a business success model launched in 1992 by the European Foundation for Quality Management (EFQM). It was based on an earlier model developed in the United States and linked to the Malcolm Baldrige Award for Quality. The EFQM model is shown in Figure 9.1. It distinguishes between the enablers (or drivers) of success and the results achieved. When used in the context of the annual European Quality Award the percentages in the boxes reflect the weightings used when assessing the applicant companies.

Leadership is assessed on how managers take positive steps to:

▌ communicate with staff;

▌ give and receive training;

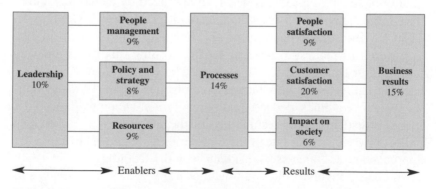

Figure 9.1   *The EFQM business success model*

▌ assess the awareness of total quality;

▌ establish and participate in joint improvement teams with customers and suppliers.

People management is judged by how the organization releases the full potential of its people by:

▌ integrating corporate and HR strategy;

▌ assessing the match between people's skills and organizational needs;

▌ establishing and implementing training programmes;

▌ achieving effective up and down communication.

Policy and strategy are assessed by how the organization's policies:

▌ reflect the fundamentals of Total Quality;

▌ test, improve and align business plans with desired direction;

▌ account for feedback from internal and external sources.

Use of resources is assessed in terms of how they are deployed in support of strategy, including:

▌ financial;

▌ informational;

▌ technological;

▌ material.

Measuring performance

Mannochehri (1999) argues that when attempts to implement new manufacturing strategies have failed to match expectations, one possible reason has been lack of appropriate performance measures. For example, some manufacturing companies still do not have any specific performance metrics for measuring customer satisfaction, which is the primary focus of manufacturing excellence. Traditional performance measures do not support and may even inhibit the implementation of new manufacturing strategies and practices.

The conventional measures in many manufacturing companies are primarily financial and are mostly generated by long-established manufacturing cost accounting systems. Cost accounting was developed many years ago and manufacturing systems and practices have changed enormously since then, particularly in the last two decades; in many cases accounting systems have not kept up. The structure of manufacturing cost elements has changed dramatically since the 1920s. At that time, labour was by far the largest cost, followed by material cost. Overhead was only a very small portion of total costs. These days, however, overhead counts for the largest portion of manufacturing cost, while the labour content of an average product can be as low as 10 per cent.

Traditional cost accounting carefully calculates and reports the labour costs and allocates the overhead costs based on direct proportion to a product's labour costs. This approach can lead to a major cost distortion, particularly if there is a large variation in the use of resources among the products of the firm. Recent developments in activity-based costing are aimed at fixing this flaw.

Activity-based costing

The key concept underlying activity-based costing is the *cost driver*. Focusing on cost drivers makes it possible to link the costs involved in activities to products, reflecting the product's demand for those activities during the production process. Typical cost drivers in manufacturing are set-up times, number of components, frequency of product order and frequency of product shipment. In traditional costing, where overhead is allocated on the basis of direct labour hours, two products using the same amount of direct labour will share the same proportion of overhead, despite the fact that one requires a set-up time of three days and the other one takes three minutes. Similarly, if one product requires 20 components, which have to be ordered from 20 different suppliers, and the other consists of just two components, both from the same supplier, if both require the same amount of direct labour, both will attract the same share of overhead, which clearly does not reflect the true cost of production.

Throughput accounting

Based on the ideas of Eli Goldratt (Goldratt and Cox, 1986), this technique focuses on the bottlenecks or capacity-constrained resources in manufacturing. The argument is that an hour lost at the bottleneck of a production process is an hour lost for the process as a whole. The key cost driver, therefore, is not the amount of direct labour a product uses, but rather how much of the bottleneck's time it requires. Overhead should, therefore, be allocated proportionately to the time taken at the bottleneck rather than in proportion to the use of direct labour.

Manufacturing strategy today must track performance in such things as customer satisfaction, quality (as defined and perceived by customers), flexibility and innovation. Such strategic goals cannot be monitored with traditional reports. Financial reports often are not relevant for operational control, either. To control operations, factory managers need information such as production rates, yield quantities, cycle time, reject rates and stock-outs.

In recent years, research evidence shows that there has been a rapid increase in the number of companies measuring aspects of performance other than purely financial ones. The companies featured in the *Fortune* list of the world's most admired companies for 2000 were the subjects of a survey by the Hay Group. The findings showed that compared with their peers the most admired companies are more likely to focus on customer- and employee-based measures of performance. Almost 60 per cent of the admired companies do so, compared with only 38 per cent of their peers. Of the admired group, 40 per cent measure employee retention, career development and other employee-related indicators – more than three times the percentage among the peer group.

> In contrast with those of their peer companies, senior executives in The Most Admired Companies believe that many of these performance measures encourage co-operation and collaboration. Many executives reported that such measures help their companies to focus on growth, operational excellence, customer loyalty, human capital development and other critical issues. The top organizations create performance measures that focus on all the drivers of their businesses – financial performance, shareholder value, employees and customers.
> (*Fortune*, 2 October 2000)

Frequency and timing of the reports is another problem. The accounting reports are typically issued monthly and are available a few days after the closing of the financial period. The data in the report are typically a few weeks old. That is often too late for operational decision making. Manufacturing excellence puts high emphasis on quick feedback and response. Also, another issue is that accounting does not consider intangibles that might be of great significance to factory performance.

The cost accounting mentality creates hurdles in manufacturing excellence implementation. Typically, any product improvement or process innovation has to be justified based on the costs, particularly labour costs. Emphasizing labour costs and ignoring intangibles (that is, whatever is not objectively measurable) blocks many sound improvement projects. For example, investing in more expensive equipment to increase flexibility is hard to justify, as flexibility may not be measured and reported. Also, the appropriate focus of cost accounting leads to some wasteful activities. The high emphasis on machine and labour utilization, for example, results in production in large batch size with the focus on production quantity, when often the need is for small lot size, synchronized production, fast changeover, zero inventory and high quality.

Motorola plays down the importance of financial measures in monitoring manufacturing performance and focuses instead on the key drivers of operations such as the manufacturing yield rate, the cycle time and operating unit productivity. It is argued that, if you manage the key drivers, the financial results will follow.

Benchmarking

In defining what to measure, some companies use benchmarking to review practices of the best in class and compare those to their own. Caterpillar recently went through an overhaul of its corporate structure and instituted performance measures appropriate for the new structure. Early in the process of defining the performance measures, Caterpillar visited companies such as Texas Instruments, AT&T and IBM to benchmark their approach.

The aim of benchmarking is to compare measures of such performance indicators as defects per million parts with measures of best practice. The comparisons are usually, but not always, carried out on an industry basis. They are well established in the automotive industry resulting in clear standards of what is meant by world-class performance. Clutterbuck, Clark and Armistead (1993) describe the approach used in Elida Gibbs, a Unilever subsidiary manufacturing toiletries and cosmetics. Initially it compared performance levels on its key processes with other companies in the Unilever group. It then followed up with studies of world-class performance levels both in other fast-moving consumer goods firms and in businesses in other sectors.

The measurement process is followed by programmes to implement performance levels so as to attain comparability with best practice.

Benchmarking breaks down into the following stages:

▌ Deciding which processes to benchmark.

▌ Deciding what measures to employ in respect of these processes.

■ Choosing which companies against which to benchmark.

■ Obtaining the relevant data from these companies. This can be done directly, with agreement, on a reciprocal basis, through a trade association, or from published sources. It is important to ensure that the data are truly comparable.

■ Measuring the competitive gap between the company's current performance level and best practice.

■ Implementation of action to close the gap.

Effective performance measurement in manufacturing

Managers can take the following steps to develop effective manufacturing performance measures:

■ *Focus on leading indicators*. Performance measures can be classified as reactive and proactive. Proactive performance measures are preventive in nature and can be called leading indicators. These measures can anticipate and impact the future desired results. Rising defect rates and employee turnover often precede lower customer satisfaction. In contrast, the reactive or lagging indicators are descriptive of what has happened in the past. They show the results of the completed performance of a system. Traditional financial measures such as revenue, profits and ROI are lagging indicators. Though they are needed to show the company's performance to the shareholders, creditors and government agencies, they are not typically helpful in operations decision making regarding future decisions and action. In order to focus attention on the future, the UK company Reckitt and Colman uses the term 'development measures' rather than 'performance measures'.

■ *Focus on measures that are controllable*. The purpose of using performance measures is to monitor the actual performance and compare it to a pre-specified goal in order to measure progress toward the goal. If there is a significant dispersion between the two, a corrective action is needed. But does the manager have control over the resources, inputs and processes to take the required corrective action? If not, the performance measures are useless.

■ *Focus on measures for which you can collect the required data*. Ability to collect the required data for a performance measure is a critical consideration. Some companies develop interesting and relevant measures only to discover that they currently do not collect the required data and it is not practical to do so.

■ *Focus on 'soft' issues as well as 'hard' ones*. Many companies do not set performance measures for soft issues. Despite all the rhetoric about customer care, employee empowerment and learning organizations, many companies do not measure their performance in these areas. Soft issues are harder to measure and compare, but this does not justify ignoring them. Johnson & Johnson realized years ago that financial results are essentially driven by how well executives managed key stakeholders such as customers, employees and the communities in which they operate.

■ *Focus on measuring activities and capabilities as well as outcomes*. Measuring results of a product development process such as schedule and cost might indicate that a project is late and over budget. However, that does not tell what to do differently. Measuring activities and capabilities such as the staffing level during the course of the project might indicate what went wrong.

■ *Focus on the users*. Performance measures are effective only if they are consistent with users' needs and consequently are used by them. These needs are to be explored and determined by talking to supervisors and employees who use the measures. Getting answers to questions such as 'Why is it needed?', 'How is it used?' and 'How is it related to the operating unit's performance?' can help managers understand and define the users' needs.

HUMAN RESOURCE STRATEGY

There is increasing recognition of the role that a progressive human resource strategy can play in creating world-class competitiveness.

Pfeffer (1998) argues that 'the real sources of competitive leverage' are the culture and capabilities of the organization that are derived from the way people are managed. This, he asserts, is a much more important source of sustained success than things like having a large market share or a distinctive brand 'because it is much more difficult to understand capability and systems of management practice than it is to copy strategy, technology or even global presence'. He extracted, from various studies, related literature, and personal observation and experience, a set of seven dimensions that characterize most if not all of the human resources practices of companies creating a competitive advantage via human resource management.

These are:

▌ *Security of employment*. Pfeffer quotes Lincoln Electric, General Motors' innovative Saturn and Fremont plants and the highly successful Southwest Airlines as examples of companies that offered guaranteed employment and avoided lay-offs during recessions.

▌ *Selective hiring*. This first requires a large applicant pool from which to select. In 1994, for example, Southwest Airlines received 125,000 job applications and hired 2,700 people. The second requirement is a sophisticated selection process, which relates the skills and qualities needed in the job to the qualities of the individual. The third is to use this process for all jobs at all levels. Examples of good practice include Subaru-Isuzu in respect of automotive front-line employees, Enterprise Rent-a-car in respect of customer service people and Hewlett Packard.

▌ *Self-managed teams*. Pfeffer asserts that 'organising people into self-managed teams is a critical component of virtually all high performance management systems'. As well as examples from automotive manufacturing such as New United Motor Manufacturing (NUMMI) and Chrysler, where the practice is not uncommon, he cites cases from other industries, such as Bell Telephone, Whole Foods Markets and Ritz Carlton Hotels.

▌ *High compensation contingent upon organizational performance*. 'The level of salaries sends a message to the firm's workforce – they are truly valued or they are not.' It is important, however, that a significant element of compensation should relate to the organization's performance. This element can take a number of different forms such as profit sharing, employee share ownership or various forms of individual or team incentives. Among the US companies with share ownership schemes are Wal-Mart, Microsoft and Southwest Airlines.

▌ *Training*. 'Training is an essential component of high performance work systems because these systems rely on front line employee skill and initiative to identify and resolve problems, to initiate changes in work methods and to take responsibility for quality.'

▌ *Reduction in status differences*. 'In order to help make all organization members feel important and committed to enhancing organizational operations... most high commitment management systems attempt to reduce the status distinctions that separate individuals and groups and cause some to feel less valued.' This can be accomplished in two ways – symbolically by means of language, job titles, dress, allocation of physical space, car parking privileges and the like, and substantively (and much more rarely) through reducing inequality in compensation across the different levels of the company. An example of the latter approach is Whole Foods Markets. Company policy is to limit annual compensation pay to eight times the average full-time salary of all employees. In 1995 the CEO earned $130,000 in salary and a bonus of $20,000. The CEO of Southwest Airlines earns about $500,000 a year including bonuses. When the company negotiated a wage freeze with its pilots in 1995, in exchange for stock options and unguaranteed profit-related bonuses he agreed to freeze his own base salary at $395,000 for the following four years.

■ *Sharing information*. Sharing information, particularly financial information, shows people that they are trusted. Also, if people are to contribute meaningfully to enhancing performance they need to have performance data and to be trained in how to interpret it. The systematic sharing of information as a basis for performance improvement pioneered at Springfield Re-manufacturing in the 1980s and known as 'open-book management' has been widely adopted in the United States.

Pfeffer's views are supported by research carried out by Huselid (1995). This research was based on 968 responses to a survey of the senior HR managers in a sample of 3,452 firms representing all major US industries.

Two scales were constructed from the responses:

1. *employee skills and structures* – includes a broad range of practices intended to enhance employees' knowledge, skills and abilities and provide mechanisms through which employees can use those attributes in performing their roles;

2. *employee motivation* – practices designed to recognize and reinforce desired employee behaviours, such as performance appraisal linked to compensation.

The study assessed the effects of management practices on:

▌ turnover;

▌ sales per employee;

▌ ratio of stock market value to book value.

In the analysis Huselid included a large number of alternative explanations of the results, such as size, capital intensity, degree of concentration of the industry and R&D spend as a percentage of sales. He also used statistical methods that better enabled him to assess the direction of causality, ie whether performance was driving management practices or the practices were driving performance.

The results indicated that firms in the top 16 per cent in terms of their use of these HR practices compared with the average firm, showed, on average:

▌ $27,044 per employee more in sales (productivity);

▌ $18,641 per employee in market value; and

▌ $3,814 in profits.

A study of over 100 firms in Germany in 10 industries (Bilmes, Wetzker and Xhonneux, 1997) found a strong link between investing in employees and stock market performance. Companies that place workers at the core of their strategies produce higher long-term returns to their shareholders than their industry peers. Companies that focused on their people not only produced superior returns to their shareholders but also created more jobs.

Other research evidence

There is growing evidence of the links between the commitment and involvement of employees and company performance. For example, a study by the Institute of Work Psychology at the University of Sheffield found a strong relationship between employee satisfaction, employee commitment to the organization and its goals and overall business performance. In particular they found that:

▌ 12 per cent of the variation in profitability among companies could be explained by variations in the job satisfaction of their employees and 13 per cent could be explained by differences in employee organizational commitment;

▌ 25 per cent of the variation in productivity among companies could be explained by differences in job satisfaction and 17 per cent by differences in organizational commitment.

Research in the USA by Gallup in 1998 reported that organizations with higher levels of employee satisfaction than their competitors outperformed them by 22 per cent in productivity, 38 per cent in customer satisfaction, 27 per cent in profitability and 22 per cent in staff retention.

Investors in People and business performance
A study by the Hambleden Group (1996) compared the financial performance of companies that had gained Investors in People recognition with that of other companies in the same Standard Industrial Classification (SIC) that had not gained IIP. The sample consisted of 81,000 companies that filed full accounts with Companies House.

When the results for all 20 SIC groups were combined, the results were as follows:

Return on sales	192% above the median
Return on capital employed	97% above the median
Return on assets managed	41% above the median
Average remuneration	71% above the median
Turnover per employee	106% above the median
Profit per employee	734% above the median

The study concluded: 'There is overwhelming proof that IIP recognised companies outperform their competitors.'

MARKETING STRATEGY

Marketing at its simplest is the process of winning customers for products or services. It can be approached in two ways. It may begin with a new product, one for which a market has to be created, such as the Sony Walkman or the video recorder. Or it may start from the point of an existing market and the search for a way of winning a bigger share or a more profitable share of it than competitors, as for example when Virgin entered the financial services market.

The basic elements of the process are as follows:

1. **Research**:
   - identification of the market or potential market in terms of such things as size; characteristics of the customers, their needs, aspirations, lifestyles; rate of growth etc;
   - analysis of the market in terms of its internal structure or segmentation.

2. **Decision making**:
   - determination of the precise market segment(s) on which to focus;
   - choice of distribution channel(s):
     - own retail outlets (Body Shop)
     - general retail
     - mail order
     - Web-based
     - 'parties' (Tupperware, Ann Summers)
     - house calls (Avon)
     - tele-sales (double glazing);
   - pricing strategy;
   - design of the product or service in both functional and aesthetic terms to meet anticipated customer requirements.

3. **Getting and keeping customers**:
   - attracting new customers (advertising and promotion);
   - building customer loyalty (relationship marketing);
   - brand management;
   - measuring customer satisfaction;
   - adapting product or service design, packaging and performance characteristics to meet changing customer requirements.

This list, while covering the main activities of a marketing department, includes elements that are both strategic and operational. The key strategic issue in marketing, however, is undoubtedly that of creating, developing and maintaining a position of clear product or service differentiation in a given market such that a substantial and profitable market share can be sustained. This is the process that has come to be known as brand management.

Brand management

Kotler (1993) defines brand as 'A name, term, sign, symbol or design, or a combination of these, which is intended to identify the goods or services of one group of sellers and differentiate them from those of competitors.' A brand is all these things, but it can be much more in the sense that it can convey not only a message about a particular product or service but about important qualities of the organization that supplies it. In this way the brands Virgin, Marks and Spencer or Calvin Klein can be applied successfully to a range of products or services.

According to Keller (2000) the world's strongest brands share these 10 attributes:

1. ***The brand excels at delivering the benefits customers truly desire***. Why do customers really buy a product? Not because the product is a collection of attributes but because those attributes, together with the brand's image, the service and many other tangible and intangible factors, create an attractive whole.

   He cites Starbucks as a company that focuses its efforts on building a coffee-bar culture, opening coffee houses like those in Italy. Just as important, the company maintains control over the coffee from start to finish – from the selection and procurement of the beans to their roasting and blending to their ultimate consumption. Vertical integration has paid off. Starbucks locations have successfully delivered superior benefits to customers by appealing to all five senses – through the enticing aroma and rich taste of the coffee, the product displays and attractive artwork adorning the walls, the contemporary music playing in the background and even the cleanliness of the furnishings. The company's sales and profits have each grown more than 50 per cent annually through much of the 1990s.

2. ***The brand stays relevant***. Without losing sight of their core strengths, the strongest brands stay on the leading edge in their markets and adapt their image to fit the times.

   Gillette, for example, spends millions of dollars on R&D to ensure that its razor blades are highly technologically advanced. Yet at the same time, Gillette has created a consistent, intangible sense of product superiority with its long-running ads, 'The best a man can be', which maintain relevancy to today's world through images of men at work and at play that have evolved over time to reflect contemporary taste and fashion.

3. ***The pricing strategy is based on consumers' perceptions of value***. The right blend of product quality, design, features, costs and prices is very difficult to achieve but can be critical to success.

4. ***The brand is properly positioned***. Brands that are well positioned occupy particular niches in consumers' minds. They are similar to and different from competing brands in certain reliably identifiable

ways. The most successful brands in this regard keep up with competitors by creating points of parity in those areas where competitors are trying to find an advantage while at the same time creating points of difference to achieve advantages over competitors in some other areas. The Mercedes-Benz and Sony brands, for example, hold clear advantages in product superiority and match competitors' level of service.

5. *The brand is consistent*. Maintaining a strong brand means striking the right balance between continuity in marketing activities and the kind of change needed to stay relevant. The brand's image doesn't get muddled or lost by lack of continuity in marketing efforts that confuse customers by sending conflicting messages.

6. *The brand portfolio and hierarchy make sense*. Most companies do not have only one brand; they create and maintain different brands for different market segments. Single product lines are often sold under different brand names, and different brands within a company hold different powers. The corporate, or company-wide, brand acts as an umbrella. A second brand name under that umbrella might be targeted at the family market. A third brand name might nest one level below the family brand and appeal to boys, for example, or be used for one type of product.

   BMW, for example, has a particularly well-designed and implemented hierarchy. At the corporate brand level, BMW pioneered the luxury sports car category by combining seemingly incongruent style and performance considerations. BMW's advertising slogan, 'The ultimate driving machine', reinforces the dual aspects of this image and is applicable to all cars sold under the BMW name. At the same time, BMW created well-differentiated sub-brands through its 3, 5 and 7 series, which suggest a logical order and hierarchy of quality and price.

7. *The brand makes use of and coordinates a full repertoire of marketing activities to build equity*. At its most basic level, a brand is made up of all the marketing elements that can be trademarked – logos, symbols, slogans, packaging, signage and so on. Strong brands mix and match these elements to perform a number of brand-related functions, such as enhancing or reinforcing consumer awareness of the brand or its image and helping to protect the brand both competitively and legally.

Coca-Cola is one of the best examples. The brand makes excellent use of many kinds of marketing activities. These include media advertising (such as the global 'Always Coca-Cola' campaign); promotions (the recent effort focused on the return of the popular contour bottle, for example); and sponsorship (its extensive involvement with the Olympics). They also include direct response (the Coca-Cola catalogue, which sells licensed Coke merchandise) and interactive media (the company's Web site, which offers, among other things, games, a trading post for collectors of Coke memorabilia, and a virtual look at the World of Coca-Cola museum in Atlanta).

8. *The brand's managers understand what the brand means to consumers*. Managers of strong brands appreciate the totality of their brand's image – that is, all the different perceptions, beliefs, attitudes and behaviours customers associate with their brand, whether created intentionally by the company or not. As a result, managers are able to make decisions regarding the brand with confidence. If it's clear what customers like and don't like about a brand, and what core associations are linked to the brand, then it should also be clear whether any given action will dovetail nicely with the brand or create friction.

   Gillette again provides a good example. While all of its products benefit from a similarly extensive distribution system, it is very protective of the name carried by its razors, blades and associated toiletries. The company's electric razors, for example, use the entirely separate Braun name, and its oral-care products are marketed under the Oral B name.

9. *The brand is given proper support, and that support is sustained over the long run*. Brand equity must be carefully constructed. A firm foundation for brand equity requires that consumers have the proper depth and breadth of awareness and strong, favourable and unique associations with the brand in their memory. Too often, managers want to take short cuts and bypass more basic branding considerations – such as achieving the necessary level of brand awareness – in favour of concentrating on flashier aspects of brand building related to image.

10. *The company monitors sources of brand equity*. Strong brands generally make good and frequent use of in-depth brand audits and ongoing brand-tracking studies. A brand audit is an exercise designed to assess the health of a given brand. Typically, it consists

of a detailed internal description of exactly how the brand has been marketed (called a 'brand inventory') and a thorough external investigation, through focus groups and other consumer research, of exactly what the brand does and could mean to consumers (called a 'brand exploratory').

Building a strong brand, argues Keller, involves maximizing all 10 characteristics. And that is, clearly, a worthy goal. But in practice, it is difficult because in many cases, when a company focuses on improving one, others may suffer.

In 2002 the top 10 brands in the UK were the following:

1. Coca-Cola;

2. Walkers;

3. Nescafe;

4. Stella Artois;

5. Muller;

6. Persil;

7. Andrex;

8. Robinsons;

9. Kit Kat;

10. Pepsi.

Part 3

Competitive strategy

INTRODUCTION

The next three chapters focus on the process of obtaining and maintaining a competitive advantage in a particular market or market segment.

The process basically involves matching the resources and capabilities of the organization to the needs and expectations of customers (Chapter 10).

Resources and capabilities are brought to bear on the process of building competitive advantage through two distinct approaches: (1) cost leadership; and (2) differentiation (Chapter 11).

Chapter 12 looks at these issues in an international setting.

The firm: resources, capabilities and competitive advantage

INTRODUCTION

Differences in profitability between companies in the same industry are as great as, and sometimes greater than, differences in profitability across industries. Table 10.1 illustrates this point from the automotive industry, where the margins being earned in 2000 varied from 5.4 per cent in the case of Nissan to 1.1 per cent in the case of Fiat. This is an industry in which economies of scale are important, yet a much smaller company than these, BMW, was earning around 9 per cent.

Table 10.1 *Sales, profits and margins of major automotive manufacturers, 2000*

	$ million	$ million	%
General Motors	184,632	4,452	2.4
Ford	180,598	3,467	1.9
Daimler-Chrysler	150,070	7,295	4.9
Toyota	121,416	4,263	3.5
VW	78,852	1,896	2.4
Honda	58,462	2,100	3.6
Nissan	55,077	2,994	5.4
Fiat	53,190	614	1.1
PSA	40,831	1,213	2.9
Renault	37,128	998	2.7

To understand why some firms consistently outperform others within the same industry, it is insufficient to look solely at differences in strategy. If some firms are better than others at identifying key success factors and so select strategies which are appropriate to the industry environment, then it is to be expected that poorly performing firms within an industry will imitate the strategies of successful firms. If competitive advantage is to be *sustainable* over time, then there must be differences between firms which result in some firms being able to outperform others.

The key differences between firms which we shall focus on in this chapter are differences between firms in *resources and capabilities*. *Resources* are the firm's most fundamental characteristics; they are its tools and its personality. By bringing its resources to bear, a firm displays its *capabilities*, its skills in performing productive activities.

RESOURCES, CAPABILITIES AND STRATEGY FORMULATION

For much of the 1980s and 1990s, strategic analysis concentrated on the attractiveness of the external environment and issues of positioning – market share, relative cost position, first-mover advantage and the like. This emphasis was driven in part by the influential contributions of Michael Porter (1980, 1985) and the work of the PIMS project which investigated on a systematic basis the determinants of company profitability (Buzzell and Gale, 1989). Recent examination of the firm has largely been devoted to the implementation of strategic plans. There has also been a resurgence of interest in internal aspects of the firm, and specifically in how an understanding of the firm's resources is critical to strategy formulation and sustained success. This chapter will argue that resources form the foundation for the firm's strategy and the fundamental basis of its profits.

The shift from an external to an internal view of the firm also involves a change of emphasis. Conventionally, strategy has been customer focused: the primary mission of firms has usually been viewed in terms of serving customer needs. Yet in many instances this has led to firms adopting strategies which have overstretched their resources. Saatchi and Saatchi's global expansion and diversification was driven by the vision of providing a full range of marketing and consulting services to multinational clients throughout the world.

Unfortunately, this vision took the company beyond its competence base – providing creative advertising solutions to clients' marketing needs from its London office.

One consequence of the recent emphasis on resources has been to redirect the firm's attention to what it is truly capable of supplying. The value of this perspective is exemplified by the success of certain companies which have established their long-term strategies on the development and application of a core of resources and capabilities, rather than on serving any particular product market:

▌ *Honda Motor Company* began in 1948 producing small engines to provide auxiliary power to bicycles. The company's strategy has been based on innovation and efficiency in the design and manufacture of four-stroke engines. The efficiency and reliability of Honda's engines played a major role in the company's dominance of the world motorcycle industry. Subsequently, Honda has established itself in motor cars and a wide variety of markets where its engine technology can be applied – generators, small marine engines, lawn mowers.

▌ *3M Corporation.* Minnesota Mining and Manufacturing (3M) began supplying abrasive papers. The company diversified into adhesive tape ('Scotchtape') and has gone on to develop an £8 billion group of businesses built around two core technologies: adhesives and thin-film technology. The result has been a proliferation of products ranging from 'Post-it' notes to photographic film, audiotape and computer discs.

In addition to providing an injection of reality into the firm, the resource-based view has other values. If the firm's market environment is subject to rapid change, then a strategy based on resources and capabilities may provide a more stable, long-term focus. For example, fashion design houses such as Gucci, Yves St Laurent, Calvin Klein and Chanel have defined their businesses not as clothing design – this is too fickle a market – but around their brand names. Therefore they have been prepared to exploit their upmarket names in almost any product market where a profit potential exists.

Lastly, profits are ultimately a return on the resources owned and controlled by the firm. Profits are derived from the attractiveness of the industry and the firm's achievement of a competitive advantage over other firms. Resources underlie both of these profit elements.

FUNDAMENTALS OF RESOURCE ANALYSIS

Resources are the individual assets of the firm: items of capital equipment, employee skills, patents, brand names, and the like. Capabilities are what the firm can do: they are the result of resources working together to achieve productive tasks. Figure 10.1 shows the relationship between resources, capabilities and competitive advantage. While capabilities depend on the integration and application of the firm's human, technical and tangible resources, it is through the application of capabilities that the firm also creates and augments its resource base. For example, through the application of R&D capabilities the firm develops new patents and other forms of proprietary technology. Through the application of new product development capabilities and marketing capabilities, the firm creates new brand names.

Finally, the application of capabilities within an appropriate strategy creates a competitive advantage for the firm, which then produces a stream of profits to further nourish the resource base.

Identifying and classifying resources

Listing resources is a far-from-straightforward task. A starting point is the balance sheet, which purports to show a valuation of the assets.

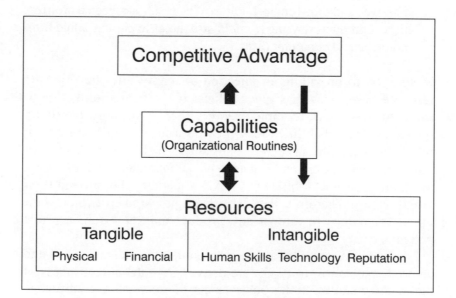

Figure 10.1   *Resources, capabilities and competitive advantage*

However, balance sheets focus on *tangible* resources: cash, financial assets, land and capital equipment. Some *intangible* resources may be included such as brands, technology and 'goodwill', but typically the valuations of these items follow accounting conventions and seldom give much indication of their true economic value.

For most firms, it is intangible resources which are both the most valuable and the most strategically important items in the resource pool. The importance of these intangibles has been increasingly recognized by investors. Table 10.2 compares the net asset values and stock exchange valuations for several British companies. It can be seen that those companies which are rich in intangible resources – such as technology and consumer brands – tend to show the greatest surplus of market value over book value.

To identify the resources of the firm it is useful to consider the principal categories of resources. Table 10.3 provides a first-cut classification.

Resource deployment

In examining how a firm deploys its resources, two issues are particularly important:

▌ What opportunities exist for economizing on the use of resources in order to undertake existing activities more efficiently?

Table 10.2   *Valuation ratios for selected British companies, 1992*

Company	Valuation ratio*
SmithKline Beecham	9.85
Glaxo	6.87
Reckitt & Colman	4.28
Cadbury Schweppes	3.89
United Biscuits	3.33
Guinness	2.89
Tate & Lyle	2.21
Allied-Lyons	1.84
British Petroleum	1.74
Hanson	1.37
Lucas Industries	1.32
Rolls Royce	1.30
British Steel	0.59

* Measured as the ratio of the stock exchange capitalization of ordinary shares to the book value of shareholders' equity.

Table 10.3   *Classifying resources*

Financial resources	Cash reserves. Short-term financial assets. Borrowing capacity. Cash flow.
Physical resources	Plant and equipment (scale, location, vintage, technology, flexibility). Resources of raw materials.
Human resources	The experience and skills of different categories of employee. Adaptability of employees. Loyalty of employees. Skills and experience of top management.
Technology	Proprietary technology in the form of patents, copyrights and trade secrets. Technology resources in the form of R&D facilities and staff.
Reputation	Product brands and their associated 'brand equity'. Trademarks. Company reputation.
Relationship	With customers, suppliers, distributors and government authorities.

▌ What are the possibilities for employing existing assets more profitably?

The first question takes the firm's existing level of activities as given and asks how they may be undertaken with fewer resources. Before it was demerged in 1996 Hanson was one of the leading British exponents of this type of management. When reviewing the businesses of an acquired company, its first task was to identify which of those businesses it wished to retain and which to divest. Its second task was to investigate opportunities for greater efficiency within the retained businesses. For example, in reviewing the Imperial Group's tobacco business, Hanson identified a host of opportunities for managing the business with fewer resources. These included a radical reduction in management and administration staff, lower inventories, reductions in capacity and employment in manufacturing operations, and more efficient use of cash within the business.

The second question begins with the resource pool and asks whether resources can be deployed in alternative ways. At 3M, for example, there is a continuing quest to use employee skills and ideas and the firm's pool of technological know-how in seeking new business opportunities. Among several of the oil companies in the early 1980s, managers took the initiative to establish venture capital and technology development subsidiaries with a view to deploying the technologies and financial resources within to build the company new technology-based businesses. Among British banks and building societies, an important strategic issue has been how to put their large retail branch networks to better use. While the banks have used their retail premises to provide a broader range of financial services, including stockbroking and insurance retailing, the building societies have expanded their range of personal banking services and offered office services (such as copying and fax services) and estate agency services.

Thus the main issues with regard to resources are how to maintain existing activities with fewer resources, and how to increase the range or intensity of activities using the same resources. Achieving these tasks requires a careful identification of the firm's resources and a thorough understanding of its performance and potential.

Strategy as stretch

Hamel and Prahalad (1993) depict strategy, not as a fit between a company's resources and its environment but as stretch and leverage. They start by pointing out that the winning companies in recent times have not necessarily been the largest players in their industry. Several large players like Pan Am and TWA no longer exist; others have been seriously challenged by smaller players, eg General Motors and Fiat by Toyota and Honda. The problem with large size is that it very often breeds complacency and an inability to contemplate radical change. (The Marks and Spencer case illustrates this very well.) Smaller companies may have greater stretch in their aspirations, but how can they, with their limited resources, aspire to take on the global giants? The answer according to Hamel and Prahalad is to 'leverage' resources. This can be done in five basic ways:

1. by concentrating resources on more focused strategic goals;

2. by accumulating resources more efficiently;

3. by complementing or combining resources with others to create higher value;

4. by conserving resources; and

5. by recovering resources from the market in the shortest possible time.

Concentrating resources entails greater convergence of resources around a single, clear goal. Hamel and Prahalad quote President Kennedy's challenge to put a man on the moon within a decade as an example. It also means being willing to make trade-offs in the short term that can improve the longer-term competitive position.

Accumulating resources refers to the ease with which companies can learn from experience and disseminate the knowledge around the organization. This is clearly closely related to the idea of the learning organization, but simply being a learning organization is not sufficient. A company must also be capable of learning more efficiently than its competitors. In order for this to happen, an appropriate corporate climate must be created in which employees feel free to challenge long-standing practices. The other aspect of accumulating resources is the ability to borrow ideas from other organizations. This means gaining access to the skills of joint venture partners.

Blending and balancing has to do with cross-functional integration and is linked to the notion of the lean enterprise. To blend knowledge effectively requires technology generalists capable of systems thinking and optimizing complex technology trade-offs. Companies should have three separate capabilities, which should be in balance:

▌ strong product development capability;

▌ the capability of manufacturing or delivering services at world-class levels;

▌ effective distribution marketing and after-sales infrastructure.

Companies that have well-developed core competences in one of these areas, for example product development, could easily come to grief if they failed to possess another, for example the ability to distribute and market.

Conserving resources includes dispersing skills and transferring technologies that are developed in one area of the company across to another area. So, for example, Honda's expertise in engines for cars can also be used in its motorcycle or outboard-motor business. Resources can also be conserved through co-opting the partners. This means attracting a potential partner/competitor into an alliance against a third party, so that, by pooling resources, the two parties are able to conserve their respective resources. The third aspect to conserving resources is referred to as shielding. Shielding means, in effect, not mounting a full-frontal assault on an established player.

Finally, recovering resources means shortening the time between when resources are expended and when a return on investment can be expected. To quote Hamel and Prahalad's phrase, 'a company that can do anything twice as fast as its competitors, with a similar resource commitment, enjoys a two-fold leverage advantage'.

CAPABILITIES

On their own, resources can achieve little. It is by working together that resources perform productive tasks and so establish competitive advantage. *Organizational capability* refers to a firm's ability to achieve particular tasks and activities. Analysis of capabilities begins with classifying the activities of the firm. Before asking: 'What does our company do particularly well?', we must first ask, 'What does our company do?' A common reason for business failure is not the absence of capabilities, but an inability to recognize what they are and put them to effective use. Hence analysis of capabilities must begin with a careful recognition of the activities which the firm performs.

There are a number of approaches which can be used to identify and classify a company's capabilities. Two common frameworks are a functional classification and the value chain.

Functions

In the same way that businesses are typically organized along functional lines, organizational capabilities can be described and classified by functional area. Table 10.4 suggests some examples of functional capabilities.

Value chain analysis

The value chain is a graphical representation of a firm's activities, arranged in such a way as to show the sequence of these activities. The value chain provides a powerful framework for identifying and appraising the resources and capabilities of a firm, in part because it emphasizes the linkages between the different activities, and also because it facilitates comparisons between firms, regarding both individual activities and the structuring of activities. The simplest representation of the chain of activities of a company is McKinsey and Company's business system (Figure 10.2). The generic value chain

Table 10.4   *Functional capabilities*

Corporate	
Strategic control	GENERAL ELECTRIC
	UNITED BISCUITS
Multinational management	UNILEVER
Acquisitions management	BTR
Marketing	GUINNESS
International brand management	COCA-COLA
Building customer trust	AMERICAN EXPRESS
Market research and segment-targeted marketing	CAMPBELL'S SOUP
Human resource management	HP
Building employee loyalty and trust	SHELL
Management development	IBM
Design	TETRA PAK ALFA-LAVAL
New product design capability	APPLE COMPUTER
R&D	IBM, 3M
Research capability	DU PONT
New product development capability	SONY
	CANON
Operations	NUCOR
Efficiency in volume manufacturing	TEXAS INSTRUMENTS
Manufacturing flexibility	BMW
Quality manufacturing	TOYOTA
Management information systems	
Timely and comprehensive	THE GAP
communication of information	AMERICAN AIRLINES
Sales and distribution	
Efficiency and speed of distribution	WAL-MART
Order processing efficiency	LL BEAN

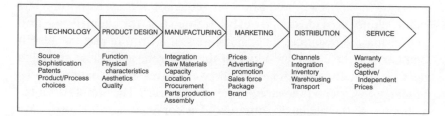

Figure 10.2   *McKinsey's business system value chain*

developed by Michael Porter analyzes the activities of the firm in greater detail, distinguishing between operational (or 'primary') activities and support activities (Figure 10.3).

APPRAISING CAPABILITIES

Identifying what an organization can do is straightforward. The difficult task is to assess capabilities, particularly with a degree of objectivity. When a company is showing satisfactory performance, it is easy to perceive distinctive capabilities where none exist. Equally, when a company's financial performance is dismal, it is easy for a cloud of pessimism to obscure those areas where the firm does possess distinctive competence.

One of the most powerful techniques for assessing a firm's capabilities and setting targets for improving capabilities is *benchmarking*. Benchmarking involves establishing performance measures for different aspects of performance (product failure rates, production yields, production cycle times, speed of distribution, new product development times, and so on) then, for each performance measure, selecting another company which is perceived as an 'exemplar' against which to make comparisons. Benchmarking has proven immensely popular and effective in both Europe and North America.

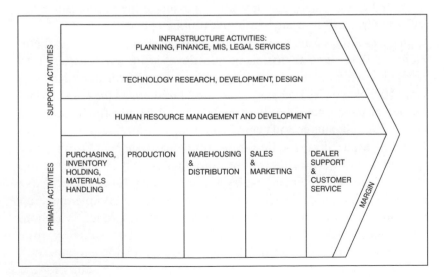

Figure 10.3 *Porter's value chain*

At Xerox, for example, benchmarking is seen as a critical element in the company's performance turnaround in the 1980s.

MANAGING CAPABILITIES

Identifying and assessing capabilities is easier than creating them. Organizational capabilities are typically the result of complex patterns of co-ordination between a number of employees offering a range of specialist skills and knowledge, and integrating skills and knowledge with the other resources of the firm. Nelson and Winter (1982) introduced the term *'organizational routines'* to describe patterns of co-ordinated behaviour within firms which are repeated over time. Virtually all the capabilities of a firm are exercised through organizational routines. The significant feature of such routines is that they are regular, predictable patterns of behaviour in which individuals co-ordinate their activities with fellow employees, typically relying on a variety of signals which govern the sequencing of activities and variations in the repertoires. Capabilities are typically the result of a series of interlinked organizational routines. Thus, Toyota's 'lean' manufacturing system, UPS's system of express delivery and Microsoft's software development process all involve a number of closely co-ordinated routines.

Yet *managing* these routines is exceptionally difficult, in part because individual routines and networks of routines develop over time, and it is unlikely that any single person in the organization has full knowledge of how any particular routine operates.

In general it is easier to destroy capabilities than it is to create them. Hence a first stage in fostering and developing capabilities is to recognize which of the firm's capabilities are critical to its success. Gary Hamel and CK Prahalad (1994) refer to these as the *core competencies* of the corporation: the capabilities which are fundamental to competitive advantage and central to strategy formulation. Hamel and Prahalad argue that, for long-run competitive success, firms must recognize and nurture their core competencies; it is vital that top management view their companies as a set of capabilities rather than a portfolio of products. Products are the vehicles for commercializing the company's capabilities. An example of this approach is Canon, whose product development capability involves a meshing of three technologies: micro-electronics, optics and precision engineering. Canon's stream of new products has involved the integration of these technologies (Table 10.5).

Table 10.5 *Canon's application of technical capabilities to new products*

| Product | Competencies | | |
	Precision mechanics	Fine optics	Microelectronics
Electronic cameras	✓	✓	✓
Video cameras	✓	✓	✓
Laser printers	✓		✓
Bubble jet printers	✓		✓
Basic fax	✓		✓
Laser fax	✓		✓
Plain paper copier	✓	✓	✓
Colour laser copier	✓	✓	✓
Laser imager	✓	✓	✓
Excimer laser aligners	✓	✓	✓

FROM RESOURCES AND CAPABILITIES TO COMPETITIVE ADVANTAGE

If a firm possesses resources and capabilities which are superior to those of competitors, then as long as the firm adopts a strategy that utilizes these resources and capabilities effectively, it should be possible for it to establish a competitive advantage. But in terms of the ability to derive profits from this position of competitive advantage, a critical issue is the time period over which the firm can sustain its advantage. The sustainability of competitive advantage depends on three major characteristics of resources and capabilities: *durability, transferability* and *replicability*; while a firm's ability to earn profits from its competitive advantage depends upon the *appropriability* of these returns.

Durability

The period over which a competitive advantage is sustained depends in part on the rate at which a firm's resources and capabilities deteriorate. In industries where the rate of product innovation is fast, product patents are quite likely to become obsolescent. Similarly, capabilities which are the result of the management expertise of the CEO are also vulnerable to his or her retirement or departure. On the other hand, many consumer brand names have a highly durable appeal. If capabilities are managed carefully and employee training is effective, then capabilities can be maintained even when there is a change in the employees on which those capabilities depend.

Transferability

Even if the resources and capabilities on which a competitive advantage is based are durable, it is likely to be eroded by competition from rivals. The ability of rivals to attack positions of competitive advantage relies on their gaining access to the necessary resources and capabilities. The easier it is to transfer resources and capabilities between companies, the less sustainable will be the competitive advantage which is based on them. Physical assets and skills associated with individual employees are among the more readily transferable. If a company's cost advantage is based on its investment in state-of-the-art automated equipment, so long as the equipment is supplied by a third party, other companies can acquire the same advantage. If Opel's efficiency in purchasing components was dependent on the unique skills of its purchasing boss, José Ignacio López de Arriortúa, then by bidding Mr López away in April 1993 Volkswagen was able to acquire the same purchasing capability. Other resources are likely to be specific to companies, corporate reputation for example, while capabilities, to the extent that they are dependent on groups of people working together, are also difficult to transfer.

Replicability

If resources and capabilities cannot be purchased by a would-be imitator, then they must be built from scratch. How easily and quickly can your competitors build the resources and capabilities on which your competitive advantage is based? In some businesses replication is easy: in financial services, innovations lack legal protection and are easily copied. Here again the complexity of many organizational capabilities can provide a degree of competitive defence. Where capabilities require networks of organizational routines, whose effectiveness depends on the corporate culture, replication is difficult. McDonald's unique system which permits it to serve millions of hamburgers every week from thousands of outlets spread across the globe is a case in point. Often, there are many subtle factors underlying the success of complex organizational routines such as JIT or quality circles, where societal norms in addition to corporate culture are critical to success.

Appropriability

Even where resources and capabilities are capable of offering sustainable advantage, there is an issue as to *who receives the returns on these resources*. This is particularly the case with human skills and the capabilities based on them. While a firm owns its physical assets and proprietary technology, employees own their skills, and to the extent that a major part of the surplus (or 'rents') earned by the firm is a return on know-how, how is this surplus to be divided between the firm's owners and its employees? *Appropriability* refers to the ability of the firm's owners to appropriate the returns on its resource base. The 'division of spoils' is likely to depend on the ability of an individual employee to identify his or her contribution to productivity and that employee's bargaining power relative to that of the firm. To the extent that CEOs such as Michael Eisner of Walt Disney and Lou Gerstner of IBM can identify improvements in their companies' profitability as the result of their own efforts, they are in a powerful position to claim remuneration packages which take a substantial share of these performance improvements. Similarly with football players: any football club chairman hoping to enhance the club's financial performance by hiring star players such as Rio Ferdinand or Ronaldo is likely to find it difficult to earn a surplus over the pay and fees needed to acquire such players.

The problem of highly skilled individuals appropriating the major part of the rents associated with their skills is particularly important in businesses such as management consulting, financial services, advertising agencies, film production and advertising. The reason that so many professional service firms are organized as partnerships rather than corporations is partly a desire to prevent this conflict of interest and to tie professionals to the firm. The wish to avoid strategic dependence on individuals has encouraged several management consulting firms and advertising agencies to organize themselves around teams where capabilities are team based rather than individually based.

SUMMARY

Differences in profitability between companies in the same industry are as great if not greater than differences in profitability across industries. The primary determinant of business success is the firm's ability to achieve and maintain a competitive advantage in the market or markets in which it operates. To a considerable extent the ability to sustain a competitive advantage is a function of the resources a company is able to deploy and the capabilities it possesses. Examples of companies that have been able to sustain their strong position in their respective markets as a result of having developed a strong core of resources and capabilities include Honda, BMW, 3M, Shell and Diageo.

A firm's resources include not only those that appear on the balance sheet – its physical and financial resources – but also its intangible assets such as brands, technological expertise, goodwill and exceptionally talented employees. It is often the intangibles that are strategically the most important. It is not just a question of what resources a firm has at its disposal; the more critical issue is how well it manages them. Hamel and Prahalad have stressed the importance of 'leveraging' resources so as to increase their impact on performance.

The task of managing resources effectively leads naturally into the issue of capabilities or competences. These are the things that companies do well and which are related to the key success factors in the industries in which they operate. Examples include Coca-Cola's capability in international brand management, 3M's track record in new product development, BMW's competence in high-quality manufacturing, Hewlett Packard's success in building employee commitment and Unilever's skills in multinational management.

The sustainability of a competitive advantage depends in particular on the following major factors:

▌ *Durability*. The ability of a company, through investment, training and continuous learning and improvement, to maintain the quality of its resources and capabilities.

▌ *Transferability*. The extent to which other companies can acquire a firm's resources or capabilities, for example by 'poaching' key personnel or copying key processes or systems.

▌ *Replicability*. The ease with which competitors can build comparable resources or capabilities from scratch.

▌ *Appropriability*. This is the issue of who receives the returns from the key resources or capabilities. In the case of Premiership football clubs it is clearly the star players and not the shareholders!

Strategies for cost advantage and differentiation advantage

INTRODUCTION

Superior profitability can be achieved by a firm in one of two ways: by locating in an industry where an attractive structure leads to subdued competition and high overall rates of profits, or by establishing a competitive advantage over rivals. In Chapter 10 it was observed that the overwhelmingly important determinant of a company's long-term profitability is its ability to establish a sustainable competitive advantage. Over time it seems that industry environment is becoming a less and less important determinant of profit performance, while the ability to establish a competitive advantage is becoming increasingly important. Deregulation, increased global competition, the effects of technology and diversification in breaking down industry boundaries have all had the effect of intensifying competition within industries which were once considered attractive because of muted competition.

The principal components of competitive advantage have already been discussed. In Chapter 5 *key success factors* were introduced: the conditions for establishing competitive advantage within a particular industry. Then in Chapter 10 *resources* and *capabilities* were discussed; these are the sources of competitive advantage *within* the firm. Competitive advantage is the result of the combination of the two. A strategy will be successful in creating competitive advantage when it deploys a firm's resources and capabilities to match the key success factors within the industry environment (see Figure 11.1).

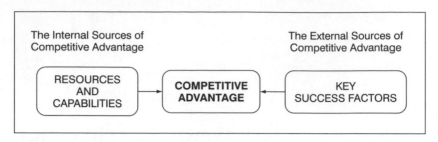

Figure 11.1   *The determinants of competitive advantage*

CREATION AND EROSION OF COMPETITIVE ADVANTAGE

Chapter 10 discussed some of the characteristics of resources which are conducive to sustaining competitive advantage. This section will consider more broadly the conditions under which competitive advantage is created and then eroded.

Creating competitive advantage

Competitive advantage is typically the result of some form of disturbance. Such a disturbance may be external or internal to the firm. An external disturbance may be any change in the external environment which alters the competitive positions of firms within an industry. Thus the rise in oil prices following Iraq's invasion of Kuwait in 1990 provided a temporary boost to the competitive positions of petrol distributors which marketed blends of petrol and alcohol ('gasohol'). The competitive position of Intel in integrated circuits was greatly enhanced by IBM's selection of Intel's microprocessor for its first PC launched in 1981.

Alternatively, the disturbance which creates a competitive advantage may be internally generated through innovation. Such innovations may be in the form of:

■ *new products*, such as Philips' development of the compact disc, Searle's *Nutrasweet* or Turner Broadcasting System's *Cable News Network*, a global, 24-hour, all news TV channel;

■ *new processes*, such as Pilkington's float glass process, Toyota's 'lean manufacturing' system, NASDAQ's computer-based system for quoting and trading company shares;

▌ *strategic innovations*: new approaches to doing business within a market, such as Federal Express's system of nationwide, next-day, express delivery, Body Shop's approach to marketing and retailing toiletries, Dell Computer's direct-mail approach to the marketing and distribution of personal computers.

If establishing competitive advantage means responding either to external opportunities or to internally generated innovation, this implies that firms must be opportunistic and creative. The successful companies are those which are quick in recognizing the opportunities which change provides, and those which are able to develop new ways of better meeting customer needs.

Recognizing opportunities requires environmental scanning. Such scanning is not simply a case of gathering and analyzing information such as in conventional, statistically based market research. If environmental scanning is to recognize opportunities for creating competitive advantage, then the key input is not so much information as *insight*. The main elements are a thorough understanding of customers' needs and the product and performance characteristics which customers value and are willing to pay for. In addition, firms must be aware of new opportunities for serving customers through changes in technology, legislation and communications infrastructure.

Environmental scanning is primarily a deductive art. If a firm is aiming to be the source of change through innovation, deductive reasoning must be augmented, possibly supplanted, by imagination and creativity. This enters the debate over the role of analysis in promoting, or possibly suppressing, creativity and innovation. As will be explained, the value chain can provide a framework for helping to recognize opportunities for strategic innovation. Hamel and Prahalad (1993) have argued that the success of upstarts against better established rivals (Sony against RCA, Toyota against GM, British Airways against Pan Am) reflects the ability of the upstarts to overcome initial advantages through 'breaking managerial frames'. Important in innovative approaches is setting strategic ambitions which 'stretch' performance and 'leverage' resources. For a business to excel in a highly competitive environment, resources need to be creatively manipulated. Like the keys on a piano, resources at any point of time are finite, but there is no limit to what can be achieved if they are utilized creatively and effectively.

Erosion of competitive advantage

Once created, competitive advantage is eroded through competition. If a firm is achieving superior profitability as a result of having established a competitive advantage, then it will attract imitators. Thus, if a firm is to sustain a competitive advantage over time, there must exist some form of *barriers to imitation*. In the absence of such barriers, competitive advantage will be fleeting. Consider financial and securities markets, which are described as being *'efficient'* precisely because competitive advantage can neither be established nor sustained. If the prices of securities and financial instruments reflect all available information, then returns are random; it is not possible to 'beat the market' on any consistent basis.

Most markets, however, are *'inefficient'*, in the sense that imperfections of competition exist which prevent the competitive process from equalizing expected returns to all firms. These imperfections in the competitive process take the form of barriers which prevent competitive advantages being imitated. These barriers may arise from a number of sources:

1. *Information barriers*. In order to imitate, would-be imitators must be able to identify firms which possess a competitive advantage, and also to diagnose the sources of their success. Neither of these problems is trivial. In many industries, and for many firms, it is not easy to detect success. Where firms are privately held (eg family owned firms, partnerships and the like), it may be far from obvious which firms are exceptionally profitable. Even if success can be identified, diagnosing the sources of success may be subject to *'causal ambiguity'*. Why was M&S so successful over such a long period? Was it its quality management, supplier relations, customer service, human resource management, or a complex combination of these? Even among senior managers there are likely to be differences of opinion as to the sources of M&S's success. As a result, it was not only difficult to imitate M&S but it was equally difficult for M&S directors to understand why they lost competitiveness in the late 1990s.

2. *First-mover advantages*. It may be impossible for the success to be imitated, simply because the first mover has advantages which are unattainable by a follower. Investment opportunities, otherwise open to rivals, can be pre-empted by saturating the market with additions to capacity, vertical expansion, and proliferation of the product range. First movers may also be able to attain advantages from experience and the ability to set industry standards.

3. ***Resource-based advantages***. Even if rivals can diagnose the sources of success of the leader, and even if the leader has not pre-empted all the opportunities, the would-be imitator still needs to assemble the resources and capabilities required for imitation. As we discussed in Chapter 10, there are two characteristics of resources which are critical to determining the ability of rivals to obtain the means to imitate. First, are the required resources and capabilities *transferable*, ie can they be purchased? Second, if they cannot be purchased, how easy is it to *replicate* them?

Firms which are able to sustain competitive advantage over the long term are typically protected by a combination of these barriers. Consider BMW's competitive position in the luxury car market. Its emergence during the 1960s as a successful manufacturer of high-performance saloon cars was based on outstanding engineering capabilities, meticulous manufacturing, and extremely well targeted marketing. Despite the weaknesses of small company size and aggressive competition from US and Japanese car manufacturers, BMW has maintained and strengthened its competitive position within its narrow market niche. Although other automobile companies possess greater technological resources, more advanced manufacturing systems and greater marketing resources, the combination of engineering capabilities, reputation and highly effective distribution and marketing has made BMW very difficult to dislodge within the luxury car market.

COST AND DIFFERENTIATION ADVANTAGES

One firm can outperform another by one of two means: either it can supply an identical product at a lower cost, or it can produce a product that is differentiated so that the customer is willing to pay a price premium which exceeds the cost of the differentiation.

These two sources of competitive advantage define a dichotomous approach to business strategy. The goal of cost advantage is to be the cost leader in the industry. If a firm can establish a position of cost leadership then it can use its cost advantage to undercut its rivals on price. In many cases cost leaders are also market share leaders: Boeing in commercial jets, General Electric in turbine generators, McDonald's in hamburgers. However, this is not always so. In many industries, such as printing, carton manufacturing and construction, the lowest cost firms are small operators who use low-cost, non-union labour and second-hand capital equipment, and keep overheads to a minimum. Differentiation advantage may be achieved in a myriad of different ways from mass-market branding such as Coca-Cola, to the engineering quality of Mercedes or the exclusiveness of the Ivy restaurant. A third option is to compete by virtue of a focus strategy, occupying successfully a small niche in a large market. Morgan cars provide a good example as does the *Financial Times* relative to the mass-circulation daily press.

On the basis of these sources of competitive advantage and a firm's choice of market scope, Michael Porter has distinguished three generic strategies: cost leadership, differentiation and focus (see Figure 11.2).

This raises the issue of whether these strategies are mutually exclusive or whether it is possible for a firm to attain both cost leadership and differentiation advantage. Some kinds of innovation can result in a product which offers the advantages of both lower cost and differentiation. Pilkington's float glass was much cheaper to produce than traditionally made rolled and machined glass and was made to tighter tolerances. One of the most interesting outcomes of Total Quality Management is the recognition that techniques whose goals are to increase product quality can also have the effect of lowering costs through reducing waste and rework, and improving co-ordination and work design.

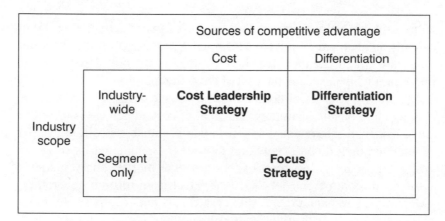

Figure 11.2   *Generic competitive strategies*

SOURCES OF COST ADVANTAGE

To understand why one firm has unit costs which are different from those of a competitor producing a similar product, we need to examine the role of different *cost drivers* – factors which determine the level of unit costs within a particular industry. These are described below.

Economies of learning and scale

In business, as in life, repetition can be an excellent teacher. If you observe the price trends of almost any new product: microcomputers, compact disc players, DVD players or flat-screen television sets, you observe a decline. One of the main factors is learning. As more and more of a product is manufactured, individual workers become more adept at their jobs and improvements are made to product organization. As a result, employee time per unit of production falls. Economies of learning are more pronounced in more complex operations, and learning is the result of the refinement of organizational routines.

During the early 1970s, the Boston Consulting Group took this kind of analysis a stage further, by proposing a more or less fixed relationship between unit cost reduction and increases in cumulative volume. The BCG *experience curve* postulated that: *whenever cumulative volume doubles, unit costs fall by a constant amount* (normally between 20 and 30 per cent). This is illustrated in Figure 11.3.

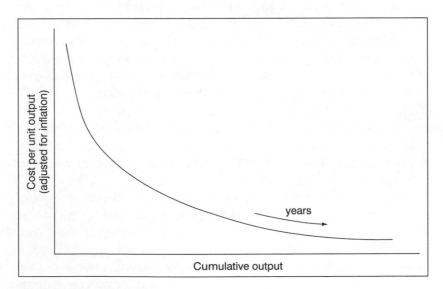

Figure 11.3 *The experience curve*

The implication of the experience curve for strategy is that, if a firm can expand its output faster than its competitors, it is able to move down the experience curve more rapidly than its rivals and can open a widening cost differential or margin. To out-accelerate rivals in output expansion requires the firm to achieve market share leadership. Hence the emphasis of BCG's experience curve doctrine was the pre-eminence of market share as a strategic goal.

In the three decades since BCG introduced its experience curve, the concept and the strategy recommendations associated with it have come under increasing criticism:

▌ The relationship between unit cost and cumulative volume at the level of the firm is far from automatic. Learning depends on will-ingness to learn and mechanisms for learning. New companies may be able to access the learning of other companies without having to start at the top of the experience curve.

▌ The recommended strategy of competing aggressively for market share is hazardous when several firms are pursuing the same strategy. In the European steel and chemical industries for example, the excess capacity of the late 1970s and 1980s has been partly a result of competing firms all seeking market share lead-ership through price cutting and investment in new capacity.

Economies of scale exist whenever proportionate increases in the amounts of inputs employed in a production process result in a more than proportionate increase in total output. Economies of scale have conventionally been associated with manufacturing activities, espe-cially those which are capital intensive (oil refining) or complex assembly tasks (motor vehicles). However, scale economies are increasingly important in other functions. In manufacturing indus-tries, new product development costs are the principal source of scale economies. Developing a new model range of motor cars typically costs over US $1 billion. As a result, smaller car manufacturers such as Rover, Jaguar, Renault, Volvo and Saab have sought either merger or collaboration. Jaguar and Volvo cars are now owned by Ford. General Motors owns Saab, while Renault owns 38 per cent of Nissan. Rover, having been first acquired and then divested by BMW, is pursuing joint ventures in China. Important scale advantages also exist in marketing and distribution. The cost of producing and broad-casting TV commercials means that, in most consumer goods indus-tries, smaller players are at a substantial cost disadvantage if they attempt to compete on the basis of brand advertising.

The most important source of scale economies is the presence of *indivisibilities*, fixed costs which must be incurred irrespective of the output being produced. Developing a new product, launching a national advertising campaign, or installing a catalytic cracker at an oil refinery, all involve some minimal level of expenditure. The greater the sales volume of the firm, the lower the unit costs of these items are likely to be.

COST DRIVERS

Input costs

In many cases the largest source of differences in input costs arises from differences in labour costs. In the steel industry, the success of the 'minimill' operators comes partly from lower wage, non-union labour; the advantage of South East Asian companies in assembling consumer electronic goods is traditionally based on their low labour costs. Cost advantage also occurs in relation to other inputs. In the oil industry, Exxon, Texaco and Mobil benefited for decades from the so-called 'Aramco advantage': access to low-cost Saudi oil. Lower input costs may also arise through the exercise of bargaining power. The increasing dominance of food retailing by a handful of supermarket companies is partly a result of their bargaining power in relation to the food manufacturing companies.

Process technology

The development or adoption of new production technology can be an important source of cost advantage. Cost leadership requires constant technological advancement, often through such incremental process innovations as flexible manufacturing systems and computer-integrated manufacture.

Product design

Manufacturing costs vary with product design. A key source of the cost advantage of Japanese manufacturers of electronics and vehicles has been *design for manufacture*. A significant theme across a wide range of industries has been redesigning products in order to reduce the number of components and to facilitate automated assembly. Increasingly design engineering is performed *concurrently*, so that designers, engineers, marketers and customers can collaborate in all production phases from conception to sale.

Capacity utilization

Where production capacity is costly to install and remove, cost efficiency depends on utilizing capacity to the full. Some businesses' costs are almost entirely fixed. Airlines, cinemas, amusement parks and spectator sports are 'bums on seats' businesses – total costs are much the same at 1 per cent or 100 per cent capacity. Hence the ability to operate close to capacity is critical to lowering unit costs and earning a profit. The economics of capital-intensive industries such as steel and chemicals are similar; costs and margins are highly sensitive to capacity utilization. Efficient capacity utilization requires accurate demand forecasting before and after expansion, together with the flexibility to close surplus capacity during troughs in demand.

Managerial factors

Even after taking account of these various 'cost drivers', there are still likely to be unexplained differences in cost between competing companies. Some firms are better than others at leveraging resources and capabilities for greater efficiency. To explain why Ford is able to build cars at a cost which is almost 10 per cent below that of General Motors, despite no obvious differences in wage rates or scale, attention must be directed to operational efficiencies associated with the effectiveness of management.

ANALYZING COSTS

Using the value chain to analyze costs

'Cost drivers' are useful for categorizing differences in unit costs between competing companies. Cost drivers and relative costs are likely to be different, however, when the different activities within the firm are considered. Value chain analysis provides a means of disaggregating the activities of the firm to provide a better understanding of the basic elements affecting cost. The procedure is as follows:

1. Disaggregate the firm into its principal activities, using the kinds of generic frameworks shown in Figures 10.2 and 10.3 in the previous chapter.

2. Make a rough estimate of the allocation of total costs between different activities. This permits (a) attention to be focused on

those activities which account for a large proportion of total costs, and (b) comparisons to be made with competitors, eg do administrative costs account for a higher proportion of total costs in company A compared with company B?

3. Identify cost drivers for each activity. For example, market costs per unit of output are likely to depend on the size of the budget for advertising and promotion and the total number of units sold.

4. With reference to these cost drivers, explain any cost differences between company A and its competitors.

5. Identify opportunities for cost reduction. For example, in order to reduce marketing costs it may be possible to find ways of reducing the advertising budget by changing media, by pressuring TV stations for bigger discounts, or by redesigning marketing campaigns. Or it might be possible to maintain the advertising budget and seek to spread it over a bigger sales base through expanding distribution outlets.

Producer costs and buyer costs

If the goal is to achieve a cost advantage in the market, it is important to distinguish between low cost to the producer and low cost to the customer. Few products are consumed directly and independently by customers. When products require further processing by the customer or are consumed with other goods and services, cost advantage is likely to require that the firm is aware not only of its own producer costs, but also the overall costs to the buyer. In the case of a motor car, for example, the purchase price of the car is only one element in the overall buyer cost which takes account of depreciation costs, repair and maintenance costs, fuel and insurance costs. The failure of several low-cost car companies (Yugo, for instance) reflects the fact that a low purchase price did not correspond to a low overall buyer cost.

Dynamic versus static sources of cost efficiency

The analysis has included both static and dynamic sources of cost efficiency. Static sources include lower wage rates, access to scale economies, increased capacity utilization and the like. Dynamic sources include learning and innovation. Much traditional management emphasized static sources of cost reduction. However, the evidence from many Japanese companies and companies such as Nucor, Motorola and Hewlett-Packard suggests that sustained improvements in cost efficiency are likely to be those which stress dynamic efficiency through emphasizing learning, innovation and flexibility in responding to changing circumstances.

DIFFERENTIATION AND DIFFERENTIATION ADVANTAGE

'Differentiation' describes the uniqueness which a firm incorporates into its offerings. Differential advantage occurs when a firm is able to obtain a price premium from its differentiation in the market that exceeds the cost of providing differentiation.

Virtually any product can be differentiated. While complex products and those that do not have to comply with strict regulatory standards offer the greatest potential for differentiation, even so-called commodities still offer opportunities. If the product itself cannot be differentiated, a firm may still be capable of offering superior customer service in the form of efficient order processing, speedy delivery, customer financing opportunities or reliability. Under these conditions, imagination is the only limiting factor. The success of differentiation rests on the firm's commitment to and understanding of the customer, its knowledge of its capabilities, and its innovative skills in bringing the two together.

Because differentiation is about creating a perception on the part of the customer of something special and distinctive, it is complex in nature and not amenable to generalization. Since all offerings from supplier to customer tend to involve a package of goods and services, the opportunities for differentiation are very wide, including product features and performance characteristics; ancillary items such as accessories, credit and pre- and post-sale services; and intangible factors which influence customers' perception of the product, such as packaging, promotion, the retail context of the product, and the image of the supplying firm. For most consumer goods and services, and some business services as well, social, emotional, psychological and aesthetic considerations play a large role in purchase decisions.

In terms of sustaining competitive advantage, differentiation is typically a more reliable basis for competitive advantage than cost leadership. Cost advantages tend to be more easily imitated than differentiation advantages, and cost advantage is highly vulnerable to changes in exchange rates and the emergence of competitors from low-wage countries. Since the 1980s, competitive advantage based on quality, brand loyalty and product innovation has been more secure than cost advantage founded on low input costs, scale economies, or superior process technology.

ANALYZING DIFFERENTIATION

The demand side

Successful differentiation is rooted in the firm's ability to understand customer demand and to match the customers' demand for something special with its ability to supply unique product and service features. Marketing research is rich with methods of investigating and analyzing customer demand. However, the most difficult and challenging issues are not identifying the features and performance which customers want, but determining the price premium that differentiation will support. Typically, however, the most innovative and successful differentiation arises not from market research but from *insight* into customer needs and from *experimentation*. The Macintosh personal computer, Chrysler's people carriers, and Mars' chocolate ice-cream were born out of imagination and trial and error in which insight rather than market research findings played the critical role.

The supply side

To identify the firm's potential to supply differentiation it is necessary to examine the activities of the firm and consider the opportunities for each activity to add uniqueness in the offering to customers. Some possibilities are listed in Table 11.1.

TANGIBLE AND INTANGIBLE DIFFERENTIATION

The discussion thus far has tended to emphasize the 'real' or 'tangible' aspects of differentiation. Certainly, most of the items in Table 11.1 relate to differentiation opportunities which involve some form of objectively identifiable adaptation of the product or service that enhances performance in some measurable way. However, once the importance of customers' psychological and social motivations is recognized, then the realm of 'intangible differentiation' is opened up. Most consumer goods, and many producer goods and services, are

Table 11.1   *Opportunities for creating uniqueness within the firm*

Activity	Differentiation opportunity
Purchasing	Quality of components and materials acquired

Design	Aesthetic appeal
	    Robustness of performance
	    Ease of maintenance

Manufacturing	Minimization of defects
	    Conformity to design specifications enhances
	    performance in use

Delivery	Speed in filling customer orders Reliability in meeting promised delivery items
Human resources management	Improved training and motivation increases customer service capability
Information systems	Permits responsiveness to the needs of specific customers
Financial management	Improves stability of the firm and firm's reputation as a stable supplier
Marketing	Building of product and company reputation through advertising
Customer service	Providing pre-sales information to customers

differentiated by the image which they project. Image is not created directly, it must be 'signalled' to customers through various forms of subtle differentiation. For example, packaging is a powerful and tangible signalling vehicle in product marketing. Services acquire their image through the appearance of the service facilities and the behaviour and attitudes of the employees. Advertising is an especially important mechanism through which firms signal quality and the relationship between the product and its consumer. Consistency in signalling is important if the differentiation is to be convincing in establishing a credible image of the product in the eyes of the customer.

The role of such signalling is related to the observability of product performance. For those goods where quality is observable prior to purchase – fresh flowers, for example – intangible differentiation through signalling is unlikely to be effective. However, for *experience goods*, where quality is only observable after consumption, intangible differentiation is capable of being more effective. The greatest opportunities are for those goods and services where, even after consumption, it is difficult to assess product performance objectively – baldness treatments, medical services and education fall into these categories.

THE COSTS OF DIFFERENTIATION

Differentiation adds costs. Differentiation involves added features, greater customization to meet individual customer preferences, the addition of ancillary services, increased expenditure on training and increased advertising and promotion. Some of these costs may be modest: it has already been observed that in many manufacturing activities improvements and quality and cost efficiency can be achieved simultaneously. Yet, despite Crosby's dictum tuat 'Quality is Free' (1989), at some point improvements in quality inevitably lead to higher cost. The indirect costs of differentiation are also significant. The rationale for Henry Ford's standardization ('You can have any color so long as it's black') was to maximize scale economies. To the extent that differentiation requires segmenting markets and customizing products, it also limits the potential for exploiting scale economies. Also, experience curve economies are sacrificed for innovation and frequent variations or new models.

Reconciling differentiation with cost efficiency involves managing a difficult trade-off. One approach is to seek standardization of components and the basic design parameters, while postponing differentiation to the later stages of the value chain. For example, Harley-Davidson offers over a dozen models of motorcycles and a number of variants of each model. However, this differentiation is principally through differences in accessories, styling features, and paint and trim. It has one basic engine in three different cylinder displacements, two styles of petrol tank, two types of final drive, a single gearbox type, and so on. In service industries such as airlines, hotels and rental, the objective appears to be to offer a fairly standardized product, but with personalized service.

Some new approaches to production have reduced differentiation costs. This is most dramatically demonstrated in manufacturing where technology has permitted unprecedently high rates of 're-tooling' that economically support rapid, yet efficient, procedure and product changes. Computer-aided manufacturing is the most outstanding example of a modern technology whose cost is more than offset by increased customer demand and the ability to reduce costs in other production areas, such as labour.

In some instances, differentiation and cost efficiency can work hand in hand. Where advertising expands market demand, for example, it can facilitate the exploitation of scale economies.

VALUE CHAIN ANALYSIS OF DIFFERENTIATION ADVANTAGE

The success of differentiation advantage depends on matching the firm's opportunities for augmenting and adapting its offering with the preferences and needs of customers. One approach to matching the supply and demand for differentiation is to use the value chain as a framework for analysis. By constructing a value chain both for the firm and for its customers, *linkages between the two sets of activities* can be sought. The issue here is to identify those activities where the firm can create some form of uniqueness which also creates value for the buyer. Figure 11.4 provides an example relating to a supplier of ready-mixed concrete. Having identified opportunities for differentiation, the critical task is to establish the profitability of such opportunities. Considerations are the cost of the differentiation, the price premium which the differentiation will support, and the sustainability of the differentiation advantage in the face of possible competition.

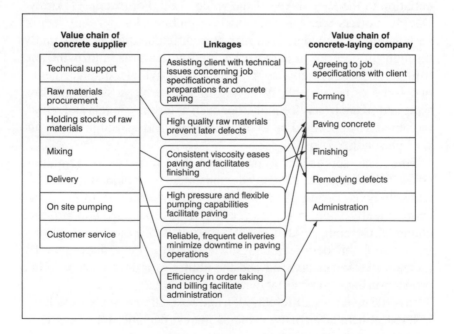

Figure 11.4   *Using the value chain to identify opportunities for product differentiation*

SUMMARY

A competitive advantage can be initially established in a variety of ways including the launching of a new product (for example, the Apple computer), new-process technology (Pilkington's float glass process) or innovation in the way of doing business (Body Shop).

Once created, however, a competitive advantage can be lost to the competition. The sustainability of the advantage is a function of a number of factors, such as:

▌ barriers to imitation – competitors either cannot determine the reasons for the advantage or fail to imitate them successfully;

▌ first-mover advantages, enabling the setting of industry standards (Microsoft, for example);

▌ resource-based factors – competitors unable to assemble the resources and/or capabilities required to compete effectively.

In the absence of significant product or marketing innovations of the kind that lead to significant changes in industry structure, firms compete by two means – being the lowest-cost producer or producing a product that is differentiated in ways that result in customers being willing to pay a premium price. The drive for cost leadership is exemplified by McDonald's, while an extreme example of differentiation is the Concorde Division of British Airways.

Even in such extreme cases, a cost leader cannot afford to ignore differentiation and a differentiator will seek to keep costs under control. McDonald's differentiates itself in outlet design and ambience and in aspects of service, while Concorde operations are subject to close control of costs.

Cost advantage comes from such things as economies of learning and of scale, access to cheap labour, use of advanced technology in manufacturing and information processing, product design, process re-engineering and capacity utilization.

Differentiation can be achieved in an almost infinite number of ways, some concrete and some intangible. For example, a restaurant can be differentiated in the following ways:

▌ quality of the cuisine;

▌ décor;

- availability of parking;
- quality of service;
- ambience;
- reputation.

Competing in global markets

INTRODUCTION

Worldwide business and trade, sparked by competition, fanned by potential cost and market share advantages, and fuelled by modern communications and transportation, continue to expand, despite the impact of inevitable periods of stagnation or recession. Yet, despite the pervasiveness and power of the drive towards internationalization in the world of business, national and local factors remain important. Globalization is hampered by trade restrictions, government regulations and differences in standards (as anyone who travels with a hairdryer or portable computer has come to know). More fundamental are cultural and language differences which inevitably make international business more complex and risky than domestic business.

Internationalization of the world economy is associated with two main developments: the growth of international trade and the growth of international investment. During the post-war period world trade has grown far more rapidly than world output, with the result that all the industrialized countries' export/sales ratios and import penetration ratios have increased substantially. Second, the growth of international direct investment is reflected in the growing dominance of national markets by multinational corporations. The interesting feature of Ford Motor Company, Unilever and Shell is not just that they sell in most of the countries of the world, but that they also produce in many of them. The consequence of the growth in both trade and direct investment is that it is increasingly difficult to associate companies with particular countries. The problems encountered by Los Angeles in attempting to enforce a 'Buy American' policy when purchasing trains for its Metro railway system is instructive. After awarding the contract to Komatsu it subsequently offered the business to an American firm, Cummins, only to find that the 'Japanese' trains were built in the United States, while the Cummins 'American' trains were built under licence in Korea. The pattern of companies' international activities is becoming increasingly complicated by the number and diversity of international joint ventures and other forms of strategic alliance. Some companies have long used joint ventures with overseas partners: Xerox set up Rank-Xerox and Fuji-Xerox to develop the European and Japanese markets for its copiers during the 1960s. For other companies, international alliances are a much newer phenomenon. (Alliances were discussed in Chapter 8.)

Analyzing the international aspects of strategy formulation and implementation concerns issues of both business strategy and corporate strategy. Business strategy is concerned primarily with issues of competitive advantage within individual markets. As we shall see, the internationalization of markets and companies has fundamentally affected the business environment of companies and has enormous implications for the means by which companies can establish and sustain competitive advantage – even within their domestic markets. At the corporate level, we are concerned primarily with issues of *scope*. What should the geographical range of a company's activities be? Through what mechanisms should a company seek access to overseas markets? What are the relative advantages of producing overseas as compared with producing at home? And what types of organizational structure and management systems are appropriate to the multinational corporation?

Despite the fact that trade and direct investment open up a whole new set of opportunities and problems which greatly complicate the formulation and implementation of company strategy, the following analysis of strategic management from a global perspective will utilize many of the principles discussed in previous chapters. The focus is on the consequences of increasing international competition for business strategy formulation and a firm's ability to sustain competitive advantage. Two questions are of particular interest:

▌ What threats does the internationalization of business pose to the competitive positions of particular businesses?

▌ What opportunities does globalization provide for firms to gain competitive advantage over domestically based rivals?

IMPLICATIONS OF INTERNATIONALIZATION FOR INDUSTRY STRUCTURE AND COMPETITION

The internationalization of business has implications for virtually all companies in almost all industries. Even companies which use domestic sources of inputs and supply their domestic market can be heavily affected by international forces. Consider the example of the Sheffield cutlery industry below.

THE DECLINE OF THE SHEFFIELD CUTLERY INDUSTRY

From the Middle Ages into the 1960s, the city of Sheffield was the world's largest centre for the manufacture of cutlery. For much of the 20th century the industry was in decline; yet in 1973 there were still about 120 manufacturers employing some 14,000 people. During the next few years, output halved and employment declined to a little over 7,000.

Despite the fact that over 90 per cent of the industry's output went to the home market, and most purchases of materials, machines and components were from other British companies, the industry was devastated by the international changes of the 1970s and 1980s.

Low cost imports arrived, initially from Japan, later from South Korea. At the beginning of the 1980s, it was observed that the price of stainless steel cutlery (per tonne) imported from South Korea was below the cost charged by the British Steel Corporation for the stainless steel needed to produce one tonne of cutlery. Meanwhile in the other sectors of the market, such as silver cutlery and pocket knives, entry into the European Community was increasing the intensity of competition from manufacturers in France and Germany.

The ability of Sheffield producers to fight back was hampered by several other international factors. Speculation by the Hunt brothers had caused turmoil in the world silver market at the beginning of the 1980s. At about the same time, the pound sterling rose sharply against other currencies as a result of the North Sea oil boom and the Thatcher government's interest rate policies – the result was to make British exports dearer and imports cheaper.

Of the six largest Sheffield cutlery companies at the end of 1973, only two survived until 1983.

The key feature of the internationalization of business has been the growth of international competition. International competition occurs whenever customers are willing to look to overseas as well as to domestic suppliers, and whenever producers are willing and able to supply overseas as well as the domestic market. The growth of international competition has resulted in industries which were once sheltered from strong competitive forces becoming highly competitive. It has been a key factor in depressing return on capital throughout the industrialized sectors of most Western nations. Internationalization has also increased the intensity of competition within national markets through its impact on industry structure. In terms of the structural determinants of competition and profitability which were discussed in Chapter 5, the following are most affected by internationalization:

I **Seller concentration** falls as overseas companies participate in national markets. Consider the US car industry. At the beginning of the 1970s, the market was dominated by the Big Three (General Motors, Ford and Chrysler), and a small market share was held by importers. By the end of 1993, there were many more car companies with plants in North America, including Honda, Nissan, Toyota, Subaru, Suzuki and BMW, with at least another 20 companies exporting cars to the US. The extent of this trade means that, for many industries, it no longer makes sense to draw boundaries around the national market. Once the relevant market is considered to be the region (eg the European Community) or even the whole world, inevitably seller concentration fails.

I The increasing **diversity of competitors** associated with internationalization causes firms to compete more vigorously (as stated above) while making co-operation more difficult. The London securities industry was affected by many events during the 1980s; however, the presence of financial services companies from the US, Japan and Continental Europe has had an enormous impact in stimulating competition through a reappraisal of industry norms and traditions.

▌ *Barriers to entry* are generally lessened in the international market. Except where government regulations are restrictive, established national companies can easily enter foreign markets where they can implement business procedures similar to those used domestically. Some countries invite new business through lax patent laws, and occasionally subsidize particular industries.

▌ New entry (unless it occurs through acquisition) typically involves new investment. Hence internationalization often results in increased competition as a result of *excess capacity.* The growth of excess capacity in the European car industry has partly been a result of inward investment by the Japanese and the building of new capacity in Southern and Eastern Europe by Fiat, Ford, General Motors and Volkswagen.

▌ Internationalization also increases the *buying power* exercised by large customers. All the main car companies have used their ability to 'shop the world' for components as a means of pressuring lower prices out of domestic suppliers, while retailers are especially flexible and aggressive in their use of international buying opportunities.

IMPLICATIONS OF INTERNATIONALIZATION FOR COMPETITIVE ADVANTAGE

In Chapter 10 it was noted that the competitive advantage of one firm over another depends to a great extent on their relative resources. Where competitors reside in different countries, the resource position of one against the other varies with the supply conditions of different resources in each location. This idea that relative competitiveness depends on resource availability in different countries is formalized in the economic theory of *comparative advantage.* In simple terms, the theory states that:

> a country has a relative competitive advantage in those products which make intensive use of resources which are available in relative abundance within the country.

Table 12.1 offers some examples of the role of national resources in conferring competitive advantage. The most straightforward

Table 12.1 *Natural resources and national competitive advantage*

Canada	Abundant land and natural resources	Lumber, natural gas, fish
Costa Rica	Hot climate Rich volcanic soils	Bananas and tropical fruits
Switzerland	600 years of political stability and neutrality Conservative and punctual national temperament Affluence	Banking and insurance
	Well-educated, well-trained population with strong traditional of mechanical engineering skills	Clocks, watches and precision engineering
USA	Abundance of fertile land Absence of rigid, traditional rural social structure	Agricultural products
	Very strong in basic research (esp. chemical research)	Chemicals and pharmaceuticals
	Communications infrastructure highly efficient Materialistic culture Commitment to free-enterprise capitalism	Financial services

examples of competitive advantage are those resulting from natural resource endowments – Saudi Arabia's huge oil reserves, for example. However, some of the most interesting examples are those resources which are associated with a country's education and training, its national culture or its infrastructure. The dominance of British companies in the auctioneering of art and antiques can only be explained with reference to Britain's colonial history and the penchant for its aristocratic classes to plunder the art of older civilizations. Technological skills are also interesting. The British tend to be strong in basic research and British companies tend to do well in industries where innovations arising from research are the basis for competitive advantage (pharmaceuticals, for example). The Japanese strength, on the other hand, is much more in the application and improvement of technology and the integration of different technologies. These strengths are most apparent in products such as cameras, cars and audio equipment.

Michael Porter's study of the *Competitive Advantage of Nations* goes beyond the role of resource availability and looks more broadly at the country conditions which influence the international competitiveness of firms in different industries (Porter, 1990). Critical to the study is his recognition that most of the important resources – sophisticated labour skills, technology and advanced management systems – are created through investment by people and companies. What is it that drives this process of improvement and upgrading? Porter's findings are summarized in his '*National Diamond*' framework, where he identifies four sets of factors which influence national competitiveness (see Figure 12.1).

▌ **Resources** (discussed in the previous section).

▌ **Related and supporting industries:** an industry may derive its competitive advantage from the presence of other world-class companies which act as suppliers, customers, or partners. For

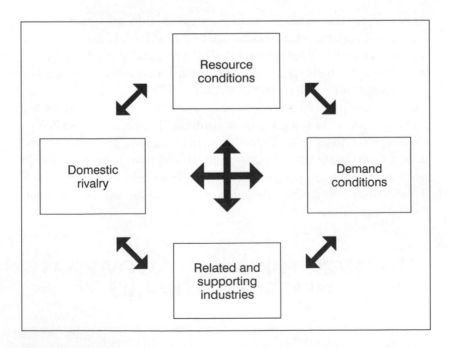

Figure 12.1   *Porter's National Diamond: the national determinants of international competitiveness*

example, the ability of the US to maintain world leadership in the computer industry owes much to the strength of its companies in software and in the manufacture of microprocessors.

▌ **Demanding home customers.** If domestic customers are discerning and demanding, pressure exists to invest and improve. German dominance of the world market for luxury, high-performance cars is related to the Germans' passion for quality engineering and their eagerness to drive on the *autobahns* at 180km per hour. Japanese firms' dominance of the world camera industry is probably related to the fact that the Japanese are such inveterate photographers.

▌ **Domestic rivalry.** Where domestic competition in an industry is strong, there are powerful forces for investment in quality and innovation. The Japanese car industry comprises nine fiercely competitive companies, and Japanese success in copiers and facsimile machines has also been associated with intense domestic rivalry. US dominance of the world markets for films and TV shows is also associated with an intensively competitive Los Angeles-based industry.

A key issue for strategic management within an international industry is that the firm's resources and capabilities exist within a national context. When competing internationally the firm has to establish a competitive advantage against firms whose resources and capabilities are determined within a different national context. This has profound implications. For example, Alcoa is one of the most efficient and lowest cost aluminium producers in the West. However, no matter how much it improves labour productivity and invests in efficient capital equipment, it will always be undercut in price by aluminium producers in the former Soviet Union which benefit from low labour costs, low energy costs, and lax environmental regulations.

STRATEGIES FOR EXPLOITING OVERSEAS MARKET OPPORTUNITIES

The primary motivation for internationalization is to exploit market opportunities outside the domestic market. This objective may be achieved through many different types of entry strategy into a foreign market. Table 12.2 identifies a number of options which range from exporting to direct investment in a stand-alone overseas subsidiary.

Direct exporting

It is possible to serve overseas markets without any need for direct investment in those markets. For certain standardized products it may be possible to sell overseas on a 'spot sales' basis. Through the Rotterdam market, an oil refinery in Germany can sell a barge-load of diesel fuel to a Belgian distributor quite simply. Where products are differentiated or where customer support is required, the exporter must establish more stable marketing and distribution arrangements. A common method is through appointing a Company in the overseas country to act as an agent. Thus until 1991 all Toyota cars sold in Britain were supplied through an exclusive agent. Alternatively, the exporting company may choose to make sales directly to its customers through its own export sales department.

Licensing

In order to exploit its competitive advantage in overseas markets, a company does not need to sell its goods and services; it can simply *license* the use of its resources and capabilities to companies in those countries. Walt Disney Company has no equity interest in Tokyo Disneyland. Walt Disney Company licensed the use of Disney's trademarks, characters and technology to the Oriental Land Company and receives a 10 per cent royalty on revenues. General Foods Corporation of the US did not export its 'Birds Eye' frozen foods to Britain after

Table 12.2 *Alternative strategies for exploiting an overseas market*

Direct Export
▌ Spot sales to overseas customers
▌ Long-term agency agreement
▌ Develop long-term arrangements with individual customers

Licensing
▌ License the use of the brand or technology
▌ Franchise

Direct investment
▌ Establish marketing and sales subsidiary
▌ Joint venture with a local partner
▌ Establish subsidiary to produce and sell

the Second World War, nor did it set up a British subsidiary to produce frozen foods; it licensed its brand name and quick-freezing process to Unilever.

Franchising agreements are a contractual relationship which embodies such licensing agreements. In service industries, such as fast food, speciality and business services, companies such as Pizza Hut and The Body Shop have expanded internationally by selling franchises to overseas operators.

Direct investment overseas

The establishment of business operations in foreign countries is termed 'direct investment'. Such direct investment may take a number of forms, the most limited being the establishment of a marketing and sales subsidiary in the overseas country. Thus Honda of America was established first to import and distribute Honda motorcycles, and it later expanded into a manufacturer of cars and bikes. A greater degree of involvement is inherent in the establishment of a joint venture under which a new company is established in which the equity is owned jointly with a local partner (or partners). Finally, a company may establish a wholly owned subsidiary in the overseas market. This may be done through new investment (eg Ford Motor Company established Ford Great Britain Ltd in 1923), or by acquisition (eg General Motors Corporation's acquisition of Vauxhall Motors Ltd and Adam Opel AG in 1925 and 1929 respectively).

Criteria for entering overseas markets

What criteria should be employed to determine the strategy for entering an overseas market? Several considerations are important:

1. *Is the product transportable and at what cost?* The ability to exploit an overseas market by direct export depends first and foremost on tradeability. If transport is difficult (fresh cream cakes) or expensive relative to the value of the product (cement, bricks), then exporting to a distant market is probably not feasible. Exporting may also be difficult in the presence of trade barriers such as tariffs, quotas, national standards, or domestic preferences in public procurement.

2. *The transferability of competitive advantage.* The attractiveness of exporting as compared with direct investment depends critically on whether a company's competitive advantage can be transferred

from the home country to another location. This in turn depends on the resources and capabilities which support the firm's competitive advantage. If competitive advantage is based on national resource advantages, such as low cost labour or the quality of the infra-structure, then that company's competitive advantage is location specific. If a company's competitive advantage is dependent on its internal resources and capabilities, their transferability depends on the ability to transfer these within the company. Technology, brand names and most organizational capabilities can usually be recreated in a new location given sufficient time, although differ-ences in national environments may create problems – Federal Express encountered huge difficulties in replicating its express delivery system in Europe.

3. *Inter-firm transferability of resources.* The issue of whether to license resources in preference to exporting or direct investment rests on whether the resources on which the firm's competitive advantage is based can be exploited directly through the market. If property rights are legally enforceable (as with most brand names and patents) then licensing provides an attractive way of exploiting overseas market opportunities without the investment costs or risk of either exporting or directly investing. Pilkington exploited its float glass process in overseas markets primarily by granting licenses to overseas glass producers. Visa International exploits its credit card brand and system primarily by selling franchises to banks and financial services companies.

4. *The need to adapt to local market conditions.* The less a product, or its means of marketing and distribution, needs to be adjusted to local market conditions, the easier it is to service an overseas market by direct exports. Conversely, the more a product needs to be adapted to meet the requirements of the local market, the more a company will need access to additional resources in order to be successful in the overseas market. The resources which are most critical to success in an overseas market are most commonly market information and distribution channels. To gain access to these resources a company will typically seek either to license its technology or brands, or to form a joint venture with a local partner.

GLOBAL VERSUS MULTINATIONAL STRATEGIES

One of the most active and heated debates in international business in recent years has been whether the world is a single market or an assembly of individual national markets. The principal proponent of the '*globalization of markets*' view is Theodore Levitt of the Harvard Business School, who argued that companies that compete on a national basis are highly vulnerable to companies that treat the world as a single global market. His argument has two strands. First, firms which produce standardized products for a global market are capable of reaping great benefits from scale economies. Second, customer preferences are increasingly converging across nations (Levitt, 1983).

In addition to the competitive cost advantage afforded by the global approach and its scale economies, Hamel and Prahalad (1985) point to the strategic advantages of an international scope. Varying competitive conditions in different countries allow the global firm to use its strong position in some national markets to improve its position in countries where it is weak. In particular, the global competitor can attack nationally based rivals in specific countries using the cash flow from less competitive markets (a practice called '*cross-subsidization*').

Yet evidence supporting the superiority of uncompromisingly global strategies is weak. The principal proponents have been the Japanese. But even Honda and Matsushita have been careful to adapt their marketing and distribution practices, and in several instances their products, to local requirements. Coca-Cola and McDonald's both make substantial concessions to local conditions in adapting their products, business practices and marketing strategies to national markets.

Bartlett and Ghoshal (1989) argue that different industries are positioned very differently with regard to the relative advantages of global integration and local adaptation (see Figure 12.2). Global products suitable for a 'single global market' approach are those which offer substantial scale economies and where national market preferences are minor. National products suitable for a 'multinational' strategy are those where scale economies are relatively unimportant, but distinct national preferences exist. Telecommunications equipment scores high on both dimensions: scale economies are very important, but also national telecommunications authorities have very different standards and requirements. Cement scores low on both: it is standardized, but its weight means that it must be produced locally.

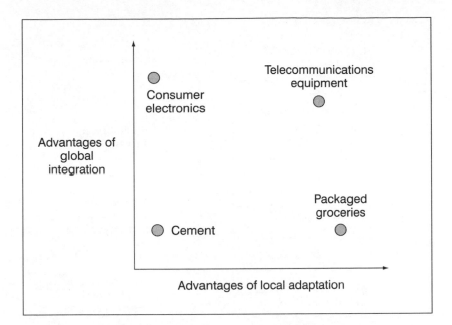

Figure 12.2   *The relative advantages of globalization and localization*

LOCATION DECISIONS AND THE VALUE CHAIN

To take the logic of globalization one stage further, issues of where in the world to market products can be considered quite separately from issues of where in the world to manufacture them. Moreover, production does not need to occur all in the same place. We can undertake a value chain analysis and, on the basis of the different resource requirements of each value chain activity, determine its optimal location. Consider, for example, the spread of Nike's activities (Figure 12.3).

However, this notion of selecting the best location for each activity considered independently ignores the potential advantages from locating activities in close proximity to one another. Where there are benefits from close links between activities – eg concurrent engineering, just-in-time scheduling, and the ability to respond swiftly to new market opportunities – dispersed activities and long supply chains may be costly.

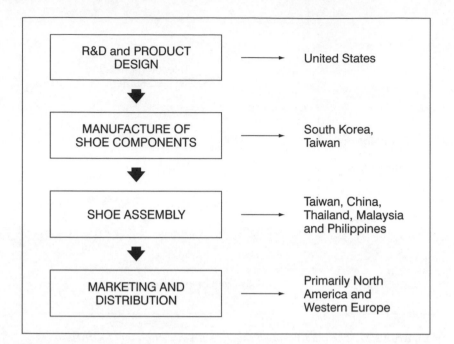

Figure 12.3   *Nike's international value chain*

ORGANIZING THE MULTINATIONAL CORPORATION

Organizational structure and management systems must be adapted to serve the needs of the strategy being pursued. In practice, however, both the strategies and structures of multinationals have been determined by what Chris Bartlett (1986) calls the 'administrative heritage' of the multinational corporation.

This view points to considerable inertia in the strategies and structures of large corporations to the extent that, even as mature corporations, they continue to reflect the conditions which existed at the time of their international development. Three principal patterns are evident (see Figure 12.4):

1. *The European multinationals.* Companies such as Unilever, Royal Dutch/Shell and Philips can trace their origins to the days of European colonialism. Typically these companies could obtain little in the way of global integration because transport and communication links were poor, hence their national

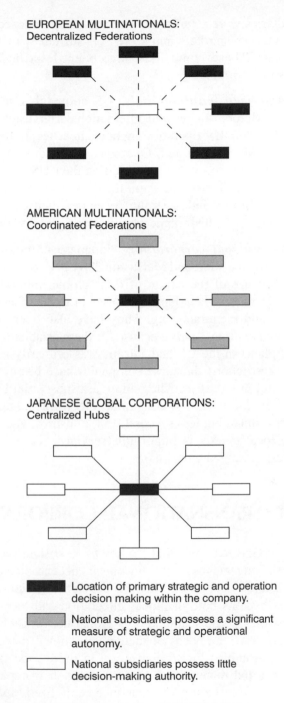

EUROPEAN MULTINATIONALS:
Decentralized Federations

AMERICAN MULTINATIONALS:
Coordinated Federations

JAPANESE GLOBAL CORPORATIONS:
Centralized Hubs

Location of primary strategic and operation decision making within the company.

National subsidiaries possess a significant measure of strategic and operational autonomy.

National subsidiaries possess little decision-making authority.

Source: R.M. Grant. *Contemporary Strategy Analysis.* Basil Blackwell, Oxford, 1991.

Figure 12.4 *Multinational strategies and structures*

subsidiaries were stand-alone entities which focused on serving their national markets and were self-sufficient in virtually all functions. These companies have been described as *'decentralized federations'*.

2. **The American multinationals.** US companies such as Ford, General Motors, Singer and International Harvester were dominated by their US operations where most technology and new products were developed. Overseas subsidiaries typically had significant autonomy, but depended on their US parents for most technology and also for capital. Thus Ford's subsidiaries in Germany, Britain and Australia developed their own models and manufactured for their domestic markets right up to the 1960s.

3. *Japanese global corporations.* Japanese companies such as Honda, Toyota, YKK and Matsushita have been called *'centralized hubs'* because of the extent of their global integration and the dominant role of their Japanese bases in terms of product development and manufacturing. They have also been described as *'reluctant multinationals'* because for them establishing manufacturing plants in the US and Europe was primarily a response to import restrictions. Japanese companies have been exceptionally successful in industries where there are substantial benefits from global integration (eg consumer electronics, cars, copiers, cameras, ships) but less successful in industries where adaptation to the local market is important (services, retailing, toiletries, clothing, packaged groceries).

THE 'TRANSNATIONAL' CORPORATION

Bartlett and Ghoshal argue that the key to success in the 1990s is to combine the advantages of the European 'decentralized federation' and the Japanese 'centralized hub' to develop a structure which can exploit the benefits both of global integration and local adaptation. Their view of the 'transnational' is a global network where national subsidiaries serve the needs of their own national markets but also explore opportunities for specialization in those aspects of product development and manufacture that best suit their capabilities (see Figure 12.5). Evidence suggests that once-centralized Japanese corporations and once-decentralized European and US corporations are both converging.

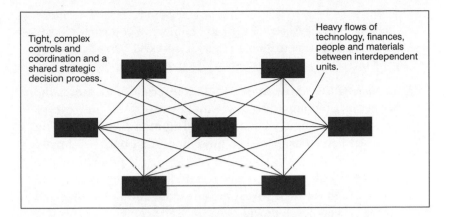

Figure 12.5   *The transnational corporation*

Thus at Ford national subsidiaries continue to adjust marketing, distribution and dealer support to the particulars of their national market, but also achieve much greater integration of design and manufacture. Ford Europe, for example, concentrates on the design of small cars and Detroit on large cars. Engine plants are increasingly focused on either four or six cylinder engines with components being globally sourced.

SUMMARY

In recent years international trade and the globalization of economic activity have expanded rapidly, stimulated by the World Trade Organization. International direct investment has become a major feature of the economies of most nations. In consequence there are few domestic companies that are now sheltered from international competition.

Globalization affects both corporate and business strategy. At the corporate level the issues are to do with major investment decisions, the assessment of risk, geopolitical factors and complex organizational arrangements.

At the level of the subsidiary the issues are to do with the particular characteristics of local markets and the resources and capabilities needed to operate successfully in them.

▌ *Industry structure.* The impact of globalization on industry structure is considerable. Competition is intensified by such factors as the presence of a greater number of companies in any given market, international rivalries, reduced barriers to entry and increased power of buyers who can source supplies globally.

▋ *Comparative advantage*. In the international arena the concept of comparative advantage refers to the role of national resources – material and human – in conferring competitive advantage. The most important ones – a highly skilled labour force, advanced technology and sophisticated management systems – are created by governments and companies through investment in education, training and research and development.

▋ *Exploiting international opportunities*. Opportunities in international markets can be exploited in a number of ways – exporting, licensing or direct investment. The right approach depends on such factors as costs of transport, the transferability of resources and capabilities and the extent to which local markets have distinctive requirements.

▋ *Global markets*. The case for treating the world as a single, global market is strong when the nature of the product is such that local matters of taste are either irrelevant (eg Intel) or have been overcome by shrewd marketing (Coca-Cola). In such instances the value of economies of scale is very considerable.

In other cases – for example, in food retailing – local tastes and preferences are strongly rooted and a standardized approach is unlikely to be successful.

▋ *Global organization*. Three approaches can be seen in operation. The 'decentralized federation' is characteristic of European multinationals and is a relic from the colonial era. National subsidiaries are highly autonomous. At the other extreme is the 'global hub', characteristic of Japanese companies; in this case the centre is dominant and all major decisions are taken by the home company. US companies are closer to the European model, but tend to provide more in the way of financial and technical support.

There is a tendency nowadays for these approaches to converge, resulting in a global network, the so-called 'transnational' model with centres of excellence located in different parts of the world.

Part 4

Implementation

Managing strategic change

INTRODUCTION

There are degrees of organizational change. At one end of the continuum lies incremental or tactical change, a process that is ongoing in all organizations, as part of the action being taken to control costs or improve quality, or reflecting adjustment to such things as simple growth or changes in key personnel. The objective here is limited – to achieve marginal improvements in productivity or quality or to make a one-time shift in response to a particular event. It is certainly not the intention to bring about a change in the organization's fundamental strategy.

At the other end of the continuum is strategic change. Here the purpose is to reorient the organization in terms of its strategic goals and thereby to achieve a step change in its competitive position. This latter type of change is the subject of this chapter. One important way in which it differs from incremental change is that it can rarely be achieved without significant changes in the underlying beliefs, values and established patterns of behaviour of the organization's members – in other words without a change in culture.

The most commonly recognized signal of a need for strategic change is an acute crisis signalled by financial losses, a significant fall in market share and a rapidly falling share price. In the case of many companies, poor financial performance is the outcome of poor quality of product or service, lack of true employee commitment, uninspiring leadership from the top and a traditional culture inhibiting creativity and innovation. In such cases tinkering with the organization by such means as improvements in communications, introducing suggestion schemes or introducing a new incentive scheme is rarely enough to turn the business round. The increasingly common approach of down-sizing the organization has been shown by research as seldom leading to lasting performance improvement.

It is stating the obvious to point out that it is better to tackle the underlying problems in an organization before they show themselves in loss of custom and deteriorating financial results, but it requires great vision and courage to see the need for a fundamental rethinking of strategy and exceptional leadership skills to bring it about in advance of a serious crisis, financial or otherwise.

One thing above all else has led to the growing focus on the need for strategic change. This is the growing acceptance of the belief that it is clearly the case that in most industries the competitive edge lies with the quality and level of commitment of an organization's people. We now know that the successful businesses of the 21st century will be those that attract, retain, motivate and develop employees to harness their talents and energies in the interest of the firm.

Siddall, Willey and Tavares (1995) point out that in the oil industry, for example, the strategies adopted to date by the major companies have been largely similar, but 'there is little doubt that the growing intensity of competition will signal a change of mood over the next few years'. They believe the economic drivers and formulae for approaching markets are well understood by the major players and that diversity in strategy in the future will be more likely to take the form of differences in organization structure and culture.

This change in priorities, reflected in many other businesses large and small, has resulted in a new, more strategic role for the personnel function – increasingly referred to as human resource management (HRM).

CHANGE OBJECTIVES

The most common strategic change objective in the UK in recent years has been to achieve a step change in competitiveness by means of radical improvement in standards of quality of product and customer service. This is often referred to as reaching world-class standards. This approach also frequently includes achieving a more competitive cost base and building greater flexibility or capacity for innovation.

Sometimes the need for change is associated with the reorganization and the merging of corporate cultures that is called for following a major acquisition. In other instances the focus is on the strategic changes called for in the transition from the public to the private sector following privatization.

In practice the actual changes that take place can be grouped under the headings of adoption of a new approach to mission and purpose, structural change, adoption of new systems and processes, and culture change.

Changing mission and purpose

Under the heading of mission and purpose, more and more companies have been moving recently from statements of objectives focusing exclusively on the creation of shareholder value to statements that acknowledge responsibilities to society and to the organization's stake-holders or to 'aspirational' mission statements. This tendency reflects growing public pressure for companies to adopt policies of corporate social responsibility (CSR) amid heightened concern about the ethics of big business following the scandals of Enron and Worldcom.

Back in 1993 the UK's Royal Society of Arts (RSA) initiated an 'Inquiry into the Nature of Tomorrow's Company'. The inquiry began by bringing together 25 of the top businesses in the UK under the chairmanship of Sir Anthony Cleaver who at that time was chairman of IBM UK. The objective was to develop a shared vision of tomorrow's company. The subsequent report, published in 1995, challenged business leaders to change their approach. It focused attention on the issue of how to achieve sustained business success in the face of profound social and economic change.

The report stated: 'As the world business climate changes, so the rules of the competitive race are being rewritten. The effect is to make people and relationships more than ever the key to sustainable success.' The report called for companies to adopt what was termed an 'inclusive' approach: 'Only through deepened relationships with – and between – employees, customers, suppliers, investors and the community will companies anticipate, innovate and adapt fast enough, while maintaining public confidence.'

Inclusiveness, as defined by the RSA report, involves the following aspects:

▎ A clearly stated, widely communicated and shared purpose or mission, together with a vision of the company's future, couched in other than purely financial or commercial terms. In particular, creating shareholder value is not seen as the sole *raison d'être* of the enterprise.

▌ A set of shared values, which form the basis for the actions and decisions of the company and its agents.

▌ A success model, which is based on a deep understanding of the drivers of long-term business success, and a balanced process of measurement of performance based on this, which is forward-looking not merely historical.

▌ The building of mutually trusting relationships with the company's business partners and key stakeholder groups, such as investors, employees, customers, suppliers and the community. (The nature and number of stakeholder groups will vary from one company to another.)

▌ Acceptance of the need to win 'a licence to operate' in the context of a society increasingly demanding in terms of ethical standards and corporate social responsibility.

Structural changes

These include:

▌ moving from a functional structure to one based on products or market segments;

▌ flatter structures – removing layers of management;

▌ the creation of highly autonomous, multi-skilled work teams;

▌ the introduction of more project-based, cross-functional work groups;

▌ changes in the role of the first-line manager or supervisor;

▌ greater delegation – pushing decision making closer to the shop floor or the customer interface (often referred to as 'empowering');

▌ smaller organizational units;

▌ breaking down functional 'silos', creating internal profit centres.

The process of changing an organization structure inevitably involves bestowing position power, status and potentially high financial rewards on some individuals, while diminishing the power, status or potential earnings of others. This is one reason why changing the structure arouses much more interest and involvement by top management than redesigning business processes or the intangibles associated with culture change. The members of top management who are in a position to influence the change process may be tempted to put their own interests and career prospects first and the achievement of a structure fully aligned with strategy second. This is a powerful argument for involving external consultants in the decision-making process. It also emphasizes the importance of the consultant's ability to remain objective and to be politically adept.

Changes in processes and systems

The redesign of processes is often referred to as 'business process reengineering'.

Among the most common changes are the following:

▌ seeking accreditation for the achievement of internationally accepted standards in such fields as quality and environmental management;

▌ the introduction of 'just-in-time' inventory control;

▌ the identification and elimination of activities along the value chain that do not add value.

Changes to systems or the introduction of new ones can include:

▌ changes in payments systems;

▌ launching employee share ownership schemes;

▌ introducing regular employee attitude surveys;

▌ continuous monitoring of customer satisfaction and service levels.

Cultural change programmes

These involve a quite different set of actions and usually include some combination of the following:

▌ developing fresh statements of mission, vision and values;

▌ designing training focused on changing values and attitudes, eg achieving a commitment to total quality;

▌ team-building processes;

▌ relaunching corporate identity.

Some issues involved in changing organizational culture

To change the corporate culture involves persuading people to abandon many of their existing beliefs and values, and the behaviours that stem from them, and to adopt new ones.

The first difficulty that arises in practice is to identify the principal characteristics of the existing culture. The process of understanding and gaining insight into the existing culture can be aided by using one of the standard and properly validated inventories or questionnaires that a number of consultants have developed to measure characteristics of corporate culture. These offer the advantage of being able to benchmark the culture against those of other, comparable firms that have used the same instruments. The weakness of this approach is that the information thus obtained tends to be more superficial and less rich than material from other sources such as interviews and group discussions and from study of the company's history.

In carrying out this diagnostic exercise, such instruments can be supplemented by surveys of employee opinions and attitudes and complementary information from surveys of customers and suppliers or the public at large.

In KPMG the process of investigating the existing culture involved asking members of the organization to imagine that they were giving advice to a close friend about how to get on in the company. They were asked to say what specific advice they would give under the following headings:

▮ What must you do? Responses included 'Be linked to prestigious clients', 'Understand the politics', 'Be seen to work long hours' and 'Have integrity and honesty.'

▮ What can you get away with not doing? Responses included 'Being on time for internal meetings', 'Conducting counselling sessions or annual appraisals on time', 'Sharing knowledge and information' and 'Most administrative tasks.'

▮ What must you absolutely never do? Responses included 'Break ethical guidelines, be dishonest or unprofessional', 'Divulge client confidentiality', 'Dress scruffily or unconventionally' and 'Show disloyalty.'

It is at this diagnostic stage that companies may need the assistance of outside consultants whose fresh insight, objectivity and absence of vested interest in the status quo may be helpful in reaching valid conclusions. Ed Schein, in his account of his own experience as a culture change consultant (1992), provides an excellent role model for this type of consultancy. Schein describes how he uncovers what he calls the 'levels of culture'. These are:

1. *Artefacts*. These include all the things one sees, hears and feels when encountering a new group with an unfamiliar culture. Examples are the physical architecture; the language in use; the technology; the products; the organization's style as reflected in clothing, manner of address and displays of emotion; published statements of values; rituals and ceremonies. This heading also covers the visible behaviour of the members of the organization and the organizational processes they have developed. Schein says of the artefacts that they are 'easy to observe and very difficult to decipher'.

2. *Espoused values*. These are the things that people say they believe in, the assumptions that they are conscious of making. Knowing what they are makes it possible to predict what people will say in a given situation but not necessarily what they will do. Where there are contradictions between the espoused values and actual behaviour, it is necessary to dig deeper and to try to understand the basic underlying assumptions.

3. *Basic assumptions*. These are the beliefs that have come to be so taken for granted that people would regard any alternative way of thinking as inconceivable. An example would be the commonly held assumption in the past that anyone in a position of authority in industry would be masculine in gender. Such deeply held assumptions or mindsets are scarcely ever confronted or debated and are, in consequence, very difficult to change.

IMPLEMENTATION

The process of implementing strategic change and doing so in such a way that it endures is one that calls for intense, persistent and dedicated effort in the context of close collaboration between company personnel and any external consultants involved.

The actual business of redrawing organization charts, rewriting job descriptions, drawing up a new incentive scheme or redesigning the performance appraisal forms is a relatively small, albeit vital, part of the process. The greater part lies in bringing about changes in people's actual behaviour and in the values, beliefs and attitudes that underlie the behaviour. The following are some of the most commonly used implementation techniques:

■ Direct, face-to-face communication involving, where feasible, the entire workforce, but in groups of manageable size so as to facilitate exchange of viewpoints and provide opportunities for feedback.

■ Role-modelling – here, again, leadership comes in, as top management sets an example by behaving in ways that are consistent with the changed standards, practices and behaviours that the new strategy calls for. Such phrases as 'putting customers first' come to life if the top team are seen to be doing so themselves.

■ Written communications – a whole arsenal of newsletters, posters, stickers, badges etc, all carrying the messages associated with the reasons for change, help to reinforce motivation to accept the need and act accordingly.

■ Appropriate human resource policies, which support the desired changes – these can include:
   – revised performance criteria and methods of performance appraisal;
   – revised remuneration systems;
   – special schemes for rewarding and recognizing appropriate behaviours;
   – investment in training – there will almost always need to be a very substantial investment in training, not simply to impart new skills but also to influence attitudes and values;
   – symbolism.

The importance of symbolism lies in the way it provides a clear message of a break with the past. Such actions as moving to open-plan offices, abolishing reserved parking places, moving to single-status catering arrangements or abolishing such traditional job titles as 'supervisor' can have a disproportionate impact in creating a climate that is receptive to change. In recent years a number of companies have gone so far as to make a name change – although not always successfully, as in the case of Consignia.

Resistance to change

Top management tend to see change in its strategic context. Rank-and-file employees are most likely to be aware of its impact on important aspects of their working lives.

Some resistance to change is almost always unavoidable, but its strength can be minimized by careful advance planning, which involves thinking about such issues as: *Who* will be affected by the proposed changes, both directly and indirectly? From their point of view, *what aspects* of their working lives will be affected? *Who should communicate* information about change, *when* and *by what means*? What *management style* is to be used?

The politics of organizational change

The legitimate power of the board of directors, appointed by the shareholders, is not the sole power base in a complex organization. In the process of managing strategic change it is important to be politically astute and to identify potential powerful sources of resistance.

Common sources of power include:

▮ organized labour;

▮ the power held by employees who possess highly valued expertise, knowledge or talent;

▮ the power of charismatic leadership;

▮ the power that comes from exercising control over key resources;

▮ the power held by those who act as the guardians of the organization's cherished traditional beliefs and values.

Any one, or indeed all, of these power sources can be used as the base from which resistance to organizational change is waged. It is a great mistake to believe that such powerful counterforces can be ignored and that the backing of the board of directors will be sufficient in itself to ensure a successful programme of implementing change.

Potential sources of resistance of this kind must be identified in advance and, if possible, their commitment to the proposed changes secured. Where this is not possible a power struggle will inevitably follow – a struggle that the board must win without the kind of compromise that will jeopardize the objectives of the change programme. If necessary, powerful individuals must be moved from the positions of power in the process.

Where to begin

With the foregoing principles in mind, and given top-level awareness of the urgent need for change, it is clear that an action plan is needed, setting out the steps to be taken in sequence, an overall timetable and the allocation of responsibility.

Undoubtedly the most difficult aspect of devising such a plan is deciding where to start, choosing the right kind of intervention that will get things moving. Among the many points of departure that companies have adopted in recent programmes of change, the following are the most common:

■ Conducting a survey among employees, which focuses on the issues facing the business, its strengths and weaknesses, and which is so designed as to point to clear priorities for action. The results can then be fed back to employees with the message 'This is your diagnosis of what is wrong with the organization and of what needs to be done – let us work together to take the needed remedial action.'

■ Carry out a series of presentations or 'roadshows' at which, over time, representatives of top management meet with large numbers of the workforce (ideally with all employees), present their views of the current situation, outline a vision for the future and seek to enthuse the audience to 'buy into' the vision and become motivated to bring it about.

■ Set up a series of cross-disciplinary or cross-divisional task forces to investigate aspects of the company's operations and report back with recommendations for change.

■ Pick an issue (the most common ones in recent years have been quality of product or standard of customer service) and focus energy on this using a wide range of tactics such as ISO 9000 accreditation, quality circles, customer surveys etc.

■ Using a wide basis of consultation across the organization, develop and publish a fresh mission statement, a vision of the company's future and a set of shared values.

■ Bring in a team of strategy consultants, ask them to review the organization's current situation – its competitiveness, strengths and weaknesses – and use their report as a trigger for change.

There are many other possibilities. There is no one way of getting started that will guarantee success. As with so many aspects of decision making at the highest level, it is a question of judgement rather than of seeking for a formula to apply. Much will depend on the degree of urgency involved, the size of the organization, the extent to which the workforce is dispersed over many sites, the extent to which the current organization is one of strong traditions deeply rooted in the past, and the involvement or otherwise of strong trade unions.

It is vital to bear in mind that organizational change is not an intellectual process concerned with the design of ever-more-complex and elegant organization structures. It is to do with the human side of enterprise and is essentially about changing people's attitudes, feelings and – above all else – their behaviour. Where the organization has a strong and well-developed personnel or human resource management function – one that is represented at board level – the process of managing change will often involve a natural partnership and close working relationship between the chief executive as the leader of change and the personnel or HR director as its leading organizer and facilitator. It is, of course, vital to success that the HR expertise available to the company should be fully exploited. At the same time problems can arise if the programme is seen as being 'owned' by personnel rather than by the line. For this reason it is important that other executive directors in line positions should be allocated clear and responsible roles in the management of the change process and that they are clearly seen to be strongly identified with it. Equally, it is very important for any external consultants to be clear about who the client is.

EVALUATION

It is essential to establish a system for evaluating the extent to which change is actually taking place. This can be done in two ways.

The first is by monitoring shifts in attitudes, beliefs and values. The starting point for many programmes of cultural change is a survey to measure attitudes and beliefs of employees and/or customers. These surveys can be invaluable tools in arriving at an objective diagnosis of pre-existing strengths and weaknesses, but their value is further enhanced if they are repeated at intervals, so as to measure the shifts that have taken place – both the shifts in the values and beliefs of employees, and the perceptions of the behaviour of employees on the part of customers.

A second approach is to evaluate success in terms of results. This calls for a long-time perspective, since the aim of strategic change is to achieve *sustainable* levels of world-class performance, not the financial equivalent of a shooting star that climbs rapidly and then fizzles out.

RECENT TRENDS IN ORGANIZATIONAL CHANGE

Pettigrew and Shaw have reported the results of a major international research project looking at recent practice in change management and the outcomes in terms of improved performance (*European Business Forum*, 1, Spring 2001). The research was jointly funded by PricewaterhouseCoopers and the UK Economic and Social Science Research Council and involved a four-year project from 1996 on and a network of research partners from around the world. Surveys of changes in companies were carried out in Europe, the United States and Japan. Eighteen in-depth case studies were conducted. In 1997, 1,500 UK firms were surveyed plus another 2,000 in Western Europe, all with at least 500 employees. There were 448 usable replies. The results revealed some clear trends in three areas:

▌ structure: delayering, decentralizing and project-based teams;

▌ processes: horizontal and vertical communications, investment in IT and new HR practices;

▌ boundaries: outsourcing, strategic alliances, downscoping.

Only a few companies are adopting all three types of change simultaneously. Those that do are among the highest performers:

> Taking just a few, isolated initiatives (e.g. outsourcing and downscoping) generally yields little benefit and can lead to worse performance, except for implementation of IT strategies which tends to produce some benefits irrespective of whether other initiatives are also taken.

Coherent programmes of complementary changes in all appropriate aspects of structure, processes and boundaries produce the best results. The full benefits of changes in one area are only achieved if they are reinforced by complementary changes in other key areas.

The high-performing companies are characterized by a distinctive set of new ways of organizing, which include:

■ *Autonomy*. Giving managers autonomy except in a few key areas where the corporate centre has a clear role in creating value.

■ *Collaboration*. Use of project teams, using IT to facilitate knowledge sharing and building the behaviours, attitudes and values that help embed a teamworking culture.

■ *Scope*. Focusing on those activities that create the most added value and coping with other activities by outsourcing or partnering.

■ *Vision*. Articulating and communicating a sense of the meaning and coherence of the programme of change in the above three areas.

The authors conclude by posing a number of key questions:

■ *Autonomy*: Which activities and decisions are best controlled from the centre? How should the corporate centre be designed and managed so as to provide maximum support to top management at the centre as well as those in the operating companies or divisions?

■ *Collaboration*: What are the key needs for communication and collaboration across internal boundaries? How far are these being met? What are the barriers? Are current IT systems adequate?

■ *Scope*: Are there opportunities to improve performance by outsourcing, or by accessing expertise or know-how that the company cannot develop in house?

■ *Vision*: Has the leadership articulated the vision and values underpinning the programme of change? How far are people aware of and committed to the vision and values? How can the level of commitment be increased?

SUMMARY

Few companies that have attempted to bring about lasting strategic change have done so successfully. Just a few years ago British Airways under Colin Marshall and ICI under John Harvey Jones as well as the Rover car company were held up as examples of success in achieving true, lasting strategic transformation, but all three have had severe problems since. To succeed involves learning the lessons derived from the experience of many companies. These are:

▮ Strategic change can be driven, but only so far. In the end it needs employee commitment and involvement to be fully successful. Successful organizational change needs to be driven simultaneously from above and below.

▮ Whether the style is directive or facilitating, the utter and sustained commitment of top management is vital to success.

▮ The leader need not be someone brought in from outside. Indeed an insider with a deep knowledge of the company's history and culture – one who has been a 'loyal critic' in the past – is probably the best choice to lead the change. In the Stanford University study 'Built to last' nearly all the chief executives in the United States' most consistently successful companies were promoted from within.

▮ It takes a very long time to complete the transformation, and even then the process of continuous improvement is still vital. Jack Welch began changing GE in 1981 and was still pushing for change 20 years later.

▮ The change process calls for simultaneous initiatives on many fronts. The coordination of all this requires a full-time champion at board level and an adequate supporting structure.

▮ There is no 'cookbook' solution. Each organization is unique and needs a carefully tailored approach.

▮ The process is essentially messy – trying to stick to a strict schedule is usually futile.

▮ It is important to emphasize the concrete, the practical and the potential pay-off. This is particularly important when dealing with culture change, which can so easily be dismissed as woolly or 'touchy-feely' stuff.

▮ Excitement, drama and performing do have a part to play.

▮ People who are both influential and obstructive need to be moved.

Cases

TESCO: CONTINUITY IN STRATEGIC MANAGEMENT – FROM DISCOUNT STORE TO UK MARKET LEADER TO GLOBAL BUSINESS

The industry environment

In the early 1990s food retailing in Britain was dominated by six chains, of which the oldest and largest was Sainsbury's. Conservatively managed by the Sainsbury family, the company did not come to the stock market until 1973. Tesco, with the second-largest share, began as an aggressive discounter but from 1977 shifted market position and set about attracting a more affluent customer base. Number three in market share at this time was Gateway (now Somerfield), followed by Argyll (now Safeway following its purchase of the UK shops of the US Safeway Corporation), Asda and Kwik Save. Asda pioneered large out-of-town stores and carried a higher proportion of non-foods than the others. It began as a discounter but also sought to move upmarket, leaving Kwik Save as the remaining large-scale discounter. The other smaller store groups were Morrison's, Waitrose (a subsidiary of the John Lewis Partnership) and Budgens.

At this time Kwik Save was the fastest-growing group and the one that was giving the best return to shareholders. On a 10-year basis, however, the outstanding performers had been Argyll and Sainsbury's.

In the last decade, fortunes have changed dramatically. Tesco is now not only the leading company in market share and profits but has put considerable distance between itself and its nearest rival, Sainsbury's. Its sales were £15.6 billion in 2002 compared with £6.4 billion. In third place was Asda, followed by a new entrant to the top six – Morrison's – with £3 billion, Safeway with £2.6 billion and Somerfield with £0.5 billion.

The other significant players include Waitrose with its comfortable niche at the top end of the market, and the foods division of Marks and Spencer. Both Sainsbury and Safeway generated earnings in 2002 that were lower than their 1992 efforts, and the purchase of Kwik Save caused Somerfield to record two years of heavy losses.

Management talent has played a key role. Archie Norman turned round Asda, while Sir Peter Davis, Carlos Criado-Perez and John von Spreckleson are currently doing their best to bring about a step change in performance at Sainsbury, Safeway and Somerfield respectively.

The strategic issues are challenging. Food retailing is a very competitive sector. When a number of companies sell more or less the same goods it makes it hard to create a *sustainable competitive advantage* for the long term. To a large extent, supermarket boardrooms have to maintain a constant process of innovation in their service offering. In consequence, the last few years have seen supermarkets move into clothing and electrical goods retailing, start selling petrol and financial services, expand their own-label product range, introduce loyalty cards and launch online delivery services, as well as consistently overhauling their core food retail operations.

The main changes in the supermarket competitive environment since 1990

Briefly, the main changes have been:

▋ Supermarket chains (such as Sainsbury's, Tesco and Asda) achieve national coverage for the first time.

▋ Continental discount retailers (Aldi, Netto, Lidl) begin to arrive in the UK.

▋ Sunday opening legalized.

▌ Supermarkets become leading petrol retailers and branch out to other forms of retailing including financial services.

▌ Twenty-four-hour opening in some stores.

▌ Some UK retailer chains expand overseas, while Wal-Mart, the world's biggest retailer, acquires Asda.

▌ Rapid uptake of the Internet prompts the launch of new home-shopping services.

▌ Merger of CRS and CWS, two leading cooperative retailers.

▌ Iceland merges with Booker and Somerfield acquires Kwik Save.

▌ Tesco expands overseas operations.

▌ Rapid growth of non-food product ranges in Asda and Tesco.

▌ New technologies prompting the development of new products, eg spreadable butter, liquid detergents, microwaveable meals, new-formula shampoos, ice-cream chocolate bars, low-fat product variants, chilled soups.

▌ Improvements in efficiency across the supply chain reducing the real cost of food.

▌ Increasing demand for convenience foods – both part-prepared and fully prepared meals.

▌ Increasing automation and importance of information technology to the industry.

▌ Increasing range and variation of products available to the UK consumer, eg exotic fruit and vegetables, patisserie, dairy products, wines, soft drinks, health and beauty items.

▌ Consolidation of every sector (ie the trend towards fewer, larger businesses), including agri-supply, farming, manufacturing, wholesaling, retailing, catering and distribution.

▌ Increasing geographical coverage of companies and products and the gradual evolution towards a global market-place.

▌ Increasingly cosmopolitan consumer tastes, eg Chinese, Indian, Italian, Thai and Mexican food.

The figures in Table A.1 are evidence of the industry's intense competition. Every one of the major supermarkets currently has an operating margin below the level seen in 1992.

Table A.1   *Company operating margin*

	2002 %	1992 %
Tesco	5.63	6.76
J Sainsbury	3.81	7.09
W M Morrison	5.40	5.60
Safeway	5.03	7.30
Somerfield	0.60	2.33

Without doubt, Tesco and Morrison are performing well above the rest of the sector. Table A.2 shows the average rates of growth for both firms between 1992 and 2002.

Table A.2   *Average rates of growth*

	Tesco	Morrison
Sales (%)	12.8	13.4
Operating profit (%)	10.8	13.0
Earnings per share (%)	6.7	12.5
Dividend per share (%)	10.3	20.7

Other factors in Morrison's favour are:

▌ *Cash in the bank*. Morrison's latest annual figures showed net cash of £11 million. Tesco has £3.8 billion of net debt, although interest payments are covered a reasonable six times.

▌ *Scope for growth*. At their latest year ends, Tesco had 729 stores (covering 18.8 million square feet) in the UK, while Morrison had 113 UK outlets (covering 4.0 million square feet). While Tesco already has a sizeable international presence, the greater opportunity for growth in the more predictable domestic market lies with Morrison.

▌ *Quality of management*. Executive chairman Sir Ken Morrison has run Morrison for 46 years, which, coincidentally, is the age of Tesco chief executive Terry Leahy. Leahy has only been in the Tesco top job for five years. In a sector where boardroom talent is key, investors are very pleased with Sir Ken and his 'no-nonsense' approach to delivering 'the very best for less'.

Although the growth rate of UK food retail sales value has been slowing, there is real volume growth taking place as the UK market has been affected by negative inflation in the food sector. This negative inflation has been driven by the so-called 'Wal-Mart effect', ie downward pressure on prices from Asda/Wal-Mart's aggressive 'Every Day Low Price' (EDLP) strategy, and also by concerns over the possible findings of the UK's Competition Commission investigation into the UK grocery retailing market. The investigation, now concluded, has vindicated the UK supermarkets of excessive profiteering. Nevertheless, following concerns raised regarding costs passed back to the supplier, there will now be a legally binding code of practice to govern relationships between retailers and suppliers.

For UK retailers, value growth is expected to remain slow, with continuing pressure on prices and fierce competition for share leading to retailers trying to position themselves in the market-place through differentiation (using marketing angles such as supporting organic food, British farmers and other ethical concerns).

Demographic changes (ageing population, increase in working women) and declining meal preparation (eating out is now the UK's favourite leisure-time pursuit) mean that the UK retailers are also focusing on added-value products such as the booming 'food-to-go' sector, premium products, increasing own labels' share of their business mix, and supply chain and other operational improvements to drive costs out of the business. This includes supply chain consolidation: UK retailers are increasingly reluctant to take on new suppliers.

Almost every major food retailer in the UK has experimented with home shopping, home delivery and/or e-tailing. Order fulfilment is proving to be very costly whether centrally based or store-based. Also, many customers have found the experience of Web-based grocery shopping dissatisfying, with software problems and general unreliability of the Web causing frustration. Tesco's home delivery and online schemes have proved the most successful, while Somerfield and Budgens have recently announced cancellation of their programmes.

The beginnings

After World War II, Tesco's founder, Sir Jack Cohen, expanded his business based on a slogan that later became famous: 'Pile It High, Sell It Cheap.' He understood that the greater the volume of goods, the bigger the discount he could offer.

In the decades following the war, Sir Jack and his management team built Tesco into one of the largest supermarket chains in the UK. Yet by the late 1980s the company appeared to have lost its way. In the more affluent and upwardly mobile Britain that was emerging, Tesco seemed increasingly out of touch. In Porter's terms it was 'stuck in the middle', providing neither the quality of goods upscale customers wanted nor the deep discounts that price-conscious buyers demanded. Sainsbury's and Waitrose became the food shops of choice for the UK's AB social groups, while CD groups shopped at Asda or Kwik Save where Tesco was consistently beaten on price.

However, when investors accused Tesco of losing touch with its changing customer tastes, instead of going into denial it took the unusual step of conducting a large-scale marketing survey of its current and potential customers. The most common responses were lower prices, better service, more selection and more non-food products.

Tesco management stuck with its belief that the company could reach both bargain hunters and premium shoppers on the grounds that it was in the 'middle market' that the greatest mass of customers was to be found. In the early 1990s, the company began to accelerate its construction of superstores, bigger than its traditional supermarkets, to allow for greater selection at lower prices. To satisfy upper-end shoppers, it introduced organic food products. The group also launched a wide range of house-brand goods differentiated by price or quality, first under the Value brand and later under the Finest Gourmet label.

Tesco paid close attention to service, as well. For example, Tesco adheres to a strict rule at the checkout. If customers find more than one person in front of them in the queue, the company promises to open another register. Also, if a customer asks the location of an item the staff member is required to conduct the customer to that location, not just point the way.

Also in the 1990s, under CEO McLauren Tesco began to experiment with new products and channels. It moved into petrol retail, placing convenience stores by the pumps. Through a joint venture with the Bank of Scotland, Tesco also started offering a wide range of financial products, including car and pet insurance. In 1996, it launched a dotcom delivery service. Tesco.com has not only endured but become profitable.

Tesco overtook Sainsbury in 1996 to become the biggest food retailer in the UK. With its 25 per cent market share – compared to 14 per cent in 1997 – Tesco has put considerable distance between it and Sainsbury's 17 per cent share and Asda's 14 per cent share.

Going global

CEO Terry Leahy, who joined the retailer as a marketing executive 23 years ago, has increased Tesco's sales 50 per cent in the four years since he succeeded McLauren to become CEO. He has done so by both continuing to grow core domestic sales and by expanding internationally. At home, Tesco has grown non-food retailing, introduced house brands for value-conscious and more indulgent shoppers, and focused on customer service. The cornerstone of its international strategy is exporting culturally customized versions of its marketing formula for hypermarkets, the popular department store/supermarket combination that sells massive amounts of food and household goods in a single store.

So far, the strategy has been successful. In April 2001, the company announced it had broken through the £1 billion ($1.4 billion) mark in annual profits. Only one British retailer, Marks & Spencer PLC, has ever accomplished that, and only for a brief interlude from 1997 to 1998. Last year, when other UK retailers' sales were relatively static, Tesco's earnings per share rose 11 per cent.

Leahy recently set a goal for Tesco to have more physical selling space outside Great Britain than inside by 2003. About 37 per cent of the company's physical floor space is already located overseas, as the company moves toward that goal. In the financial year 2001, non-UK sales reached £3 billion ($4.4 billion).

Tesco is, however, not alone in its mission to become a global food retailer. Many of the big-name retailers, including the United States' Wal-Mart Stores Inc, France's Carrefour SA and the Netherlands' Royal Ahold NV, are also expanding into foreign markets world-wide. Although the world has grown accustomed to the omnipresence of global brands like McDonald's, Volkswagen and Coke, retailers – particularly those that cater to daily household needs – have been slow to reach out to consumers outside their own country. Retailing is still a very local business around the world and globalization is in its very early stages especially in foods.

Retailers are moving overseas now because domestic growth is limited. It took decades for stores to evolve from the classic chain of corner shops to superstore enterprises with a national reach. When there was plenty of room for expansion in the United States, Wal-Mart, for example, saw little reason to go abroad. Even now, its global push is tentative for a company of its size. The group is in only nine foreign countries, and still makes about 85 per cent of its profits from US sales.

If retailers restrict themselves to their domestic markets, they must resign themselves to operating as mature businesses in mature markets. Tesco has reached 25 per cent market share – close to market saturation – in UK food retailing. The company's moves into other areas such as clothing sales and Internet shopping are unlikely to give it the kind of growth shareholders expect.

The hazards of foreign expansion are considerable, as Marks and Spencer discovered to its cost. Globalization means complexity and increased overhead. To succeed, a company has to stretch its resources, learn new skills and add to its capabilities.

Although adapting merchandising in foreign markets to local tastes and customs makes a lot of sense on the surface, the history of globalization indicates that this strategy is risky. The pioneer global branders – McDonald's, Boeing, Coke, Gillette and others – succeeded overseas by following a one-size-fits-all-cultures strategy. The reason the first global companies built their brand empires through standardization is that it is by far the most cost-effective way to export a successful domestic product to multiple countries and deliver consistent quality at an affordable price. The less adapting that multinational corporations do, the more they can spread overhead costs. By appealing to local consumers' appetite for Western goods, moreover, a multinational corporation can distinguish its products and avoid competing directly with local groups that know the market better – Marlboro cigarettes sell better in China when they are shown in the hands of an American cowboy.

Tesco, however, has adopted a different approach to globalization. By seeking to blend into the local scene, Tesco argues that shopping at a hypermarket should not be a strange or alien experience. Europeans who will happily eat at McDonald's once a week or drink a Coke once a day will probably go elsewhere if they can't find culturally familiar staple goods, whether they are food, clothes, or other items.

Recognizing this, Tesco is taking the 'think global, act local' strategy to a new level. Its approach is based on a deep understanding of and responsiveness to the lifestyles and habits of consumers in other countries.

The group plans to open 140 stores overseas within the next few years, one of the biggest commitments to globalization in the industry.

When Tesco was invited by the government of Hungary, in 1994, to purchase a piece of Global, a troubled Hungarian grocery retailer, Tesco executives agreed to send a team to assess the situation. In Hungary, they saw a very different retail picture from that which existed in France where a previous Tesco investment had not succeeded. Also, in the region generally, they saw the kind of growth prospects Tesco was seeking. Central Europe had a population growing in affluence that was clearly open to fresh shopping experiences. And unlike France, the region had few large domestic retailers, leaving the field wide open to foreign competitors.

In 1994, Tesco purchased a 51 per cent stake in Global. The next year, it followed its move into Hungary by opening stores in Poland, the Czech Republic and Slovakia. Three years later, it expanded into emerging markets in South-East Asia.

In the 1990s, Carrefour had also moved into Central Europe. However, Carrefour's strategy was to spread its investments more thinly. With a presence in 25 nations, the company has no more than a 3 per cent market share in any one country outside France.

Tesco, on the other hand, is opting for depth – dominating in contiguous countries – rather than the global breadth Carrefour has sought. Tesco hopes to build regional economies of scale in that geographic proximity enables stores to share resources. Tesco stores in Slovakia and the Czech Republic, for instance, import up to one-third of their products from each other. The company has also calculated that it needs 15 stores in any single country to be profitable.

For the time being, Tesco has limited its regional expansion to Central Europe and South-East Asia, where it now has more than 139 stores. International sales were up 46 per cent to £1.7 billion ($2.5 billion) in the first half of 2001.

Thailand became Tesco's first Asian base in 1998, and was followed by South Korea and Taiwan. In 2003, the company plans to open 18 new stores in Asia, including one in Malaysia. Management is also seriously considering the Chinese market.

The Hungarian operation, which is now profitable, recently inaugurated a 160,000-square-foot hypermarket. Tesco's largest store so far, it's about four times the size of the average UK supermarket. The company predicted that Thailand, Poland, Slovakia and the Czech Republic would all be profitable in 2001.

The Marks and Spencer failures in overseas markets infected the UK retail industry with caution. Tesco understood that part of the M & S problem was being too British, and it set out to avoid this mistake. What was needed, Tesco decided, was to combine operational efficiencies with product and service customization for each foreign market.

In the food area, a large amount of local content is to be expected. Yet even for non-food items, the company prefers to use domestic suppliers. In Slovakia, 60 per cent of non-food products are locally manufactured. In Poland, where the company has relationships with 1,300 local businesses, the number is close to 95 per cent. Furthermore, 95 per cent of employees in Tesco's foreign stores are local nationals. Tesco points out that all of Warsaw's directors are Polish, and this pattern is repeated in other countries, including South Korea, Thailand, Malaysia, Hungary and the Czech Republic.

The strategy has clear benefits. Local nationals like to see bosses from their own country: it gives them the sense that they, too, can advance. Employees say they also feel more comfortable reporting to individuals from the same culture.

Yet having a high number of foreign managers presents complexity for headquarters. Local hires are not as well versed in the Tesco corporate culture. And rank-and-file workers may have a harder time swallowing certain corporate practices. For example, Tesco slogans such as 'Ask more than tell', 'Trust and respect each other' and 'Enjoy work, celebrate success' seem overly touchy-feely for the typical Polish worker, who tends to be plain-spoken and direct. The language barrier can be a challenge, too.

Transferring best practices

What, in the globalization context, is the role of the parent company? The answer is that there is no point in reinventing the wheel. It would be prohibitively expensive for Tesco to require foreign managers to come up with entirely new ways of running their stores. To offset the costs of localization, Tesco management has focused on standardizing many aspects of management practice to achieve global economies of scale.

The stores have a similar look, both in the UK and abroad. They are located mostly on the fringes of cities, to lower costs. They offer large car parks for customers' convenience. Tesco also pushes its wide selection and distinctive service at every store. Shelves are stocked with dozens of brands, far more than at most hyper-markets. Baby-friendly shopping trolleys are available world-wide. At all its locations, Tesco stresses the same principles of good service, backing them up with training sessions that are designed at the head office in London.

Best practice transfer is not just a one-way traffic. Tesco is also applying some of the lessons of customization learnt abroad to its domestic market. Modern Britain is a diverse society, with varying concentrations of immigrants in different areas. At the company's Leytonstone store, for example, the store manager has taken care to stock items that appeal to a large immigrant customer base. For its Indian consumers, the company stocks masala curry paste; for Muslims, it offers halal meats, which meet the dietary requirements of Islamic law. Afro-Caribbean shoppers are happy to find Rubicon exotic juice, a brand they recognize from home.

So far, Tesco's foreign investment has been successful. In the first half of 2001, its world-wide sales rose 14 per cent to £11.5 billion ($16.8 billion) before taxes, on the back of a 46 per cent increase in non-UK revenues. Profits grew 14 per cent to £481 million ($701 million).

As Tesco's global expansion progresses, the company may be tempted again to try moving into even more competitive mature markets. Although management is well aware of the risks of facing formidable competitors in well-developed retail markets, successful companies also like a challenge. Tesco is seriously considering establishing a presence in Japan, and clearly hopes its joint venture with Safeway supermarkets to provide a Web-based delivery service in the United States will give the company a foothold from which to grow in America.

Tesco faces another challenge: will it be able to manage its growth abroad without neglecting its home market? One of the greatest dangers of global expansion is becoming distracted from domestic affairs. Some of the best multinationals – Coca-Cola and Gillette, for instance – have suffered setbacks on the home front as they expanded abroad.

With greater political and economic tensions around the globe, international expansion in retailing will probably slow, and reverse globalization may actually occur as companies retreat from some countries. As Marks and Spencer pulls out of Continental Europe and the United States, for example, it is clearly relying on investment in new stores, refurbishment and marketing initiatives at home to spur a revival of its business.

Exporting a high-tech business model

Tesco's dotcom delivery service, launched in 1996, has survived five years and is profitable. In 2001, the online revenues reached $450 million, and, although the Tesco.com unit lost $13 million in 2000 because of expansion into new business lines like CDs and videos, its grocery business was profitable.

Tesco moved into online slowly starting with modest investment and employing small numbers of personnel to service orders in the back rooms of existing supermarkets. It invested just £56 million to build its online business. Over a five-year period, it gradually rolled out its service to about one-third of its 692 stores in the UK.

Tesco is currently expanding its Internet services abroad. In June 2001, the company announced an Internet delivery joint venture with the number three US supermarket group, Safeway Inc. Tesco will provide the know-how for running the service; Safeway will fulfil the orders through GroceryWorks, an unprofitable start-up that is now a Safeway subsidiary and its exclusive online grocery distribution channel.

In South Korea, where it currently has seven successful super-markets and plans to open more, Tesco will launch an online shopping service in 2002. South Korea has the highest residential penetration of broadband Internet connections in the world.

(Sources: Tesco Web site; Seth and Randall, 1999; Griffiths, 2002)

MARKS AND SPENCER: LOSING SIGHT OF THE BUSINESS SUCCESS MODEL

Michael Marks and Thomas Spencer founded their business in the 1890s selling clothing on market stalls. In the 1920s, led by Simon Marks and Israel Sieff, the company expanded, becoming a national chain of shops selling mainly clothing under the brand name St Michael. Marks was chairman from 1916 until 1964 and under his leadership the company developed a set of basic business principles that became the basis of a coherent and consistent strategy over many years. Its main features were:

▌ Commitment to a combination of top quality and relatively low prices such that the customer perception was of good value for money.

▌ Rigorous cost efficiency. There were no fitting rooms in the stores, as this would have reduced the volume of sales per square foot. When credit cards were introduced the company refused to accept them. Paperwork was reduced to a minimum.

▌ A 'no-questions-asked' returns policy.

▌ Direct involvement with long-term suppliers in product development and design, quality control and production methods.

▌ A highly progressive set of personnel policies including above-average pay and conditions, a pension scheme, staff canteens and medical facilities.

During the 1970s and 1980s M & S expanded into foods, specializing in ready meals of high quality and quickly gaining a significant market share. It also moved into financial services and introduced its own storecard.

The 1970s also saw its first moves overseas. It acquired a chain of stores in Canada and opened its first store in Paris, followed by others in France, Belgium and Ireland.

The acquisition of Brooks Brothers in the United States was the most significant act of Lord Rayner, the company's first non-family chairman. In the event it turned out to be a disaster. The price paid was about twice what it was worth. In spite of considerable further investment on refurbishment, it never made a respectable return on capital.

The Greenbury era

In 1989 Richard Greenbury was appointed chief executive under Rayner's chairmanship. He had joined the company from school at the age of 17. Standing over six feet tall, with a strong, charismatic personality, Greenbury (or Rick as he was known inside the company) quickly established his dominance over the other executive directors. In 1991 he succeeded Rayner as chairman and retained the chief executive role, thus ensuring that he would have complete control over the company's destiny.

Bevan (2001) suggests that he provides a classic example of what Collins (2001b) calls a level 4 leader. These have big egos and strong charismatic personalities, but lack the distinctive qualities of level 5 leaders, who 'make great companies good'. In particular they lack sufficient humility to put the good of the company above personal ambition. In 1997 Greenbury's ambition for a peerage led him to accept chairmanship of a government-sponsored committee on executive remuneration at a time when Marks and Spencer's affairs needed his full attention. He also shows characteristics of what Kets de Vries (1994) calls the 'narcissistic personality'. He was oversensitive to criticism and prone to outbursts of rage. His burgundy Bentley carried the personalized numberplate SRG for Sir Richard Greenbury.

The company's turnover in 1990 was £5.6 billion and pre-tax profits £604 million. There were 272 UK stores. Britain was moving into a severe recession. On taking charge Greenbury's first act was to sack 850 people and, by encouraging natural wastage, to reduce the number employed within a year by over 5,000.

His second act was to call a meeting of the company's suppliers and persuade them to accept a cut in their margins.

In November 1991 he informed shareholders that half-year profits were down by 7 per cent – the first profit decline in a decade. Pundits in the City and in the press were quick to become critical. An article in the *Independent on Sunday* accused the management of making three mistakes:

I   failing to move earlier into out-of-town sites;

I   the Brooks Brothers acquisition;

I   the sackings, which had damaged morale.

Full-year profits were also down at £589 million compared with £607 million in the previous year. However, by early 1993 the tide began to turn. With the help of its suppliers the company had launched an 'outstanding value' campaign in the previous autumn and it was now paying off. The emphasis was on good design, classic cut and low prices. The fashion press applauded and *Vogue* even featured a model wearing a Marks and Spencer silk shirt on its front cover.

Pre-tax profits rebounded to £763 million in 1993 and in 1994 they were up to £851 million. Greenbury now focused on reaching the symbolically important profit target of £1 billion. He instituted a drive to cut costs. One example of the extremes to which cost cutting was taken was that only one type of hanger was allowed for all stock.

During the early to mid-1990s capital expenditure was running at some £300 million annually. By the end of the Greenbury era in 1998 it was running at over £700 million. New stores were being opened and others refurbished. At the same time a number of the smaller stores in depressed inner-city areas were being closed and others gradually deteriorated, becoming drab and shabby. Training and maintenance budgets were cut.

At this time profit growth was also being driven by the success of the company's financial services operation. Keith Oates, who had joined M & S in 1984, was the director in charge. The foods division, too, was doing well. The company entered 1995 with its reputation and share rating higher than at any previous time. By 1997 the £1 billion profit target was reached and the shares reached an all-time high of 664½p. But it was before then that things had started to go wrong. In the high street the competition in the form of Next, Arcadia and Matalan had been regrouping. Internally the pressure for short-term profitability was already beginning to eat away at the company's longer-term prospects.

The succession battle

In August 1993 Greenbury announced a new board structure. Keith Oates was appointed deputy chairman and held responsibility for finance, financial services and international operations. Three joint managing directors were also appointed. Andrew Stone was made managing director in charge of merchandising. He had, like Greenbury, come up through the ranks. According to Bevan (2001) he was regarded as highly creative but too undisciplined to head the company. Guy McCracken was put in charge of food and Peter Salsbury in charge of personnel, store operations and development.

Oates took his appointment as deputy chairman as a clear signal that he was in line to succeed and pressed his claim to be made chief executive within a short period of time. Greenbury, however, made it clear that there was no question of this.

In the summer of 1995 Greenbury, who had been due to retire at 60, dealt Oates's ambitions a further blow by obtaining the agreement of the non-executive directors that he should defer his retirement until the age of 65, subject to annual reviews from his 62nd birthday onwards. Oates knew that if Greenbury did in fact stay till aged 65 he would himself be 59 by that time and thus too old to succeed him.

Around this time things started to go wrong for Greenbury personally. His health deteriorated; he needed a hip operation and was in constant pain; his marriage to his glamorous second wife was breaking up; and the Greenbury report on executive remuneration had attracted a great deal of criticism, some of it directed against him personally.

In October 1997 a full-page profile of Keith Oates appeared in the business section of the *Observer*. The caption under his picture read 'Keith Oates is tipped to be St Michael's choice to fill Richard Greenbury's shoes'. The article praised Oates's achievements and ended by asserting that 'Outsiders certainly believe that when Sir Richard Greenbury retires, Oates, now 54, will be a front runner to step up from deputy chairman to take the top job.' Needless to say the article infuriated Greenbury and the managing directors. They saw it as a tactical move by Oates to position himself as clear choice for the chief executive role, which Greenbury was due to relinquish in 1998. Greenbury called a meeting of the non-executive directors and it was decided that two of their number, Brian Baldock and Stella Rimington, would sound out opinion among the executive directors. These soundings were spread over a number of months and eventually a consensus emerged. Everyone agreed the need to separate the roles of chairman and chief executive, but it was decided to delay this move until 1999 at the earliest. The minute of the board meeting read that Sir Richard be asked to continue as chairman and chief executive until the AGM in 2000 or until the AGM in 1999, and that he be invited to serve as non-executive chairman from the date he ceased to be chief executive until the AGM in 2001.

The fall from grace

Oates now turned his attention to supporting his case to succeed Greenbury by stating the case for a clear strategic direction for the company. He sponsored the acquisition of the 19 largest stores of the Littlewoods chain for which M & S paid £192 million or £10 million a store. The deal won universal praise in the City. However, by the time the costs of refurbishment had pushed the total bill to £450 million it did not look so attractive.

Next, Oates persuaded the board to launch a 'global vision' – to become the UK's first truly global retailer. In 1997 the international operations had made a profit of £104 million but performance was uneven. South-East Asia was doing well, but in the United States the return on sales rarely exceeded 3 per cent. Profits from Europe, too, had been variable.

At this time, too, the food side was invested in by the creation of delicatessen counters, fresh-meat counters and in-store bakeries. Oates also proposed a substantial share buy-back but Greenbury resolutely opposed this. He also did not pursue the possibility of acquiring the Safeway supermarket group.

Meanwhile, as early as spring 1997, the fashion press was becoming disenchanted with the M & S offerings. Half-year results presented in November 1997 showed pre-tax profits at £452 million, just below analysts' forecasts. Nevertheless full-year profits announced in the spring of 1998 showed sales up 5 per cent and profits 6 per cent up at £1.17 billion. Few people outside the company knew how hard the struggle had been to achieve this result. Quality of earnings was being sacrificed in favour of quantity.

In 1997 the non-executives had become sufficiently concerned to persuade Greenbury to commission a survey of customer attitudes. The results showed a serious decline had already set in in the way the customers regarded the company. Their reactions had been influenced to some extent by a *World in Action* programme that claimed that one of M & S's suppliers used child labour in its factories in Morocco. Although this was later disproved, public confidence had been shaken. Greenbury was not impressed by the report and refused to allow the director of strategic planning to present it to a full board meeting. His response was 'Look at the profits.'

The turning point in the company's fortunes came in the period August to October 1998. Clothing sales in the previous quarter were up 5 per cent and all seemed well, but now they dropped 1 per cent. The fall caught the company by surprise and in consequence the buying departments had massively overbought. A drop in profits was now inevitable, and the half-year results showed a fall of 23 per cent.

Oates's bid for power

Shortly after the announcement of the results Greenbury left for a visit to India, combining business with a short holiday. Oates now felt that the bad results would give him the opportunity he had been waiting for. Two hours later a letter was delivered by hand to every non-executive director. In it he highlighted where he thought the company had gone wrong and accused the non-executives of not realizing how serious the problem was. Brian Baldock faxed a copy of the letter to Greenbury, but advised him not to change his itinerary. However, articles appeared in the *Sunday Times*, the *Observer* and *Sunday Telegraph*, blowing the story. This press coverage was also faxed to Greenbury who decided to return to England, landing at Heathrow early on the Monday morning. That day's *Financial Times* contained another article stating that Oates was proposing that he should become chairman, with Salsbury as chief executive.

Greenbury met up with several of the non-executives in his London flat. The plan of action adopted was that the decision to split the roles of chairman and chief executive should be brought forward. A nominations committee should be set up to interview every executive director once more, with three non-executives present at each interview. By the end of the week the committee would present its recommendation as to who should be appointed chief executive.

In fact the review took three weeks to complete during which time press speculation was rife and Oates continued to lobby for support.

On 24 November the non-executives announced their decision. Greenbury would become non-executive chairman and Salsbury would be appointed chief executive. The majority of his colleagues had backed Salsbury, saying that they could work with him. Oates was informed the next day and was told that he would be expected to take early retirement.

The new arrangement did not work as smoothly as the non-executives had hoped. Far from looking to Greenbury for support and establishing a mutually acceptable division of labour, Salsbury effectively cut Greenbury out of the decision-making process.

Meanwhile, out in the real world of customers and stores things were rapidly getting worse. In January 1999 Salsbury issued a profits warning to the financial community and the shares fell by 13 per cent in a single day. The underlying reasons were to do with some of the basics of the business – quality had slipped and prices were uncompetitive.

Salsbury now set about implementing his ideas for turning the business round. His first act was to remove nearly a quarter of the top management cadre – some 34 people, including three main board directors. This was followed in March by another 200 job losses among less senior managers and in May one in eight store management jobs were cut and many supervisory staff either sacked or demoted.

The share price had been recovering but sentiment turned against the company again following an article in the *Daily Telegraph* entitled 'The Battle of Baker Street', which gave a blow-by-blow account of the succession issue. The full-year results, announced in May, showed that, while sales had remained constant at just over £8 billion, profits had fallen from £1.2 billion to £634 million. A review of the business was commissioned from consultants LEK. The main conclusion – that the company had paid too much attention to the product and had ignored the need to promote the brand – was one with which Greenbury could not agree and he tendered his resignation in June. Meanwhile sales continued to decline.

Salsbury now set about making further changes. His attack on the traditional M & S culture was symbolized by abolishing the directors' dining room with its silverware and white-gloved waiters and replacing it with more modest lunch rooms, which any executives who had visitors for lunch could use. A new, modern communal restaurant was created for all Baker Street employees to use. The medical and welfare facilities were slimmed down. Directors were no longer to enter the building through a private entrance but to enter alongside the other employees.

A new marketing director, Alan McWalter, was recruited from Woolworths and the marketing department was enlarged. More directors were fired, including Andrew Stone who, after a brief spell as head of retail, lost his job after 33 years' service. McCracken was demoted and left soon after. Morale was hit and soon some of the most talented people began to leave, including Kim Winser, director of corporate marketing.

The Kings supermarket group in the United States was put up for sale, although Brooks Brothers was kept for the time being. The long-deferred decision to accept credit cards was taken.

Perhaps Salsbury's most controversial action was the manner in which he began to move the source of the company's supplies overseas, giving William Baird, a supplier of 30 years' standing, six months' notice. As a result Baird had to close 16 factories and lay off 4,500 employees.

Following Greenbury's departure Baldock had assumed the role of acting chairman while the search for a successor proceeded. The conclusion was soon reached that really top people would not be attracted by a non-executive role and it was announced in November that the search for an executive chairman was under way. This was seen by the city as a vote of no confidence in Salsbury. The share price sank to 250p and a hostile takeover bid was mounted by Philip Green, a high-profile entrepreneur in the retail field. Media reaction was generally not in favour and the bid failed. (Green bought BHS instead and soon produced a turnround in that company's fortunes.)

In January 2000 Luc Vandevelde was appointed as the new chairman. At 48 he had previously been chairman of the French supermarket group Promodes. Like Greenbury he had gone to work straight from school and worked his way up via some years with Kraft. He announced 'If I don't deliver in two years' time then I won't be sitting here in two years' time.'

In March M & S announced an overhaul of its brand. St Michael would be played down, the shiny green M & S bags would be no more and new ones in a trendy design would take their place. A new clothing range, the Autograph collection, aimed at the more upmarket customer, was introduced. It did not, however, prove to be a success.

In May Vandevelde cut the dividend for the first time in the company's history. Salsbury asked the remaining UK suppliers to cut their margins further, upon which Coats Viyella stopped supplying Marks and Spencer with almost immediate effect, causing M & S to lose some £9 million in knitwear sales.

Vandevelde had by now lost confidence in Salsbury, who was asked to leave along with Clara Freeman and Guy McCracken, leaving only one of the directors who had been serving two years previously – Robert Colvill, the finance director.

Roger Holmes, a one-time McKinsey consultant, who had been poached from Kingfisher, was appointed to head up UK retailing and took up his post in January 2001 just as the performance monitoring company Oak Administration declared that M & S had destroyed more shareholder value than any other company in the previous three years. This announcement provoked a letter in *The Times* by Mark Goyder, director of the Centre for Tomorrow's Company, suggesting that the real story was that, although the price of the company's shares fell heavily during that period, shareholder value was in fact being destroyed in earlier years while the company's profits were still buoyant: 'Creation and destruction of shareholder value are the result of how a company is led, how it innovates, what commercial decisions it makes and how well it listens to and learns from its customers, employees and suppliers.'

Signs of recovery

Holmes's message was 'We need to get back to the product.' His first step was to recruit the services of George Davies, the founder of Next and the creator of the George range of clothes for Asda. His role was to create a new brand of women's fashion clothing under the name 'Per Una'. The rest of the clothing space would be targeted on the core customer, women from 35 to 50, producing 'classic clothes that are not boring'. To help achieve this he recruited Yasmin Yusuf, a high-profile designer. The axe was wielded on Brooks Brothers and on the 38 European stores. As the FTSE 100 fell 11 per cent in the first seven months of 2001, M & S shares rose by 35 per cent from 186p to 251p making it the best-performing share in the index over that period. There were, however, strong protests over the closing of the stores on the Continent and the manner in which it was done. This and other criticisms about the continuing poor trading performance led Vandevelde to defer his £704,000 bonus.

In the event the pre-tax profits of $481 million announced in May 2001 were 7 per cent down on the previous year on sales of £8.1 billion, slightly below the previous year's £8.2 billion. However, after exceptional charges relating mainly to the cost of the store closures on the Continent, profits were £145 million. Nevertheless the share price moved up a fraction to 259p. The first real sign of recovery did not come until the results for 2002 when profit after exceptionals rose to £335 million.

In the summer of 2002 Holmes was appointed chief executive and Vandevelde moved to a non-executive role.

(Sources: Bevan (2001); A sigh of relief at Marks and Spencer, *Business Week*, 21 January 2002; Marks and Spencer's troubles, *Economist*, 14 April 2001; Marks and Spencer's Web site)

Glossary

Accounting profit The surplus of revenues over costs as stated in a firm's profit and loss statement.

Backward integration The extension of a firm's activities upstream into activities previously undertaken by suppliers.

Barriers to entry Those factors which offer established firms in an industry a competitive advantage over new entrants, and which consequently act as impediments to entry.

Barriers to exit Those factors which impede firms from leaving an industry when profits fall below cost of capital.

Business strategy The policies and guidelines which determine how a firm competes within an industry and, in particular, the basis on which it seeks to establish a competitive advantage.

Competitive advantage The potential for one firm to earn higher profits than its competitors as a result of possessing lower costs or a differentiated product or service.

Core competences Those organizational capabilities which are critical to a company's competitive advantage.

Corporate strategy The policies and guidelines which determine the scope of the firm in terms of the product markets, geographical areas within which a firm competes and the vertical range of activities which it undertakes.

Cost drivers The principal determinants of differences in unit costs between rival firms producing the same product or service.

Diversification A company's extension of its activities across a wider range of industries.

Downsizing A reduction in company size aimed at improving profitability through reducing capacity, divesting marginal businesses, and pruning corporate overheads.

Economies of learning Reductions in unit cost over time which are associated with the increased skill of individual employees and improvements in organization and management through repetition.

Economies of scale Reductions in unit cost which accompany expansion in a firm's output capacity.

Economies of scope Reductions in total cost derived from producing *multiple* products (and/or services) within the firm, as compared with their production within separate firms.

Excess capacity A surplus of available capacity over that required to meet the current level of market demand.

Experience curve A graph showing the relationship between unit costs and cumulative output for any production process. Typically, unit costs should be a constant proportion with each doubling of cumulative output (due primarily to economies of learning).

First-mover advantage The competitive advantage gained by an innovator or by the initial entrant into a new area of business over subsequent followers.

Forward integration The extension of a firm's activities downstream into activities previously undertaken by customers.

Industry analysis The analysis of the structural characteristics of an industry in order to explain and predict competition and profitability.

Key Success Factors The principal determinants of competitive advantage within an industry.

Mission A statement of strategic goals of a company, the main themes of its strategy, and the critical features of the company's identity.

Multidivisional (or *M-form*) structure A company structure involving a number of separate divisions, each responsible for operating a different business or product area, coordinated and controlled by a corporate headquarters.

Organizational capabilities Productive tasks which an organization is able to perform. (See also **Core competences.**)

Outsourcing A firm's transition from the internal provision of an input or business service, to buying in that input or business service from an external supplier.

Partnership sourcing Establishing long-term relationships with suppliers, to mutual advantage.

PIMS (Profit Impact of Market Strategy) A database maintained by the Strategic Planning Institute comprising market and strategy data relating to several thousand business units used to estimate the impact on profitability of different strategy variables.

Porter's Five Forces of Competition Model A framework for analyzing the impact of industry structure on competition and profitability which identifies five competitive forces impacting on an industry.

Portfolio Planning Models Frameworks for appraising the strategic business units within a firm in terms of industry attractiveness and competitive position.

Product differentiation The tangible and intangible characteristics which cause one firm's product or service to be perceived as different from that of a competing firm.

Profit The surplus of revenue over cost (see also **Accounting profit** and **Rent**).

Quasi vertical integration Close supplier–customer relationships which permit the close coordination of decision making normally associated with vertical integration within a single company.

Rent The surplus of returns over and above the economic cost of the resources required to generate that return.

Resources The inputs utilized by a firm. These include materials, capital equipment, finance, technology, labour, human capital (know-how and skills) and land.

Shareholder value The value of a firm to its shareholders = the stockmarket price of the company's shares × the number of shares outstanding.

Strategic business unit A division or department within a company which is a sufficiently distinct business to be treated separately for the purposes of strategic planning.

Synergy Linkages between separate businesses within a firm whereby one (or both) derives competitive advantage as a result of the presence of the other.

Transaction costs Costs associated with negotiating and consummating an exchange transaction across a market.

Value chain The sequence of activities which a company is engaged in when it transforms inputs into outputs.

Vertical integration The extension of a company's activities into vertically-related activities previously undertaken by a supplier or customer.

References

Ansoff, H (1965) *Corporate Strategy*, McGraw-Hill, New York

Argenti, John (1996) Are you a stakeholder?, *Strategy*, 9

Bartlett, C (1986) Building and managing the transnational: the new organizational challenge, in *Competition in Global Industries*, ed M Porter, Harvard Business School Press, Boston, MA, pp 367–401

Bartlett, C and Ghoshal, S (1989) *Managing Across Borders*, Harvard Business School Press, Boston, MA

Beer, M, Eisenstat, R A and Spector, B (1990) Why change programs don't produce change, *Harvard Business Review*, November–December, pp 158–66

Bekier, M M, Bogardus, A J and Oldham, T (2001) Why mergers fail, *McKinsey Quarterly*, Autumn, p 6

Bevan, J (2001) *The Rise and Fall of Marks and Spencer*, Profile Books, London

Bilmes, L, Wetzker, K and Xhonneux, P (1997) Value in human resources, *Financial Times*, 10 February

Buzzell, R and Gale, B (1989) *The PIMS Principles*, Free Press, New York

Cairncross, F (1997) *The Death of Distance*, Orion, London

Carson, R (1962) *The Silent Spring*, Houghton Mifflin, New York

Chandler, A D (1962) *Strategy and Structure*, MIT Press, Cambridge, MA

Christensen, C M (1997) *The Innovator's Dilemma: When new technologies cause great firms to fail*, Harvard Business School Press, Boston, MA

Clausewitz, C von (1989) *On War*, Princeton University Press, Princeton, NJ

Club of Rome (Meadows, D H *et al*) (1972) *Limits to Growth*, W W III Universe Books, New York

Clutterbuck, D, Clark, G and Armistead, C (1993) *Inspired Customer Service*, Kogan Page, London

Collins, J (2001a) *Good to Great*, Random House, London

Collins, J (2001b) Level 5 leadership, *Harvard Business Review*, **79** (1), January, pp 67–76

Collins, J and Porras, J (1995) *Built to Last*, Century, London

Company Law Review Steering Group (2000) *Modern Company Law for a Competitive Economy*, Company Law Steering Group, London

Crosby, P B (1989) *Quality is Free*, McGraw-Hill, New York

Cyert, R M and March, J G (1963) *A Behavioral Theory of the Firm*, Prentice Hall, Englewood Cliffs, NJ

Drucker, P (1992) Leadership: more doing than dash, *Managing for the Future*, pp 100–03, Butterworth Heinemann, London

Foster, R N and Kaplan, S (2001) *Creative Destruction,* Doubleday Currency, New York

Gadiesh, O *et al* (2001) The 'why' and 'how' of merger success, *European Business Journal*, **13**, Winter, p 187

Goldenberg, P (1997) *Shareholders v. Stakeholders: The bogus argument*, IALS Lecture

Goldratt, E and Cox, J (1986) *The Goal*, Creative Output Books, Hounslow

Goold, M and Campbell, A (1987) *Strategies and Styles*, Basil Blackwell, Oxford

Goold, M and Campbell, A (2002) *Designing Effective Organizations: How to create structured networks*, Jossey Bass, San Francisco, CA

Goold, M, Campbell, A and Alexander, M (1994) *Corporate Level Strategy*, Wiley, New York

Grant, R M, Jammine, A P and Thomas, H (1988) Diversity, diversification and profitability among British manufacturing companies, *Academy of Management Journal*, **31**, Winter, pp 771–802

Griffiths, V (2002) Welcome to Tesco, your 'glocal' superstore, *Strategy+Business*, First Quarter

Hambleden Group (1996) *Investors in People Review*, Hambleden Group, London

Hamel, G and Prahalad, C K (1985) Do you really have a global strategy?, *Harvard Business Review*, July–August, pp 139–48

Hamel, G and Prahalad, C K (1993) Strategy as stretch and leverage, *Harvard Business Review*, March–April

Hamel, G and Prahalad, C K (1994) *Competing for the Future*, Harvard Business School Press, Boston, MA

Hertz, N (2001) *The Silent Take-over*, William Heinemann, London

Hobsbawm, E (2000) *The New Century*, Little, Brown and Company, New York

Huselid, M A (1995) The impact of human resource management practices on turnover, productivity, and corporate financial performance, *Academy of Management Journal*, **38**, p 645

Kay, J (1993) *Foundations of Corporate Success*, Oxford University Press, Oxford

Keller, K L (2000) The brand report card, *Harvard Business Review*, **78** (1), January, p 147

Kennedy, A (2000) *The End of Shareholder Value*, Orion Business, London

Kets de Vries, M (1994) The mystique of leadership, *Academy of Management Executive*, **8** (3), p 73

Klein, N (2000) *No Logo*, Flamingo, London

Korten, David C (1996) *When Corporations Rule the World*, Earthscan, London

Kotler, P (1993) *Practice of Marketing*, Prentice Hall, Englewood Cliffs, NJ

Kotter, J (1995) Leading change: why transformation efforts fail, *Harvard Business Review*, March–April, pp 59–67

Kotter, J and Heskett, J (1992) *Corporate Culture and Performance*, Free Press, New York

Le Carré, John (2001) *The Constant Gardener*, Hodder & Stoughton, London

Learned, E P *et al* (1965) *Business Policy: Text and cases*, Irwin, Homewood, IL

Levitt, T (1983) The globalization of markets, *Harvard Business Review*, May–June, pp 92–102

Mannochehri, G (1999) The road to manufacturing excellence: using performance measures, *Industrial Management*, **41**, p 7

Mayo, A and Hadaway, A (2001) A cultural adaptation: the ICL–Nokia Data merger 1991–92, *Journal of Management Development*, **13** (2)

McIvor, R (2001) Lean supply: the design and cost reduction dimension, *Organization*, **35** (2), pp 139–60

Miles, R E and Snow, C C (1978) *Organisational Strategy, Structure and Process*, McGraw-Hill, New York

Mintzberg, H (1994) *The Rise and Fall of Strategic Planning*, Free Press, New York

Mintzberg, H, Ahlstrand, B and Lampel, J (1998) *Strategy Safari*, Prentice Hall, Hemel Hempstead

Neely, Andy (1998) *Measuring Business Performance*, Economist Books, London

Nelson, R R and Winter, S G (1982) *The Evolutionary Theory of Economic Change*, Belknap Press, Cambridge, MA

Normann, R (1977) *Management for Growth*, Wiley, New York

Pettigrew, A M (1985) *The Awakening Giant: Continuity and change in Imperial Chemical Industries*, Basil Blackwell, Oxford

Pfeffer, J (1998) *The Human Equation*, Harvard Business School, Cambridge, MA

Plender, J (1997) *A Stake in the Future*, Nicholas Brealey, London

Porter, M (1980) *Competitive Strategy*, Free Press, New York

Porter, M (1985) *Competitive Advantage*, Free Press, New York

Porter, M (1987) From competitive advantage to corporate strategy, *Harvard Business Review*, May–June

Porter, M (1990) *The Competitive Advantage of Nations*, Free Press, New York

Quin, J B (1980) *Strategies for Change: Logical incrementalism*, Irwin, Homewood, IL

Rhenman, E (1973) *Organisation Theory for Long Range Planning*, Wiley, London

Royal Society of Arts (1995) *An Inquiry into the Nature of Tomorrow's Company*, RSA, London

Sadler, P (1993) *Managing Talent*, FT Pitman, London

Sadler, P (2001) *The Seamless Organization*, Kogan Page, London

Schein, E (1992) *Organisation Culture and Leadership*, Jossey Bass, San Francisco, CA

Selznick, P (1957) *Leadership in Administration*, Row Peterson, Evanston, IL

Senge, Peter (1990) *The Fifth Discipline*, Century Business, London

Seth A and Randall, G (1999) *The Grocers: The rise and rise of the supermarket chains*, Kogan Page, London

Siddall, P, Willey, K and Tavarcs, J (1995) Building a transnational organisation for BP Oil, in *Strategic Change: Building a high performance organisation*, ed P Sadler, Elsevier Science, Oxford

Sinclair, D, Hunter, L and Beaumont, P (1996) Models of customer supplier relations, *Journal of General Management*, **22** (2), Winter, pp 56–75

Steiner, G A (1969) *Top Management Planning*, Macmillan, New York

Sternberg, E (1999) *The Stakeholder Concept: A mistaken doctrine*, Foundation for Business Responsibilities, London

Sun Tzu (1971) *The Art of War*, Oxford University Press, New York

Svendsen, A (1998) *The Stakeholder Society*, Berrett-Koehler, San Francisco, CA

Tichy, N M and Sherman, S (1993) *Control Your Destiny or Someone Else Will: How Jack Welch is making General Electric the world's most competitive corporation*, Doubleday, New York

Waddock, S and Graves, S (1997) Quality of management in quality of stakeholder relations, *Business and Society*, **36**, 3 September

Wolfensohn, J D (2001) Foreword, in *The New Economy of Corporate Citizenship*, ed S Zadek *et al*, Copenhagen Centre, Copenhagen

Womack, J P, Jones, D T and Roos, D (1990) *The Machine that Changed the World*, Rawson Associates/Macmillan, London

Zadek, S (2001) *The Civil Corporation*, Earthscan, London

Further reading

On the concept of strategy:

Hamel, G and Prahalad, C K (1993) Strategy as stretch and leverage, *Harvard Business Review*, March–April
Mintzberg, H (1987) Crafting strategy, *Harvard Business Review*, July–August
Mintzberg, H, Ahlstrand, B and Lampel, J (1998) *Strategy Safari*, Prentice Hall, Hemel Hempstead
Ohmae, K (1988) Getting back to strategy, *Harvard Business Review*, November–December

On corporate strategy:

Goold, M, Campbell, A and Alexander, M (1994) *Corporate Level Strategy*, Wiley, New York

On the analysis of industry and competition:

Porter, M E (1979) How competitive forces shape strategy, *Harvard Business Review*, March–April, p 86
Porter, M E (1990) *Competitive Strategy*, Free Press, New York

On resources and capabilities:

Grant, R M (1991) The resource-based theory of competitive advantage, *California Management Review*, Spring
Prahalad, C K and Hamel G (1990) The core competences of the corporation, *Harvard Business Review*, May–June

On competitive advantage:

Baden Fuller, C and Stopford, J M (1992) *Rejuvenating the Mature Business,* Routledge, London
Buzzell, R and Gale, B (1989) *The PIMS Principles,* Free Press, New York
Ghemawat, P (1991) *Commitment: The dynamic of strategy,* Free Press, New York
Kay, J (1993) *The Foundations of Corporate Success,* Oxford University Press, Oxford
Porter, M E (1985) *Competitive Advantage,* Free Press, New York

On international management:

Bartlett, C and Ghoshal, S (1989) *Managing Across Borders,* Harvard Business School Press, Boston, MA

On implementation:

Kotter, J (1995) Leading change: why transformation efforts fail, *Harvard Business Review,* March–April, pp 59–67

Index